Amelia & Me

*On deafness, autism and parenting
by the seat of my pants*

MELINDA HILDEBRANDT

What Others Are Saying

"Melinda Hildebrandt is an incredible writer with an amazing story. One she tells with insight, humour and brilliance. You must buy this book for everyone you know. Life did not turn out the way Melinda expected. She has been on an incredible journey and she's not only embraced it and learned from it, she's woven an incredible tale. What a cracking read. Brilliantly written and fascinating as fuck. You won't put it down. This book is the book that should have been there for Melinda when she found herself expecting to go to Italy but instead touching down in Holland. How do you make God laugh? Tell him your plans. Melinda's experience of becoming a mother was not at all what she imagined. But becoming a mother made her the incredible writer she is today with a story that will bend you and fold you in ways you never would have imagined. What stands out about this book is Melinda's clarity, honesty and spirit of understanding. And boy! She can write."

— CATHERINE DEVENY, writer, comedian,
author and social commentator

"*Amelia & Me* is simply a divine love letter, from mother to daughter. Melinda's love for Amelia is evident on every page. A wonderful memoir of parenting when things don't go quite to plan. I call it the best 'mothers group you never meant to join'! It's Olympic-level parenting sometimes, but Melinda keeps stepping up, keeps pushing forward, keeps forging a place for Amelia in the world. This isn't just a 'special needs' story though, deafness and autism are merely characters. This is a beautiful insight into mothering. How we sacrifice, advocate and are ferocious in our protection of our children. Amelia is one very lucky little girl and her mum sure can write."

— NICOLE ROGERSON, CEO, Autism Awareness Australia

"Melinda Hildebrandt's incredible, no-holds-barred memoir exploring her journey of raising a daughter with hearing loss and autism is a brilliant combination of deeply inspiring, humorous and heart-wrenching. An exceptional story of one family's struggle, perseverance and triumph in helping Amelia find her voice. Witty, intelligent and completely authentic - Melinda's strength in embracing all the joys and challenges that Amelia has brought to her life - brings with it humour, connectedness and hope. This book should be mandatory reading for all families of children with hearing loss and/or autism, their families, carers, and all who interact with them."

— JULIE POSTANCE, author of *Breaking the Sound Barriers* and director of iinspire media

"Mothering is a complicated job, made twenty times more complicated when your child has a disability. Hildebrandt has turned this into an inspiring story – from love notes left on side tables to tantrums that last forever, and dolls with hearing aids (I need to order one right now, actually). There are tears in this book, there is some deep reflection on what disability and mothering means, but there is also an awesome and proud little girl starring in the show who will win you over in the end. Buy this book."

— DR BELINDA BARNET, author, Senior Lecturer in Media and Communications at Swinburne University, Melbourne and the coolest tech nerd in the world

"In this memoir *Amelia & Me*, Melinda Hildebrandt does a rare thing. She writes with a light-filled grace about her experiences as the mother of a daughter with a disability. Melinda's writing is suffused with love and poignancy about the yearnings and achievements of her deaf daughter, Amelia. She also writes with delight about Amelia's shining personality. Throughout all this, Melinda keeps an unflinchingly cool, self-regarding eye on her decisions on Amelia's behalf, fixing her compass on her hopes for Amelia's future. I belong to the generation of oral-deaf children, now adults. Some of us were lonely for mentors to guide us on our identity-pathways towards a better understanding of who we are and who we could be. While reading *Amelia & Me*, I sensed the press of Amelia's little hand in my hand, tugging me forward to still greater adventures and joy."

— Donna McDonald, *The Art of Being Deaf: a memoir*
(Gallaudet University Press. 2014)

"What does it take for a reader to want to follow the journey of someone unknown to them? This story. Melinda Hildebrandt writes with the passion of a mother who clearly loves her daughter; not so unusual, but she enables the reader to discover something of the world according to Amelia with great sensitivity and humour as they negotiate the unpredictable, painful and poignantly beautiful journey as determined by Amelia's disabilities. There are 'take home' lessons here - insights into a different view of life that make you aware of the limitations of personal perspective; that kneeling or bending for face-to-face communication can have such a significant effect on understanding, and that, in the end, it's the story of feisty and determined little girl who will perform this thing called life her way, and a mother and father who watch with love and pride, sometimes from the wings."

— Amanda Apthorpe, PhD, author and teacher

"Melinda extends a hand and takes us on a journey through the new and sometimes bewildering terrain traversed by the parent of a child with disabilities. In intimate, bite-size chunks we have a window into Amelia's life as she (and her family) becomes immersed in the deaf community. Melinda is open about the grief she sometimes feels, but the overwhelming tenor of her writing is one of powerful joy at watching her young daughter bloom."

— Miki Perkins, senior writer, The Age

"Life with a child with special needs is at times gut-wrenchingly heart breaking and yet beautiful at the same time. The story of Amelia and Melinda is a story of love, of sunshine amidst the darkest clouds. Everyone's journey is different. Melinda and I found each other online and connected because we love our children and because we are human. This book will make you cry, it will make you laugh, but most of all it will help you walk in the shoes of a Mum and a little girl who together are taking on the messy journey of life."

— Professor Jane Burns, CEO, Young and Well Digital and SynCo International; Professor of Innovation and Industry, University of Sydney

"I was captured by *Amelia & Me* from the beginning, and was completely drawn into the honesty and frankness with which Melinda Hildebrandt tells her family's story – it cuts deep. She has a fantastic turn of phrase, and a wicked sense of humour (I was laughing out loud in places), and other times she reached in and ripped my heart out. There aren't a lot of writers I've read who can do that, and I've read *a lot* of writers. There's no doubt in my mind that there will be a lot of families who will find this book inspiring, and fall in love with Amelia as I did."

— Amanda Spedding, professional editor, proofreader and award-winning author

"Melinda's writing is moving and informative and gives a real insight into deafness from a mother's perspective."

— Charlie Swinbourne, freelance journalist, scriptwriter and editor of online deaf news website, *The Limping Chicken*

For my hero, Amelia Isobel.
You have my whole heart.

And for every parent out there in
the trenches, I'm with you.

Published in Australia by
Agincourt Publishing
Postal: PO Box 944 Merlynston VIC 3058
Email: melinda.hildebrandt@gmail.com
Website: melindahildebrandt.com.au

First published in Australia 2017
Copyright © Melinda Hildebrandt 2017

National Library of Australia Cataloguing –in – Publication entry

Creator: Hildebrandt, Melinda, author.

Title: Amelia & me: on deafness, autism and parenting by the seat of my pants / Melinda Hildebrandt.

ISBN: 978-0-9946491-2-6 (paperback)

ISBN: 978-0-9946491-1-9 (epub)

Notes: Includes bibliographical references.

Subjects: Hildebrandt, Melinda.
              Autistic children--Victoria--Melbourne--Biography.
              Deaf children--Victoria--Melbourne--Biography.
              Mothers of children with disabilities--Victoria--Melbourne--Biography.
              Parenting--Victoria--Melbourne.

Dewey Number: 618.92858820092

Back cover photograph by Lynette Zeeng
Front cover photo by the author
Cover layout and design by Ronald Cruz of crucialdesigns studio
Book typesetting by Nelly Murariu of pixbeedesign.com
Printed by CreateSpace

Contents

Foreword

I am delighted that Melinda Hildebrandt has been persuaded to turn her wonderful blog 'Moderate-severe/profound… quirky' into a book. I have known Melinda for a few years now. I feel I know her well but this is a 'virtual' friendship – through the Aussie Deaf Kids online groups and through her wonderful blog. She writes about things that are so familiar, in such a way that helps us reframe our own experiences in a different light – acknowledging the hard times but focusing on the positives and progress. She is insightful, funny, and truthful.

My youngest daughter was born with a unilateral hearing loss – she could hear, but only with one ear. When she was 7, she lost the hearing in her other ear overnight. Unlike Melinda, I am no cinephile, but years before this long night, I had seen *Children of a Lesser God* – again and again. I simply loved the feistiness of Marlee Matlin. I loved how the deaf kids danced to Twisted Sister. And I loved the music William Hurt wrapped himself in when he needed space and time. It was Bach's *Concerto for Two Violins*. It is a heart-breakingly beautiful piece of music. It fed my despair while nourishing my hope.

Melinda's love of movies (her PhD thesis was on realism in British film) is a riff throughout her blog. Movies seem to help her make sense of the bad times and the good. She writes so beautifully about her love for Amelia and Tim, but I love this little insight she provides into the part of her that is not a mother of a deaf child with autism. Despite her life being different to the one she had imagined, she shows that parents of children with a disability can (and should) continue to be true to who they are.

It took me longer than Melinda to understand that labels cannot predict where our children will shine. If someone had told me that night I lay in the bed next to Bonny in hospital that she would become a chef, I would have railed that deafness would not limit her to life in the kitchen.

She was destined for bigger things. And she was – but not in a way I had ever imagined. She found her own strengths, her own passions and her own way forward. And Melinda has discovered this too. Despite us, our kids "strike out on their own path, discovering 'who they really are' on their own terms." (11 June, 2014)

Rereading Melinda's blog, I love how she has come to accept that Amelia dances to her own rhythm – a beat to be celebrated and appreciated, and the acceptance that her family life is not the one she had imagined but understanding "…this life as the real one, the one you were meant to have." (13 September, 2013)

I started an online group for parents of deaf children a few years after Bonny lost her hearing. I have got to know so many parents through this online experience and sometimes, there are parents who just *speak* to me. Melinda is one of those parents. She joined one of the Aussie Deaf Kids groups in 2011. We read little snippets of her ups and downs in her posts. The cover of the February 2013 Aussie Deaf Kids newsletter featured a joyful drawing of *Hermione Granger with hearing aids* by Amelia, aged 4. And then she introduced us to her blog. I have sent countless parents to it over the past few years as they struggle with different aspects of raising a child with hearing loss and autism. She is so honest about her experiences. She gives voice to some of our dark thoughts but also shows a lightness of being.

I think this book will be one that parents will have sitting on their bedside table – a trusted companion they can dip into or read from cover to cover. As Melinda says, "None of us is in possession of an infallible crystal ball…" (13 October, 2014) but the book is sure to provide hope.

Ann Porter AM
Founder, Aussie Deaf Kids

Introduction

Amelia in her element, by the ocean (2013)

What are heavy? Sea-sand and sorrow:
What are brief? To-day and to-morrow:
What are frail? Spring blossoms and youth:
What are deep? The ocean and truth.

— Christina Georgina Rossetti,
What Are Heavy?

Tomorrow, at dawn, at the hour when the countryside whitens,
I will set out. You see, I know that you wait for me.
I will go by the forest, I will go by the mountain.
I can no longer remain far from you.

— Victor Hugo, *Tomorrow, At Dawn*

In 2013, I stepped out onto Swanston Street in Melbourne, leaving my job at that time for good. For a few moments I felt buoyed by the change, my feet light as I walked more slowly than usual towards the train station. What was the rush anyway? I was free, wasn't I?

Leaving had been one of the easiest decisions I'd ever made. My daughter Amelia is deaf, and had just completed the intensive assessment for a cochlear implant. She wasn't a candidate but other storms were gathering above our heads. At four, her behaviour was becoming more and more challenging. More tests and dreaded appointments lay ahead. Privately, in some deep down place, I knew the answer would be found on the autism spectrum. My sense of weightlessness was fleeting. My pace quickened; I had a long way to go.

What follows is not a traditional memoir, written in a single go or with a clear purpose in mind. It began that same year as a blog about Amelia and me. I say blog, but it became more of a lifeline for me over the intervening years as I documented and shared my hopes and fears for Amelia's present and future. In the first year, I blogged with a feverish intensity I've never experienced before. I had banked a lot of grief, and I felt a sudden desperation to be rid of it, to exorcise it from within and put it on the page, then the web and out into the world. I wanted to let that pain go and celebrate and ponder the wonder of raising someone as unique as my little girl. Once I started, wild horses could not have held me back.

The response from friends and family was instant and overwhelming. They read my posts and propped me up with words of understanding and empathy. Amelia became known to them in a more profound way than seeing her could have achieved back then. People followed her progress and cheered from the sidelines. Sent their love. Laughed with me about her eccentric little ways; hoped with all their hearts for things to be better soon. Writing was a life-sustaining practice for me then as it is now. My nearest and dearest know me to be a pretty frank over-sharer, but they didn't flinch from my thoughts and words. So much pressure to explain things to people in person was alleviated by each story. The blog was a gateway to learning how to meet Amelia more than halfway. In that way, it was a gift to me and to her.

After three years I have amassed a huge number of stories about our life with Amelia. She has come such a long way and the boundaries of our world are beginning to stretch and shift outwards. With that space, our life feels more stable than ever, so it feels like the right time to bring all of my writing together into this book. I always hoped that sharing our experiences might help parents in similar situations. I have had many messages from people around the world who have expressed heartfelt solidarity with me. Those messages have meant a lot as I have peeled back the many layers of what it means to be the mother of a feisty, hilarious, and enigmatic little person with enough energy to power the sun.

Welcome to Holland?

3 May, 2013

Where wouldn't I travel for her?

The day we found out that our daughter was deaf, we were given a blue book called '*Choices*' (Australian Hearing). The first page of the book features a piece called 'Welcome to Holland' by Emily Perl Kingsley, aimed at parents whose babies are born with an unforeseen challenge or disability.

The basic premise of Kingsley's piece is that having a baby born with some kind of challenge is like planning a trip to Italy, but when you land (post-birth) you are suddenly told you have arrived in Holland.

It's not where you intended to go but it's not a terrible place, just different to what you expected.

There's nothing flippant about her use of the analogy. She's asking parents to try and adjust their thinking about their shattered hopes for their children and start to consider the special things about Holland. Because, and this is the key, you ain't going anywhere else.

But on D-Day (Diagnosis Day), I wasn't ready to be philosophical about what I was feeling, which was absolute devastation. Because I had thought we *were* in Italy for more than two years.

We'd arrived with our bags, unpacked them, explored the sights and started to put down roots in this strange but exciting place. I'd relaxed and allowed my shoulders to drop a little. It felt like home to me.

Finding out we were actually in Holland – that my cherished daughter could not hear me when I sang to her or said her name or told her that I loved her – swallowed me whole and kept me in the belly of grief for a very long time.

I couldn't contain my anger and pain at the 'lie' of our time in Italy. I felt cheated, like we'd been made a promise and sucked into the pretence that we had 'made it', when all the while the 'truth' of Amelia's deafness was lying in wait for us.

It was impossible not to feel alienated by the endless holiday stories of friends and family who took that journey to Italy with relative ease, over and over again. It stretched that distance – from Italy to Holland – between me and others, that began with infertility and, I thought, ended with IVF success.

Now the gap had widened into a bottomless hole, and I experienced a powerful sense of isolation from people. Every time I saw parents with their kids at the park or at parties bonding through incidental chatter, my heart cracked a little more.

This was more like far-flung Siberia than a nearby Western-European country.

I know this distance changed me, made me harder, and there is part of me still bruised on the inside. In a way, I chose not to heal all the way through, because this toughness is something for which I'm oddly grateful.

It keeps me strong in the fighting zone, which is where I so often have to be for Amelia: punching hard in her corner.

I have come to realise that you don't mourn forever, and the parts of you that still grieve rear their hydra heads less often. And good people keep building small bridges that reach you and help you to make it at least part of the way back.

Cos it's only Italy, right? That's what people tell me. There are plenty of other places we could have ended up. I see it in Amelia's deaf kinder class every day and it never fails to floor me and bring me back to myself.

And what of Holland? It takes a lot of work and even more time, but eventually I did accept the pain and incorporate it into new plans for the future. It's not all tulips and windmills, and sometimes the snow obscures your view of the path ahead, but it's unique and rewarding in a way I never imagined.

Recently I have found myself able to take out those pictures and memories of our time in faux-Italy. It's bittersweet but my heart doesn't ache as much as it used to. Amelia was as beautiful to me then as she is now, and nothing will ever change that.

I've also made some kind of peace with that feeling of betrayal that buried me deep for almost a year, and that is a very good thing.

We only had one shot to get to Italy or anywhere on the map as it turns out. But if we'd known before Amelia was born that we had a one-way ticket to Holland, I'm sure we would still have chosen to go.

To meet our daughter, to bring her into the world and hold her close, I know I would have gone just about anywhere.

Art therapy, session notes #1

2 May, 2013

I have lost count of the number of medical appointments Amelia and I have been to over the last two or so years. Scores of them, I guess. Hearing tests, MRI/CT scans, speech and language assessments and therapy, paediatrician check-ups, blood tests, genetics testing, more hearing tests, the list goes on.

It has been gruelling and demanding to say the least. Banking on the cooperation of your young child in testing environments is an exercise in futility. It's always a crapshoot, but win, lose or draw, we will be back again for more of the same.

With the recent addition of suspected autism to the roll call of Amelia's challenges, we are looking down the barrel of numerous meetings with a child psychologist to help us understand her better. Other intensive therapies are sure to follow.

In the face of all this, it was a strange feeling to have Art Therapy suggested to me as a way to reach Amelia and tap into her already burgeoning creative side.

After a pressure-filled six months inside the exhaustive cochlear implant assessment program, I was definitely up for something fun with a 'no harm, no foul' feel to it.

Amelia's sage paediatrician supported this kind of alternative therapy wholeheartedly: "Amelia is an artsy kind of girl, so I think it's a great idea."

My acupuncturist (I know, I know) gave me the name of an Expressive Therapist (ditto), JM, who describes her work as "the recovery, maintenance and development of self-esteem and resilience in children and adolescents.

"The main aim over four or five sessions using things like Sandplay, Relaxation, Art, Clay Work and Movement is in returning children to their healthy capacity to fully participate positively in their lives as soon as possible."

Whatever the future holds for Amelia, it was an easy decision to enter into this type of gentle therapy aimed at nurturing her, building her up and maybe helping to free her from the anxiety and rage that sometimes affects her life.

Like *Fight Club*, the first (and only) 'rule' for an Expressive Therapies session is that usually the parent does not stay with their child. Okay JM, let's see how we go.

On our way to JM's house, I continued explaining in detail to Amelia how the morning was going to work and that I would not stay with her unless she wanted me to. Amelia likes lots of preparation before most outings, so she is a little armed in advance.

We were welcomed by the delightful JM who took us into her home, which had an enormous back room set up like an Aladdin's cave of artistic delights. Amelia took one look at the shelves and shelves of fascinating 'stuff' and chose a small blue fish to hold. Then she grabbed my hand and said, "Mummy go now!"

Wow. I found myself standing on the street two minutes after we'd arrived. like a third wheel dismissed for being the boring one. But it was exhilarating. I had become so gun-shy of new experiences that I often find it hard to picture them actually going to plan. But this one did, and a new door opened for Amelia the Brave.

About an hour later, JM and Amelia came outside to greet me. My girl was the picture of happiness, spinning and laughing and relaxed in JM's presence. It was early days, and after one session

Getting in touch with her artistic side

impossible to know where things would go from here, but I couldn't have wished for a more positive start.

JM is a warm and intuitive woman. She recognised the depth of Amelia's interior world, just out of reach for now. She also detected the rage in her and perhaps some grief below it.

It wasn't easy for me to hear that, but I get that Amelia has suffered 'losses' in her own way. Every time she tries to make herself known or understood and we let her down by failing to grasp it, she is frustrated. Maybe that feels like grief inside her growing mind and body.

It was clearly a learning curve for JM too, because deafness can put people a bit on edge, as though communication stops or is hampered when verbal language is largely off the table.

But I don't think I need to step in as Amelia's interpreter. This gig is between them and I'm excited to see how they'll work it out. For once I am not required and that is a blessed relief.

The drive home was one of our most relaxed for years. No screaming from the backseat or worrying in the front over bad news just received.

I put the window down to feel the wind and the good vibes and looked forward to next week. Bring on session number two.

One little shell

26 April, 2013

Waiting in the foyer at Amelia's school for her to finish kinder is a warm and frequently special place to be.

Sitting there, in the middle of the hectic end-of-day rush to get home, I watch the kids signing to each other with awe and respect, and I love them.

The other day, a young girl, maybe six or seven years old, nudged my arm to show me a little shell she was holding in her hand. In Auslan (Australian sign language), I asked her, "What's that?"

We mouthed the word "shell" to each other, but she was desperate to show me the sign and I so wanted her to teach me.

But she needed two hands.

After a few seconds fumbling with the shell I extended my hand so she could rest it there.

Her hands now free, she lifted one to the other and rotated her right hand out from the left, like the drawing together of layers into a whole.

Ah, shell. I placed it in my lap and repeated the sign back to her.

No not quite, she wasn't happy with my signing form that time. Maybe a finger or two askew, or a motion not delivered deftly enough.

I tried again and she nodded with approval. Got it.

Then, quick as flash, she reclaimed her shell and skipped away.

And I couldn't stop smiling.

Hand in hand: small steps in speech therapy

10 May, 2013

Amelia started working with a new speech pathologist last week. Our much-loved 'speechie', MA, had to suddenly move out of the city for family reasons, so we've been scrambling to find a suitable replacement.

In general, there are lots of speech pathologists to choose from, but only a handful who have extensive experience with deaf children and, in my view, that special knack of coaxing results out of complex little people.

We chose a trial appointment with PP, a pathologist we had previously met but never worked with closely. She had always shown great affection for Amelia, but I had no idea if they would hit it off.

Over the last six months, Amelia has undergone a myriad of language tests at the Cochlear Implant Clinic (Royal Victorian Eye and Ear Hospital) to see if she would benefit from an implant. These appointments often lasted between one to two hours (with breaks) and the pressure to perform was felt by all.

Sometimes Amelia would happily look at the images put in front of her and respond to questions. Other times, frustrated by her lack of understanding or perhaps just from fatigue, she would run around and around in manic circles. As a defence strategy, it was terribly effective.

Mostly though, and this is Amelia's defining modus operandi, she played the testing 'game' according to her rules. She would dismantle activities and set them up in the corner to play with in her own way. My steps, my way, indeed.

The environment of a language test or assessment – where it's all about specific results on the day – is very different to a therapy session, which is about building understanding in the long-term, one brick at a time.

Not one to hedge my bets, when PP came out to greet us in the foyer of her building, I just knew we were in good hands. Amelia didn't remember her from their previous meetings, but she seemed relaxed and open to being in this strange, new place.

We were led into a medium-sized room with a little table set up in the centre, like so many we had been in before. I am used to Amelia rebelling against co-operation in these settings, but what a casual observer might call 'naughtiness', I have come to understand as a cover for her very real anxiety about what's expected in these endless rooms with small tables.

But not today.

Amelia did a routine check-in with me first, "Mummy stay?", "Yes baby, Mummy's going to stay with you and we're going to have some fun and play some games with PP, okay?" She took a seat and from that point on it was plain sailing with barely a hint of cloud overhead.

PP showed herself to be just the right fit for our family. She has a clear agenda for her sessions, *but* she also responds quickly and intuitively to the personality of the child, their mood on the day, their engagement with other games in the room and their stamina for each activity.

She took Amelia in hand – literally – using tactile therapy, she was constantly taking Amelia's proffered hands into her own, getting in close to teach her what a sound *feels* like (the air-movement created when we pronounce a *p* sound), to gain attention and to build trust.

It was wonderful to watch. If Amelia was desperate to play with Mr and Mrs Potato Head (it's a *Toy Story* thing), then that was no problem. When PP asked if she would look at one more card and name the objects there and was given a resounding "No", she switched promptly to the next thing.

Normally in sessions like this, I am the cajoler, the suggester (maybe we should try that game Amelia has been hungrily eyeing off for the last ten minutes…), and the go-to person if things fall apart.

But here, I only needed to sit and watch, laugh, encourage and learn. There was a lot of high-fiving, touching for support and to regain focus (so important for communication with deaf children), and no rigidity at all.

I marvelled at PP's ability to make swift transitions from one activity to the next with complete flexibility and a lot of well-honed instinct.

Amelia struggles with pronouns, so we did a lot of practice with turn-taking and saying "I want the Potato Head eyes", "I want the mouth", and so on. She really started to get it, and as the session went on, her speech became clearer and more confident.

And she never left her chair.

The whole time, PP was prompting and encouraging, she was writing notes and giving me snippets of feedback. We moved to a computer for one more activity and then, as quickly as it had all started, for Amelia it was time to finish.

When my girl has had enough, it really is ENOUGH. But this time, the meltdown was minor, just a little choppiness with the harbour safely in sight. Amelia sat on the floor and cried quietly for a few seconds and then gathered herself up.

I tentatively offered her my hand (she *hates* offers of help) and her face cleared and opened to me again with a smile. I stared in wonder at this newfound self-possession, a sign of her maturing self.

I loved PP's approach to Amelia. She got away with being bossy, when the rest of us go home in a body bag for saying "wait" or "careful" or (heaven forbid) "not yet" or "NO". At the same time, she was full of praise and warmth for Amelia and that meant a lot.

The beginning of things to come

She found a way to guide, respond and maximise the benefits of the session while making Amelia feel like she was in control.

PP and I agreed that thirty-minute appointments, once a fortnight, would be more than enough for Amelia. There was no need to push too hard when little people are putting in such intensive effort to understand and learn.

That night, while we were cooking dinner, Amelia was very talkative, and unprompted, she began saying in a sing-song voice, "I cook the egg", "I want the jam," "I make the dinner".

It doesn't seem like much, but when your child has had so many barriers to speaking *any* words, even a single 'I' is a thing to cherish.

No doubt there will come a time, as it does for most parents, where it'll be one self-centred 'I' too many, but for now I'm taking it to the bank.

Because it's the smallest things, the tiniest steps that make me so proud and filled with something that feels dangerously like *hope,* and for once it's hard to contain.

Obsess much?
A quirky child's guide
to hoarding

12 May, 2013

Hoards she has known

For Amelia, the hoarding started small. Just a few disparate objects piled on top of her bed, seemingly chosen at random.

Then, the number of objects and their apparent randomness increased while the bed held fast as the breeding ground for greater mountains of 'stuff'.

These Jenga-like structures comprised hard and plush toys, linen, cushions, whatever Amelia felt had that *special* quality, that hoard-worthy 'X factor'. Sometimes these mountains were hidden under blankets, I suppose for safe-keeping. Who the hell knows?

The 'point' of this assemblage of things eluded me, but what was not in doubt was their deep importance to Amelia. She had a clear sense of purpose on hoard-making days, even rolled up her sleeves to better get on with the hard yakka this work entailed.

I did not give this new pastime much thought except to peer into her room from time to time and think, "Hmm...weird." But the eccentricity of growing children takes on many forms and this was no more odd than a couple of other specialties like, say, chewing on a single grape for six hours or pretending to be blind (replete with 'cane') for an afternoon. Quirky is as quirky does.

At this early point, when she was about three, these pop-up installations were fairly temporary. Her attachment to them was shallow and fleeting. When the hoard-police (me) came to dismantle her handy-work, there was no problem and no argument. The piles of stuff had served some inner function, but she did not need to cling onto them then.

I'm not so sure when the hoarding ramped up into something bigger and, to me, more alarming. It was before the clinical suggestion of autism, but those words were already on my mind. Over summer, the stockpiling got bigger and its intensity ratcheted up about a hundred notches.

We visited friends at their holiday house and as usual, there was a backyard gathering centred around outdoor cricket. A handful of kids aged between three and seven fought each other for their turn at the crease, but not Amelia.

She was engrossed in the creation of a makeshift hoard inside a medium-sized, red wheelie bin, the kind used to store (just store) loads of toys. Detached from the activities going on around her, she busied herself with collecting and placing arbitrary objects (not her own) inside the bin.

No amount of persuading could distract her from her core purpose. Other children, attracted by Amelia's activity, tried to get involved but this caused her stress and she screamed at them to go away.

At my dear friend GH's suggestion, the wheelie bin came home with us (she would not have been easily parted from it) and for the next few weeks she was its most loyal sentry. Initially, I did not allow it to come inside, filled as it was with bits of concrete, dirt and lord knew what else.

Then, the hoard-creep continued with the bin appearing one day in her room, squirreled past me like a scene out of *The Hobbit* (in this I'm Gollum, I suppose, and she has most definitely stolen the ring).

Her memory of the artefacts that made up the hoard was nothing less than astonishing.

If I tried to surreptitiously retrieve my husband's wallet, this transgression was noticed immediately after Amelia had run a *Terminator*-like scan over her grouping of 'treasures'. Game over.

Why was I so alarmed? I'm the first to say you should allow children to explore their needs and desires and follow their instincts, as long as they are safe and happy.

But the hoarding had no happy quality to it. For want of a better expression, it looked to me like the play of the damned. Whatever motivated the sudden need to hoard on a grander and more intense scale – control, security, satisfaction – did not serve to connect her to the world above her eye line, least of all to us.

It seemed only to heighten her anxiety and cut her off from people in a new way; this girl we had painstakingly dragged back to us from the silence of deafness, undetected for her first two years of life.

Amelia was like the boy in *The Life of Pi*, stranded on a make-shift raft, barely tethered to the life boat of her family, with offers of shelter and food and comfort refused in favour of self-preservation. I felt vaguely horrified.

She could not be parted from her hoard without an epic tantrum. She wanted to sleep with it, take it into the car with her. If it remained at home, she would simply create new ones wherever she went, like at birthday parties while other children sat in a circle playing pass-the-parcel, Amelia would be in a corner safeguarding the paper. It was all so *obsessive* and *joyless*.

If I broached the subject with people, mostly they would tell me their children did the same thing and not to worry. Really? They won't play with others or engage in any other games or social interactions because they have to guard their 'precious' hoard? I wasn't so sure.

I didn't want to 'break' Amelia of this habit if it meant so much to her. The meaning of it in her life was unclear but I felt if I could help her to rein it in, reduce its importance in relation to other things, then maybe I could help her to re-engage with us, with life beyond the hoard.

The first thing to go was the red wheelie bin of horror. I offered her smaller receptacles (one at a time) for her chosen objects, which she came to accept. I started asking her to collect only a set number of things to put in whatever bag or box she had selected for the day.

Thankfully Amelia enjoyed these limits and it gave her a sense of empowerment to think about what items she would choose to hang onto. Far from rebelling against the new rules of hoarding, she seemed to float back down from some obsessive place that had engaged her so intensely for months on end. It was a new day.

With this approach I was trying to say to Amelia, "Have your hoarding, yes, but calm yourself and talk to me about what you like, involve me in what interests you, give me some clue about who you are." Basically, let me *in*.

The biggest breakthrough came, as it so often does for us, with art and craft. I bought bags and bags of crêpe paper, crayons, paints, brushes, play dough, glue sticks, cardboard: all the fab stuff reserved for kindergarten storerooms. "Great, more hoardable stuff," said my husband. I threw it all on the dining-room table and left it there all day, every day, for weeks.

If Amelia loves art (*Mister Maker* is like the Beatles in our house) and control in equal measure, then for a while I decided to let her have access to her favourite things, all of the time.

Suddenly, we were invited to join her for sessions of 'making'. The simple offer of being drawn into your child's play is not common in our experience, so it's like the Queen has just called you up to her kitchens to bash out a lazy batch of scones. You don't think twice; you just dive into the making.

Back in the game through making

Since then, the hoarding has not returned to its previously worrying levels of practice. It does not have that same compulsive life-or-death focus for Amelia that characterised it for some time. These days it doesn't really seem like hoarding at all.

Like most children, Amelia still likes to carry little cases and stow secret trinkets inside her backpack, but now it's an exercise that doesn't dominate her life or detach her from other activities or experiences.

Because of who she is and her profound need for space and control, Amelia will always seek some alone time where her aims are her own. But now that I know I can pull her back to where we are, waiting for an invitation to play, then a little bit of 'stash-in-the-bag' is okay by me.

My wise little monkey

14 May, 2013

A child who learns to compensate for two years (pre-hearing aids) with a less-than-turbo-charged sense of sound is, in my experience, a clever and often cunning creature. I offer two common examples of said cunning.

The first happened at a children's birthday party. Our best friends had arranged for a jumping castle in the backyard of the family's holiday house and I have never seen a happier bunch of kids playing together.

Amelia was busting out of her skin with delight. Early in the day she came over to me and put something in the pocket of my skirt and ran back to the castle. I absent-mindedly reached down and found her hearing aids tucked safely there.

I thought it was so damn cool the way Amelia did that – she didn't throw them onto the grass or 'lose' them somewhere inside the castle – instead, she removed her aids with care and deliberately placed them in my custody. Amelia is never short on surprises.

For a few hours, she lost *herself* in the abandon of seriously good play. It really was a superb jumping castle, with four walls, little cul-de-sacs and a big slide. Much later we decided to head home so I went over to sign to Amelia in Auslan that it was time to go.

She spotted me trying to catch her eye, so she turned her back. I walked around the castle enclosure to gain a better vantage point, but she dodged me and my signing hands. Then my clever little monkey moved to the far corner of the castle and faced the wall. Amelia did not agree that it *was* time to go.

What a conundrum. Without her aids, she couldn't hear me, and if I couldn't persuade her to look at me, she couldn't (well, wouldn't) read my signs either. Amelia must also have understood that it would take some physical effort on the part of tired adults to climb into the castle to drag her out. If we were engaged in a game of poker, she was holding all of the cards (as well as being a terrible cheat).

Though least favoured, the drag-and-run approach was the only thing that eventually worked. It was all so *knowing* and very, very funny.

On another occasion, Amelia was not so cautious about the location of her hearing aids. It was early evening at home and I suddenly noticed that she wasn't wearing them. It is easy to tell because Amelia stops responding to voices and sort of drifts off into her own world. And she *really* likes it there.

In Auslan, I asked: "Your aids, Amelia, where did you put them?" She 'busied' herself with a book in front of her and did not answer, but I could tell from her facial expression (with its shadow of impudence), and from her body language (shoulders turning away, head tilting down), that it was all a wilful charade.

Again, Amelia refused to look at me squarely, to respond to my oft-repeated question – she knew full well what I wanted, but there was *no way* she was going to help me.

That imperious little monkey cocked her head at me (no eye contact) and flicked a hand over her shoulder, like, "Oh, you know, somewhere over there…" Great.

Luckily her aids hiss like a two-headed banshee when they are left turned on, so I could hear they were secreted somewhere in her room (in her bedside drawer as it turns out).

Amelia skipped off with a beatific smile to busy herself elsewhere. Mini-crisis averted, my husband and I laughed and laughed at her artful, calculating ways, so much a part of her strong personality.

Frustrating, yes, but my god she's entertaining.

A letter from my mother

17 May, 2013

I've been thinking a lot about grief and loss lately, how it takes many different forms and the ways in which it alters a person who has been through a radical, life-changing event. How people cope with these events and work their way through the mire will be a recurring theme in the pages of this book.

Once I sat down and wrote a lengthy piece about the day back in 2011 when Amelia's hearing loss was first discovered, but I decided against publishing it because it was a bit too close to the bone. In that case, the writing of it – the getting-it-off-my-chest bit – was the point, not the need to share it.

The snapshots of that day – the car ride to the final appointment with dread knotted inside my stomach, the grim formality of the hearing test as my baby tried valiantly to please the assembly of adults, uncontrollable tears shed inside hospital corridors – are, I think, sufficient to describe the pain I felt back then.

During the months that followed, it was like I was split into a number of distinct selves, all coexisting inside a grieving whole.

One part – the purely physical – peeled off to meet the demands of the day: getting out of bed, having a shower, feeding my child (maybe even myself), responding to basic questions and just keeping the family engine running. Life doesn't stop just because your heart is broken.

Another part was the intellectual self, which mobilised to attack the diagnosis head on. There was the navigation of medical appointments, reams of paperwork to be interpreted and filled out and masses of reading material on deafness to analyse and dissect. My mind sought to regain control over the grief by mastering information. I devoured it all.

The final part that was left over was submerged somewhere during the day, waiting, while the business of life and the post-diagnostic reality marched on. It was that fragment of me that splintered off in the testing booth and couldn't be fused back on in a matter of days or weeks.

When the day was quiet again, I found a private place to let that shattered-self have her grief in spades.

What I also remember vividly about this time is how much I needed to be with my Mum, to just sit in her familiar house or in her arms and be a child again, free from the worries of adult life.

Inside your own grief, you don't necessarily notice the residual effects on the people closest to you. Grief is naturally selfish and mercenary like that.

Of course my Mum was suffering but what I didn't realise is that she had written her pain down in a letter to herself, the night we all stepped off the edge into Grief Town.

In the letter, she retraced her steps to the start of the day before she heard the news from me (yelled down the phone from my car). Then she wrote about the moment when I told her that Amelia was deaf, about *her feelings, her sorrow*, as she stood in a car park trying to work out how to reach me fast.

The specific contents of the letter must remain between us, but it charts my mum's own sense of loss (what the news meant for Amelia's life) and all the signs she now recognised (things about Amelia's behaviour that suddenly made sense).

She wrote 'wrong' and 'sorry' many, many times. But it ended in hope, with the conviction that our dreams for Amelia would return.

I didn't know about her letter until she mentioned it to me a little while later. Naturally I asked her if I could read it. Instead, Mum handed it to me saying it was now mine to keep, to be read in my own time.

That night, after the daily routine was over, I sat down by myself and unfolded the letter. It moved me so much to read the pain-filled words of my beautiful mother, rent across those pages in a frantic staccato that resonated so deeply.

She was trying (as I am here) to capture something difficult to nail down, to make sense of what we'd been told, to unburden herself and work it through. She did not know it then, but her words, as much as her arms around me, were the greatest gift to the part of me that was heartbroken.

Because my mum *got it*, she *understood* the meaning and the cost of what had happened to our family. I didn't have to explain my darkest, saddest thoughts because they were mirrored on the pages in front of me. They were shared.

The isolation of grief is founded on the distance between your own feeling of sorrow and others who can't relate to its depth or impact. It's not that people don't try or want to connect with you. It's just that the 'thing' is happening to you in its own, individual way and so you are essentially alone.

You can be in the same house of pain as ten other people but eventually you have to return to your own room.

My mum didn't know that when she captured her own grief, committed it to paper and delivered it into my hands that I would feel a little less isolated than I did before.

It's that same feeling I get when I communicate with other parents in similar situations to ours. There is an innate, shared understanding and in that I find great solace. I hope that anyone who has experienced grief for whatever reason finds others along the way to join hands with in solidarity.

So by way of return post, this is my response to that special letter from my mother. She didn't write it to me or for me in the beginning but it is mine all the same.

I want to tell her that I carry it with me every day, and sometimes I take it out and hold it in my hand without reading it, because just knowing that it's there, that SHE is with me, made a difference to me when I needed it the most.

Who's afraid of Amelia Woolf?

23 May, 2013

If you are lucky enough to climb down the rabbit hole of parenting, you discover the existence of a world with no end – it is the realm of child-related socialising and fraternising previously hidden from view.

And like Alice, you will feel small and big (or just right) inside this world, depending on how its axial tilt favours you and the temperament of your family.

So far on our adventure, my husband and I have discovered we share a general anxiety about social gatherings or public outings where children are 'required' to do things like sit down, be quiet, or engage on some level with any kind of activity.

Our anxiety isn't an overreaction. It's a learned response to years of incidents that have taught us to be on guard. It's an unease we've been conditioned to experience and it's now embedded in our parenting DNA.

We've spent too many parties, excursions and concerts and the like standing outside rather than in, because we can't find a way to explain to Amelia what kind of behaviour is expected of her.

The 'red mist' can be quick to descend when she is told that a) she can't take that man's guitar while he's playing it and singing, or b) purloin cake from a stranger's birthday party at the park, or c) scream and cry and hit when all these things come together and the result is "it's time to get the hell out of here." A free-wheeling, party-going, take-it-as-it-comes family we are not.

Maybe we're overly sensitive, but sometimes there's no certainty we'll make it from the car park to the shops without having to stage an emotional intervention, so forgive us our premonitions of disaster. They so often come true.

Sometimes it's hard to have a sense of humour about Amelia's (and our own) public meltdowns. Sure, no- one likes to be looked at but there are plenty of people who do stare in judgement and provide not-so-helpful commentary as you drag your flailing child across grass, carpet and assorted other surfaces.

Then again it's not always like that, and even in fraught moments there are opportunities to relax and see the funny side of our child's uncompromising ways.

Here's a case in point. Last year, we went to the annual Family Day held at the Aurora School. These were intense and wonderful days for us, where we were welcomed into the community of families like ours and told powerful stories of hope and success by deaf adolescents and adults.

Arriving amidst the hectic hubbub of registrations, we had to kill about forty-five minutes before the day opened with an Auslan performance of 'Little Red Riding Hood' by Aurora's deaf staff.

That significant timeframe of just under an hour is often all the time we have before Amelia grows tired, manic, or just plain difficult to manage.

We approached the morning with smiles of optimism, but I could see it in my husband's eyes as I'm sure he could in mine. Secretly we were already strapped in for the potential turbulence ahead.

Inside the large hall of the school, the attendees numbered at least eighty, with half of these children from newborns to toddlers and so on.

Amelia was behaving in a reasonably compliant fashion when finally we were asked to take a seat and prepare for the performance. I looked around and saw every man, woman, and child dutifully take a seat on the floor and face the stage.

With the exaggeration caused by the passing of time, I recall the scene this way – where a HUGE crowd of all ages suddenly stops mid-sentence with military precision, mocking us with their social pliability and mutual respect for amateur theatre.

Like the starter's gun had been fired, Amelia took that moment of collective obedience as her cue to jump up and start running around.

We tried in vain to explain, in sign and in speech (in anything really) that there was a fun show about to start and that she would love it, so *please, please* sit down. But she was 'gone', in body and in spirit and we couldn't get her to look at us or notice the performance commencing right in front of her.

The next ten minutes followed a very familiar pattern for us. While *Little Red Riding Hood*'s well-worn adventures were played out inventively on one stage, we performed our own pageant of harried parenting, trying desperately to 'deal with' Amelia.

We took turns taking her out into corridors, trying to calm her down and reason with her to come back and watch the show.

These interventions were clearly distressing for Amelia and that made it even harder. It was a chilly winter's day but we were both sweating bullets from the stress.

At some point she seemed to understand and to acquiesce, so we led her quietly back into the hall and found a little carpet space to sit down. It lasted all of thirty seconds.

Amelia sprang up again and with her back turned slightly away from the stage, walked through part of the set and onto the temporary 'road' set up for the fabled Wolf's travels with young Ms Hood.

I looked over at one of the deaf staff seated near me and signed 'sorry' but she smiled reassuringly and signed back that it was 'okay'. I believed her.

The theatre world's newest creative voice

At last, my oblivious child turned around and grasped that she had stepped into a new layer of reality, like Tom when he breaks the 'fourth wall' in *The Purple Rose of Cairo*.

I'll never forget the look of recognition and shock on her face when she realised there was something heavy going on between Grandma (on the floor tied in ropes) and the Wolf character (shady as this day was long).

What was most amusing was that Amelia didn't know that it *was* an act. She seemed to think the story was real and she had better do something quickly to shut this fairy tale crime scene down.

There was no need for Method acting here – Amelia's reactions and emotions were absolutely genuine and hilariously funny. Someone had to save poor old Grandma and who better than a feisty three-year-old with no regard for the rules?

Amelia started signing urgently to Grandma to 'wait' and that she would be 'okay'. For the Wolf she reserved her sternest face and her most passionate telling off in Auslan and in shouted speech. He was a "naughty Wolf", a "bad Wolf" and he had to "STOP!" The deaf performers were absolute pros and played along with this unexpected narrative hook-turn.

In true pantomime style, the audience erupted into generous laughter at this spontaneous part of the show. It was a great sound, filled with kindness, and it took a while to reach me through my clenched fists and hunched shoulders.

It made me let go of my tightly-coiled state of anxiety and not mind for once that we were centre stage. I nearly missed out on the chance to see Amelia through compassionate eyes, as a funny, quirky, expressive little person, brave enough to take on the Wolf single-handed.

This is one of my favourite stories about my daughter because it has all the colours of her atypical rainbow: her resistance to parental challenge; her intolerance of social conventions she struggles to interpret; her inflexible but undoubtedly free spirit and, most of all, her deeply-felt empathy for people in need.

While we are busy worrying about what people think of *us*, she is off living life according to *her* rules and I have a lot of admiration for that.

Hopefully we will get better at seeing the humour in the moment and finding some kind of middle ground amidst all this intractability; between the rigidity of our rules and her limitless defiance of them.

My beautiful Little Red

Amelia's Expressive Therapist, JM, explained it best when she told me that she is trying to help Amelia to be more *forgiving* when people fail to understand her and what she needs, and to be more *flexible* when the world asks things of her that she would rather not do.

In this, JM has come closest to defining the challenges Amelia faces more accurately than any diagnosis of deafness or autism ever could.

She also struck on something for me and my husband to ponder as we blunder our way through the parenting maze.

Because we need to learn how to be more forgiving when Amelia does not behave the way we would like, in public or in private. We won't always have an understanding audience to remind us to laugh when we want to run and hide.

If Amelia needs to learn to be more flexible, then so do we because we can bend more readily than the rest of the world will when she has to face it by herself.

I don't think it's such a big ask to meet her halfway.

Perhaps in a moment of compromise – of forgiveness and flexibility – we might arrive at the same destination from separate points of departure and find that it was the journey itself that made it all worthwhile.

You (quite literally) can't touch this

26 May, 2013

You can look, but you can't touch

S oon after Amelia was born I could sense my baby didn't like to be cuddled or held too close. She was content to be carried from point A to B, held for feeds or to perch on my knee. But if I overstepped some invisible marker known only to her, she would retreat from my overbearing hands.

There was a veil between us, barely perceptible and made of obscure materials, but I felt its presence keenly. I was so desperate to nuzzle, encircle and possess her – to bond – but she resisted my approaches decisively. It was hard to shake the cruel feeling of my own child's *rejection*.

Then we learned that Amelia had been born with a significant hearing loss and I thought "Aha! *that* is why my darling child and I have not bonded fully, because without sound, without her hearing my voice and recognising in it the tone of tenderness, comfort and affection, she has kept me at arm's length. I understand now."

I came to learn that touch is essential to communicating with the deaf – from the day we were told about Amelia's hearing loss, I never stopped putting my hands on her, reassuring her of my presence, alerting her to my responses and guiding her eyes to my face, my mouth, my expression.

This type of touch was no less intimate but it was coded with a greater function than mere affection. I could reach out to my daughter with this new physical 'language' and so our bonding started anew.

And yes, through sound, through crazy operatic songs belted out in the kitchen, and laughter in Amelia's hair with my head bent there, we became mother and daughter properly and fully.

But though the veil had slipped, it did not disappear.

Even now, in the warmth of a shared bed if my hand strays to her leg or her belly, she will remove it in a prompt rebuttal of unwelcome contact ("Don't touch it!"). If she is ill or falls over, bangs her head even, I am not allowed to react or offer to ease her pain. She would rather bleed than let me mother her like *that*.

But over the years we have worked hard to show Amelia what affection looks and feels like. We have never stopped modelling it and offering it, no matter how often it is refused in anger or with indifference.

Hugs are on permanent parade as are kisses, snatched from her during unguarded moments. It's intimacy by stealth, by degrees.

Lately we have discovered that our girl does not dislike being touched as much as we had thought, but the idea has to germinate in her brain and heart first. It's her dance card and she's not giving waltzes away for free. She's worked her way up to it from some shy corner, emboldened by good feelings and ever-warm responses.

In quiet moments, when she thinks we're half asleep, she might reach up to softly stroke a cheek or press a tentative kiss on our lips. We hold our breath lest we scare the horses with our need, our hearts racing inside us with fierce longing.

Two years ago, Amelia seemed not to notice that her dad had gone away for over a week. There was no childish fanfare to greet his return; there was not much reaction at all. Now, when I hear him coming through the front gate I sign to her "Daddy's home!" and she tumbles out the door in her haste to greet him and throw herself into his outstretched arms.

Most nights she will pull me close to her at bedtime in a long, passionate embrace (I never break first). We are firm couch companions, sitting shoulder-to-shoulder, with her legs slung casually over mine. I rest my hands on her jiggling feet and she does not pull away. This contact, its nature and duration, remains at her bidding, but I feel such joy whenever it occurs.

Amelia doesn't know that to us it's like electricity, like magical lightning strikes on our skin, to feel her touch offered without restraint. That we turn our cheeks away from her eagle eyes so she won't see the tears so often spilled there, because with each contact – no matter how small or incidental – we receive a strong signal of love.

First name Amelia

Surveying the road ahead

In the months following Amelia's diagnosis of hearing loss, I picked up a strange habit when introducing her to people we met in our daily travels. Like an involuntary verbal tick, I would call her 'deaf' before I said her name or anything else about her.

This new tendency was the result of many obsessive days spent reading about what the diagnosis meant. Suddenly a host of alien words had intruded on our lives and I drove myself mad trying to work them out.

At first I wasn't sure what term to use to describe the diagnosis itself. There was the medical vocabulary: it was a sensorineural, (most likely) congenital, bilateral, moderate-severe/profound hearing loss. To the lay-person, this roughly equates to 'nerve deafness' in both ears from birth.

These definitions were cloaked in the mystery of a clinical world we had arrived in but did not yet understand. They were cold and impersonal but I found I could practice saying them, turn them over in my mind and get used to their presence.

The words I was really scared to speak out loud were the more commonly used descriptions like 'hearing impaired', 'hard of hearing', 'deaf' (people who have a physical condition of hearing loss) and 'Deaf' (people who use Auslan; identify as members of the signing Deaf community).

Or *disability* – that one was like acid on my tongue.

I tried them all on for size, testing the degree of pain they elicited in me. It only took one syllable to break me back then.

My fixation on nomenclature was really just my way to grapple with what was happening to us. Our situation felt more real (and not like some nightmare starring Max Schreck) if I could give it a name.

I settled on 'deaf' because 'hearing impaired' is regarded negatively by members of the Deaf community who prefer the terms 'Deaf' and 'hard of hearing' (and I am *such* a stickler for the rules).

'Hard of hearing' just brought forth the image of an old man straining to hear through an ancient ear trumpet. We did not yet use Auslan and had no ancestral or existing links to the Deaf community.

So in the end it was deaf with a little 'd' that felt about right to me.

Amelia had just turned two, so no-one asked her what she thought about this. She couldn't have told us anyway because the terms that so consumed me were simply lost on her.

I am a little ashamed to admit that once I decided I was okay to call Amelia deaf to myself, I just couldn't stop flinging the word at complete strangers, usually without necessity or context.

I was probably a little deranged by grief, but I gave little to no thought or consideration for my girl – the deaf one – and how it shaped her identity.

One day we walked into the chemist and the saleswoman leaned over the counter to look at Amelia tucked in her pram.

"Oh, she's so sweet! Hello little girl, what's your name?"

Like a Venus fly trap, I snapped her question in half with, "She can't hear you, because she's *deaf*…"

I said it callously, as though she should have known it just by looking at Amelia. It made the woman flustered and uncomfortable and on some sick level I was glad.

It was a perverse thing to do but I repeated this routine often with people who were new to us. It was my conversational trump card. I used it to provoke sympathy, to disconcert people, or to neutralise their judgement (she's not naughty, she's just *deaf*). One more time for the cheap seats.

What I think I was trying to do in my desperation was prove that I was not ashamed of Amelia's deafness. I pushed it into people's faces so they would have to deal with the fact we could not escape ourselves. I might as well have propped a sign on her pram saying 'deaf child on board'.

For a time, I simply forgot to encourage people to see Amelia beyond the feature that was actually invisible to them – her deafness. Inadvertently, I boxed her up and labelled her because I was the one who couldn't see past it.

Thankfully it was just a phase I was going through to deal with the shock and the grief, and it didn't last. I explained my behaviour to Amelia's Deaf Educator, AH, and she seemed to understand what was happening and why.

She gently told me not to worry about other people and to think of Amelia and her needs first, before the deafness, before anything. That was all that mattered, not words.

The fact is I *was* (and am) extremely proud of Amelia's deafness. It's anomalous that the thing that almost destroyed me was the same thing that made her more special in my eyes. But I realise I did a huge disservice to her to have made 'deaf' the opening number, before people had a chance to hear other songs in Amelia's repertoire.

There are many ways to honour that unique part of who she is, through learning Auslan and establishing relationships with deaf adults and children, without consigning her to an all-encompassing label.

In some situations, it is absolutely necessary to let people know that Amelia is deaf to maximise her social interactions (background noise is too loud, don't stand behind her and speak).

If someone asks about her hearing aids or her sign language then I am happy to go there, but there's no reason to keep assailing people with her deafness on a regular basis.

While I have made a decision to use one word among many to describe Amelia's hearing loss, this may not be her preference later on. In my experience, not all young people with a hearing loss identify as 'deaf' or even 'hearing impaired'; it's a complex choice based on many factors I'm only just beginning to comprehend.

One day, Amelia might tell me that she has a different way of explaining her deafness (and herself).

I have no idea what that discussion will be like, but I want to be sure to tell her that I now see her deafness as only *one* important part of who she is: my girl who is blonde, powerfully strong, mischievous, and loves to dance even when she can't hear any music.

When she is old enough, I also want her to watch a brilliant video posted on YouTube by Bethany, a teenage girl with a cochlear implant called 'MUSINGS ABOUT BEING WHO I AM – Deaf or Not.' It says so much about the limiting effects of labels we don't choose for ourselves, the genuine pride that leads parents to insist on them and the need to take ownership of how we present ourselves as individuals to the world.

Bethany says: "So this is me. I am deaf. So guess what? I can still do anything. So why should it change your opinion of me?"

Why indeed.

Of rocks and hard places

3 June, 2013

Iam reading Andrew Solomon's brilliant *Far From the Tree: Parents, children and the search for identity* at the moment. It's about how families cope with having a child with a disability (mental, physical, social) and the loaded choices that sometimes result in crises of identity and domestic turbulence.

Naturally I jumped ahead to his chapter on deafness and it was, in many ways, a tough read. The stories of the families, particularly the personal accounts of the deaf children now grown up, are inspiring but often heart-breaking.

The stories describe so well the cost of the long-term battle waged around the two prevailing deaf education philosophies – 'oralism' (an emphasis on spoken language) and 'manualism' (sign language), and historical attitudes to deafness that have ranged from pride to shame.

Many of the deaf adults interviewed about growing up in this context had suffered exclusion, isolation, depression, and real deprivation.

The book reaches back into the early-mid part of last century to today, proof that the tension between advocates of both approaches still exists, even if the rights of deaf people to use sign language and access deaf education in this 'manual' mode have significantly improved.

Solomon also tracks the splintering effect of identity that occurs with the majority of deaf children being born to hearing adults.

Something like ninety per cent of deaf and hard-of-hearing children are born into families with little to no experience of deafness.

What do these unsuspecting souls know of Deaf culture? Of sign language? Of the complex mores and communication methods specific to a community they have had no exposure to, either socially or in the media? Virtually nothing.

It's almost like some invisible hand decided to take all of the children born with a shared identity and scatter them far and wide, too far for that community to properly reach them and form cohesive bonds.

At the family level, it's about something far more personal than that, as parents try to work their way back from the shock of the unknown to some kind of understanding. They have to make hard decisions in the dark and live with them. There's no right or wrong here.

There are, of course, many echoes of our personal story. We have no history of deafness in our family and yet we have a deaf child. We've been told there's probably some genetic cause but it's very difficult to know for sure. The 'why' of it is mostly a pointless exploration and offers no comfort.

Amelia can find out, when she is ready to start her own family, if she herself is carrying a recessive gene she could pass onto her children. Already her little hands are laden with heavy baggage.

We were also faced with a choice, not of labels, but between diametrically opposed types of early intervention for deaf children, namely the oral language approach or a bilingual or bimodal philosophy which offers exposure to sign language, speech therapy and an introduction to deaf culture and communication. In essence, speech only, or sign and speech together.

No one held our hand through this philosophical maze, we just had to wing it and hope for the best. My family took the bilingual road, which is neither high nor easy, but let me explain what led us there.

When I found out Amelia was deaf, I had this odd feeling that part of her no longer belonged to me, but to something bigger, a hidden tradition I knew nothing about.

I also felt, almost instantly, that we needed to give her every possible avenue of communication available to her. She had lost more than two years of language, a time during which other children would have absorbed words and learned to process them. Instead, my girl had been stuck in a bubble, hearing sounds (at best) as though underwater.

Sign, speech, gesture, touch – whatever – I wanted her to have it all.

I refused to accept that sign language would hold her back in some way. This instinctive choice came up trumps because Amelia took to Auslan immediately (she's not short of expressive gestures) and was suddenly able to translate her thoughts and feelings into something meaningful. And she could *learn*.

Speech, language and listening skills take much longer to develop and we just didn't have any more time to waste. Developmental windows were closing, so we jumped on through with two languages to give Amelia the boost she so desperately needed.

I also wanted Amelia to be a part of that 'bigger something', that other family I suspected had at least a partial claim to her. If we were to embrace her difference I thought we could also open a door to a place where she was the same, just one of many in a crowd.

My thoughts about Amelia's so-called 'otherness' were brought home to me in a bittersweet moment when my mum and I took her to her first Early Learning Group run by our early intervention service.

It was terrifying, really. We entered a room where everyone seemed to know some sign language and there was a Deaf Educator, JC, co-running the sessions. How would we talk to her? My mum and I were like rabbits caught in blinding headlights but we pushed through our sizeable fear. For Amelia.

JC was quite aware of (and probably used to) our discomfort, so she didn't approach us directly at first. Instead, she strode confidently towards Amelia, then only two years and a few months old. Amelia was not a trusting child then and we had never been to this place before so I did not expect her to be relaxed about this approach.

I was so wrong. JC tapped Amelia softly on her arm to get her attention and signed at her to follow. Amelia held her gaze, watched her hands avidly and then followed her like she was caught in a tractor beam. I watched this from the safety of a corner and felt a curious mix of emotions wash over me.

It's hard to explain, but I felt tears well up in my eyes at the pain of seeing Amelia bond so quickly with this stranger, the first deaf person she had ever met, and with thankfulness and relief that she had been so welcomed by one of 'her people'.

However strange or overstated that sounds, I have witnessed the positive evidence of Amelia belonging to a culture other than her own family's many times over.

JC became Amelia's kinder teacher last year and they were soon inseparable, often found working together on some secret craft project or sharing a story in Auslan.

Amelia showed a clear preference for her non-verbal communication with JC. She spent very little time with the hearing teacher or even with the other children. Amelia learned a lot from JC, about how to express (and explain) herself through sign and how to touch another deaf person to get their attention.

I see the same easy bond when Amelia watches adults signing in the Cochlear Implant Clinic waiting room – there's a spark of recognition as she watches their hands moving through the air in rapid-fire conversation. She smiles as though reassured by their presence.

When she walks into her deaf kinder class I can tell she is truly at home. Because in that room, all of the children are deaf and she is not the only one who signs. Amelia likes her mainstream kinder okay, but after a term the votes are in and she never stops asking me when she's going back to 'lunch kinder' (so named because we make her lunch together and pack it in her bag).

At pick-up time, Amelia does her routine farewell to the teachers in sign and comes home to me, full of confidence and something not far from elation. Because she belongs.

It's a great feeling to see your child settling in so well at a new kinder or into a way of being that feels right to her. But I do still feel a little wistful that she is experiencing that powerful sense of fitting in with people other than us.

Amelia watches JC with rapt attention

On this clash between Deaf identity and family, Andrew Solomon quotes one of his deaf interviewees (Cheryl Heppner), saying: "Deaf people feel ownership of deaf children... I really struggle in not wanting to interfere with a parent's right to parent, at the same time knowing that they have to accept that the child can never be one hundred percent theirs." [1]

I think I have accepted this idea, at least in theory, but surrendering any part of my child's life will never be easy, no matter what the future holds. Every parent understands that.

But I hope that our choice of a bilingual education might allow us to move between both worlds, rather than having to give Amelia away to one, or hold her in another.

We chose Auslan so that Amelia could tell us straight away what she needed and also to give her a passport into the Deaf community if she decides to visit later. Her enculturation into this world is well on its way.

---

1 Solomon, Andrew, *Far From the Tree: Parents, children and the search for identity* (electronic edition), Chatto & Windus, 2013, pp. 141-2.

For us, that choice sits in harmony alongside our hopes that she will learn to speak fluently too, and be able to participate in the hearing world as far as she wants to.

If ever I worry about the decisions we have made on Amelia's behalf, I remember the teenager I once spoke to about her story, which included profound deafness, cochlear implants and an intensive oral language education – she was the quintessential poster girl for oralism.

She blanched at my question about whether she identified as 'deaf' and was justly proud of her ability to speak and excel in the hearing world. When I said to her that Amelia was learning to sign – something she herself was just starting to try – she said, "Oh yes, give her sign, give her everything."

As a parent, that's really all I'm trying to do – give her everything to help her now and prepare her for later.

"Because deaf children have a right to all worlds, not just deaf, not just hearing." [2]

2   Madden, Maree, "Early exposure to sign language: an advantage to parents and children", Aussie Deaf Kids, accessed 23 November 2016, <www.aussiedeafkids.org.au/early-exposure-to-sign-language.html>

Going the distance

7 June, 2013

Parenting sometimes feels to me like an extended relay race with multiple batons – let's call them challenges, diagnoses, worries, crises, whatever fits. You think you can hand one off as you grab for the next one but it just doesn't work like that.

No, you end up carrying them all in a messy jumble and hope like hell they don't come crashing to the floor.

Over the last four years, every time my husband and I have thought we could genuinely release one of our worries, we have gained a new one. The load lightens for a minute and then our hands are full again. We never know what hurdle is waiting for us around the next corner.

I am a keen recreational runner in my spare time, but this parenting race I'm running feels like a gruelling marathon I've barely trained for. There's only so many times you can 'hit the wall' before you feel like stopping.

It's not always lonely – there are other people on the same track – but ultimately it's your legs and willpower that must carry you over the line (if you can find it). Sharing your burdens might halve them, but you still feel their weight on your back, in your chest and on your mind.

To re-cap, our experience as Amelia's parents has so far included a minor kidney defect identified in-utero, developmental delays (gross motor, speech and language), deafness, and the newly identified autism.

And I used to think running up Anderson Street next to Melbourne's Royal Botanic Gardens was hard.

From birth to her second birthday, doctors and nurses planted seeds of worry in my mind about Amelia's achingly slow progress to crawl (thirteen months) and then walk (twenty-one months). Though more than fashionably late, she found her feet eventually and I let out a long, slow breath of relief. I remember the thought, 'Now they'll leave us alone to get on with living.'

When Amelia was two, we went to see her paediatrician for a final kidney check-up. I distinctly recall how great it felt when he gave her the all-clear – her kidneys had grown to their proper size and the minor defect had corrected itself naturally.

So, no more ultrasounds or trying (and failing) to get urine samples when she had a high temperature. Consider that baton passed.

In the same appointment, the paediatrician asked Amelia to come over and talk to him at his desk. He was holding a rabbit toy and he wanted her to tell him where the eyes, ears and mouth were.

At first she was happy to stand and look at the rabbit but she became confused by his questions and quickly ran away to the safety of the play corner.

That's when he said to us, "Well, I don't think she's autistic, but there is something wrong with her."

At the time, the suggestion of autism seemed absurd; this was a happy, engaged child who made eye contact and seemed to have great empathy for others. It was a part of our child's future we were not at all ready to face.

But despite his sledgehammer approach, I knew the paediatrician was right. There was something wrong – Amelia was two and she could hardly speak – but I had no earthly idea what it might be.

I feared yet another developmental delay but he referred us to a speech pathologist and flagged the need to test her hearing (routine for speech and language assessments).

We'd handed off one baton and gained another, all in the space of five minutes. I think we deserved a rest stop or at least a drinks break or something.

After talking to a GP, I was convinced Amelia had too much fluid in her ears from infections and would only need grommet surgery to free up her middle ear and allow the clear passage of sound.

This type of temporary hearing loss (conductive) can be as catastrophic for speech and language acquisition in infants as the more permanent kind. I grasped onto the idea a little too tightly and put all my hopes in it.

I thought we would go to the hospital and our problems would all be sorted out in a matter of months. Then, my family would be back on track.

Sadly, this was not what was proven by the Ear, Nose and Throat Surgeon or the audiologists who tested Amelia. She had no fluid. Her hearing loss was discovered to be permanent and irreversible.

I've covered in detail how this diagnosis affected us and the decisions we made as a result of it. It's just the hand she was dealt. We can help Amelia to carry this baton for as long as she needs, but in the end it's her race to run.

But sometimes batons aren't thrust upon you when are looking the other way. There are occasions when you run after them, chasing down the truth with hands outstretched.

For about a year I have been the one pushing us headlong towards the unveiling of another challenge – one more problem below the surface as yet unnamed.

In this, I've been like Chief Brody in *Jaws*: I knew there was something else in the water even if sceptical mayor-types kept telling me the beaches were safe. No really, send the children in with the shark because everything's fine.

I had watched Amelia for a long time and I knew that deafness, even with her lack of speech, was not the reason behind her rage, social isolation, meltdowns, obsessiveness and curious anxieties.

We needed urgent help if we were going to get through the next stage of the race without the wear-and-tear of life's pressures taking its toll.

It took us more than six months to get in to see the only paediatrician I thought might have the answers. She has vast professional experience working with both deaf and autistic children, so she seemed uniquely placed to guide us.

Her expertise and popularity made her nearly impossible to see, but our early intervention service wrote a letter on our behalf and we were fast-tracked to the top of the waiting-list for exceptional cases.

It was a killer letter but the picture it painted of Amelia's struggles (and ours) was not easy to read, even if it was true.

I sat in the paediatrician's office the first day and said, "Are we right to be here, do we need your help?"

I asked this because I still have this peculiar feeling – maybe it's just plain old hope – that one day a doctor will look at me and say, "What are you doing here? Your child is fine." It's hard to explain how I can still think this way after the catalogue of trials we have faced, but I do.

Our new specialist just smiled at my question and said, "Oh yes, absolutely."

We handed her our concerns and she took them from us and turned them into something useful, a diagnosis we can work with. The race isn't over but at least now we know which way to go. Even if it's towards more appointments and steep learning curves, we are closer to understanding Amelia now than ever before.

So we keep on running, from checkpoint to checkpoint, trying to refuel when we can and stay fit for the long haul. It's not about the fastest time per kilometre, and it's never been about winning. It's about stamina. And getting up to a decent pace each time you are passed another baton and making it. Just making it.

Parent or advocate?

You are the best advocate for your child.

You are the expert on your child.

14 June, 2013

If I've heard these weighted expressions once, I've heard them a thousand times over the last two years. Sometimes they are like straitjackets, pinning my arms to my sides, suffocating me. No matter how hard I struggle against the bonds, they will not break.

When I am not so angry and more accepting of my job as an externally appointed parent-advocate-expert (a triple threat, if you will), I find I can walk the line and just cop to the fact that I have to keep my eyes peeled and my sleeves rolled up. You know, all the time.

Because there's no choice between one role and the other – not at my end of the parenting game. I can't just say "yeah, you know, today I don't feel like being an advocate for you Amelia, I kind of just want to run away to the movies and hide."

My responsibilities would find me there anyway, up to my shiny eyeballs in popcorn and lust for Mads Mikkelsen.

Generous people tell me I'm doing an amazing job at it, because I'm tough, because I have fought so hard for my daughter and, I guess, because I'm still standing. This is reassuring to hear because I don't really know what the hell I'm doing most of the time.

But in all honesty, I didn't want to have to be a pugilistic parent/advocate. Not at all. It doesn't really come naturally to me, this so-called toughness. I just wanted to be a simple parent, an ordinary mother.

When I was going through IVF treatment, I didn't dream of much more than the birth of a healthy child. My hopeful mind dared to stray to thoughts of long, slow walks with the child of my future – I would hold her little hand and whisper secrets about the world into her ear.

Now I want to laugh in the face of that woman who thought the realisation of that dream was the one battle she had left to fight. That poor woman who was so deluded she put her boxing gloves away and let her guard down. I do not recognise her in myself anymore.

But resistance is futile when you become the mother of a child who needs so much more than nappies and lunches and lullabies. If you don't take on the mantle of advocate and close the gap between your child's challenges and other people's understanding of them, then they will fall into a crevasse the size of Western Australia.

So get over yourself and get on with it. That's my personal mantra. It's not very poetic as mantras go, but it'll do for what I have to get done.

If you are wondering how advocacy works in my situation, as the mother of a deaf child with additional needs, well here's a list of some of the essential gap-closing things I tell people who interact with Amelia:

1. Amelia has a moderate-severe/profound hearing loss, which means that without aids she can only hear fragments of words or really loud noises like a vacuum cleaner, a motorbike or a stereo cranked up to eleven. Australian Hearing has a handout that perfectly illustrates this information (I gave this document to lots of people in the early days and still carry a worn copy in my bag);

2. With hearing aids, in a quiet room, when you are close by, facing her and have her full attention, Amelia can understand you very well;

3. If you want to get Amelia's attention, you can touch her on the shoulder, tap the table in front of her or stamp your foot nearby (I also have fact sheets about how to communicate non-verbally with a deaf child that I have distributed when necessary);

4. Please make sure Amelia can see your face when you are trying to talk to her because she relies on the cues she reads in your expression and lips to follow what you are saying. Kneel down at her eye level and make sure you don't cover your mouth;

5. If Amelia is not wearing her aids and you are talking to her back or from across the room, SHE CANNOT HEAR YOU;

6. Well-lit rooms are the best for maximising how much of your facial expression and lip movement Amelia can see when you are speaking to her;

7. Background noise, like booming televisions or loud music will radically reduce how much Amelia can hear (her hearing aids are powerful but with competing sounds, they will not be able to pick out and make sense of softer conversational tones from the wall of noise). That kind of noisy room is an acoustic mess for Amelia, so please turn the sound down or off;

8. Amelia is a visual thinker and learner, so even if you don't know any sign language, lots of gestures to communicate with her are welcome;

9. Amelia's hearing loss was diagnosed very late, so her speech and language is delayed. But she can understand a lot of what you are saying, so please don't stop talking to Amelia just because she can't necessarily answer your questions or speak like other children her age;

10. Amelia is highly fearful of certain situations, such as doctor's examinations or tests, so please be understanding if her behaviour seems manic and a bit naughty – it is only because she is afraid and stressed.

I figure if you know these things about what it's like to be Amelia and cope with a significant hearing loss in environments that are often set up to think of her needs *last*, then maybe she'll have a fighting chance to access the world on a more level playing field.

But you have to meet her where she is, not the other way around.

You can never assume that people will know anything about deafness, its complexity and how it affects an individual child, either through experience or instinct. Even if you meet someone who knows a little bit about some of the issues involved, they won't have any idea what they mean in Amelia's case.

That's precisely why it's my job to pave the way and educate. I've had to learn so much myself, about audiograms, hearing loss, hearing aids, sign language, and cochlear implants, not to mention how my daughter's life is impacted by her challenges and what strategies might serve to help her.

In certain situations or with particular people I find I have to repeat myself many times. I'm sure that can be annoying, but I can't afford to care.

Other times I grow weary and give up after restating the same message in different ways (gently, incidentally, directly) when it just isn't being heard and taken on board.

In those moments I feel like I am failing Amelia by not pushing past my own emotions and hammering home these messages more forcefully.

I'm no expert on Amelia – she defies being pinned down or defined – but I know that when we go to have her hearing tested every eight weeks, she will only tolerate soft headphones (not the tube phones inserted into her moulds or the bone conduction ones with their hard edges) and we have to warm up with the marble game first (try it, it's tremendous fun).

If someone forgets these little details, I'm there to remind them and I always ask to wear my own pair of headphones because I know this makes Amelia feel like we're in it together. And we are.

We used to have inexperienced graduates assisting our main audiologist with the testing. By the time they had worked out the equipment and how to set up the games, Amelia was half-way out the door.

After a few conversations with the clinic, we now have two senior audiologists with us every time a test is conducted. It's harder to find a time-slot, but getting regular and accurate hearing test results is too important to settle for anything less than the best.

Amelia and me, we're in this together

At the moment, Amelia attends both a mainstream kindergarten (one day per week) and a deaf kindergarten (two days). At the latter, I can for the most part take my advocate's hat off, because her teachers understand deafness (or are deaf) and so I don't have to explain anything about the big ticket items on our list.

I know some things get missed at her other kinder, based at a local childcare centre, like hearing aids not turned back on after a nap, music played too loud or conversations held around Amelia rather than with her. But by and large the people there have been amazingly inclusive of my girl and her needs.

More than one child-care worker over the last two years has paid their own way through Auslan courses and worked with our Early Intervention service so that Amelia can make the most out of her time with them. The staff took the education process to another level on their own initiative and I truly love them for that.

It is also a nice surprise when I come into contact with a person or organisation, equipped with my advocate's bag of explanations, and find they are already primed to meet Amelia where she is.

Exhibit A: I called a local youth theatre the other day to talk about a Drama Play program for three-five year olds. Our paediatrician had told me they often work with deaf kids so I should see what they might have for my 'artsy' Amelia.

I was quickly transferred to their Access Officer (already a promising start) and told her about Amelia and that we wanted to try the program in term three. She was so positive and excited about welcoming Amelia into the program, which she said would be perfect for her.

She said, "Does she use an FM?"

"Um, yes, she does sometimes."

"Great, bring it with you, we use them all the time. I'll set up a meeting with our artistic director running the program so you can come in and tell us all about your little girl. If we need to organise for an interpreter or any extra support, we can do that at any time."

Me, "………………………."

I didn't need to say anything else because she had closed the gap of understanding before I needed to leap in and unfurl my list of 'stuff' about Amelia.

This type of interaction is rare but when it happens you have to sit back and appreciate how liberating it is when someone just 'gets it' and you don't have to endlessly explain. I'm told it's not my default setting, but I really do like shutting up when others cover the bases ahead of me.

So for a few blissful minutes on the phone, I was just a mother who was neither an advocate nor an expert, and in my experience those moments are worth their weight in gold.

Playing from the
bottom of the deck

17 June, 2013

It took me a while to start writing about Amelia's diagnosis of autism. I spoke a lot about the related behaviours but I wanted to wait a while before I started speaking the diagnosis out loud.

I'm reluctant to be too definitive about it because the diagnostic progress takes a long time and we are currently stuck in the no-man's-land between one stage and the next.

Since March, when our paediatrician first put the words autism and Amelia in the same sentence, we have spent an agonising four months waiting to see the next specialist in the queue to assess and confirm the diagnosis.

While we have been in this frustrating state of diagnostic stasis, Amelia's red-flag behaviours have persisted and some have begun to escalate beyond our reach.

As parents, we are running out of strategies to alleviate how far these things impinge upon Amelia's generally happy day-to-day existence. We needed help at least a year ago, so July seems so far away, even if it's nearly upon us.

I am trying not to worry, to smother my anxieties as they creep up my spine and into my harried mind. But it's hard to hold onto the distant promise of answers to the question I ask my husband every night after we turn out the light: "Do you think she's going to be okay?"

Last week, my mum and I decided it would be fun to teach Amelia some card games. It was cold and rainy outside, so we thought some old-fashioned parlour games would keep us all entertained.

We opted for 'Snap', because it's easy to teach and is great for learning about matching pairs and turn-taking. The three of us made a little circle on the floor and my mum dealt us cards from the deck.

After a quick précis of the rules, the first game of Snap kicked off without a hitch. Initially, Amelia seemed more interested in her cards than the object of the game, but she was so happy to be hunched on the floor with us, thick as thieves, that it didn't matter.

Then she warmed up and started to appreciate the simple joy of smacking your hand down over a jumble of cards with a pair on top.

It made me laugh that she kept playing her cards from the bottom of her little deck, almost unconsciously. She would have made the long line of wily card players in my family terribly proud.

I have to admit my mum and I are outrageously loud and competitive people when we are fired up and this day was no exception. We were really getting our Snap-groove on, leaning intently over the cards, and screeching like banshees when a match was made.

We forgot to yell "Snap" and instead went with a sort of barbaric "Yaaaaaaaaaaaaaaaaaah!!!" when a King fell onto a King or an Ace met its match on the carpet deck.

This should have been a simple and fun thing for us all to share on a rainy afternoon, and Amelia used to love joining us in moments of care-free hilarity. But this time she became deeply distressed by our laughter, by the volume of our voices and the changes to our facial expressions, caused by the ecstasy of winning. By our happiness.

This type of distress has been happening a lot lately. As soon as voices are raised in excitement or people are talking in higher volumes or laughing loudly she is gripped by a terrible anxiety and starts yelling "No laughing, no laughing!"

Amelia runs at us and puts her hands over our mouths, desperate for the change in atmosphere to cease. We have to hug our girl to reassure her that everything is all right.

Her fingers will frantically pull at my mouth as she shouts at me to "smile, smile, Mummy!" There's something comforting or recognisable Amelia wants to see restored in my expression, volume and tone.

She watches my face incessantly but her wires are all crossed so the signals that should tell Amelia that I'm happy/pleased/relaxed are being received as a mixed message that is both negative and scary.

This extreme reaction now intrudes on many conversations or occasions of spontaneous laughter both at home and when we're out visiting people. It is upsetting and baffling to watch and experience.

The rainy day card game was no different. Amelia just couldn't handle the raucous play going on around her, even though we tried to explain that laughing is good and we were only having fun. But she didn't understand.

There was something so dreadful about the gulf between the collegial laughter my mum and I were so enjoying and her absolute terror – and that's what it was – at the sound and sight of us.

We fought hard to control ourselves, like naughty schoolgirls confronted by a forbidding teacher who definitely does not get the joke. But in this case, it was my poor daughter, who was now sobbing and begging us to hold her so she would know that everything was fine in the world.

But it's not, is it? How can it be when a game of cards and shared laughter can reduce Amelia to an emotional wreck? What is happening inside her to make her so increasingly confused and upset by these shifts in the behaviour of people she knows so well? How can the sounds of merriment be so lost in translation that they become threatening to a child?

How did we get here? And how on earth do we find our way out?

July cannot come soon enough for the number of questions we have and the answers we so urgently need.

Dance like no-one's watching

19ᵗʰ June, 2013

Busting some sweet moves

I marvel at her,
The way she moves,
The angle of her head
As it tilts inwards and out

The thrust of her hands
And the awkward grace
Suggested by the arc
That is sketched in the air,

Just there.

When she dances
It's like all the light
Held in the sky turns to her,
A beacon to her moment of joy

To her dancing,
Forever dancing
Like no-one's watching
But me.

To cochlear or not to cochlear, that is the question

25 June, 2013

It's not exactly a Shakespearean proposition, is it? I mean, Hamlet was preoccupied with epic matters like the meaning of life, murder and betrayal. As big decisions go, the gloomy Dane had heavy burdens to grapple with, so our little box of trials can hardly compare.

But the weight of the decision – whether to agree to a cochlear implant, or not, for my four-year-old daughter – has had me standing in shadowy courtyards talking to ghosts and pondering the slings and arrows of outrageous fortune.

It hasn't driven me mad (yet) and it's not an Elizabethan tragedy, but it ain't no fun-fest either.

It all started late last year with a surprising hearing-test result for Amelia. Every check-up since the beginning of 2011 had shown the same level of hearing loss, averaged across both ears: moderate- severe, sloping to profound in the higher frequencies.

At this level of loss – the final frontier before cochlear implant candidacy is considered an option – hearing aids can still work very well to give a child sufficient access to sound; enough so they can learn how to listen and how to speak.

Of course aids cannot close the gap entirely and many sounds detectable to our ears, like birdsong, will mostly elude her forever. But with them, Amelia is able to hear and repeat speech sounds that would not otherwise be accessible to her.

A child will only need a cochlear implant if they have a permanent severe-profound hearing loss, and hearing aids are shown to provide little to no benefit at all.

If I have been thankful for anything since Amelia's deafness was diagnosed, it was that we did not have to go down the road of cochlear implant surgery, with its intensive (re)habilitation and the added visibility of the processor that attaches to the receiver near the back of the head.

We had settled comfortably into life with hearing aids; they had fast become a natural part of our existence. At first it was hard to adjust to their intrusion in our lives, that when I got close to Amelia's face or brushed against the aids, I would hear the horrible buzz of feedback created by the contact.

But it's funny how quickly you do adapt and also how fiercely protective you can be of the new space you're in. For us, hearing aids and a stable level of hearing loss were important threads in the security blanket we'd wrapped around ourselves to weather the change.

It's no wonder that I did not ever want my baby girl to need a cochlear implant or any other kind of intervention that would cast us into yet another vortex of the unknown.

So, when I took Amelia to her regular check-up in October 2012 and it showed that her deafness was now testing at profound levels, I felt like the sky was falling. It was a vast, bleak sky and it covered me in darkness. And fear.

I looked at the pen-lines that snaked across the audiogram in front of me, tracking Amelia's hearing levels across four frequencies. They were steady at first and then jagged downwards sharply like a plane diving into the red zone, from 75 decibels to the depths of 110 (the scale is 0-120, with 0 representing 'perfect' hearing).

Not even the mighty Chuck Yeager could have turned this tailspin around, and that guy broke the sound barrier.

The result shocked the audiologists too – I could see it in their troubled eyes. We all just sat there looking at each other, hoping there was another explanation for the sudden catastrophic change.

Had Amelia been distracted during the test? No, we all agreed she had been unusually calm and engaged, making her responses the most reliable to date. They had been able to capture four frequencies for both ears for the first time ever in one sitting.

I remember feeling so proud of her effort that day, but the result cast a pall over it. There was nothing to rejoice in here.

Perhaps it was some other kind of obstruction in Amelia's ears. I have never wished so hard for poor ear health. No, they performed the standard tympanometry test and her middle-ear function was free and clear. There was no wax or fluid to blame for this alarming result.

We were told that the next step was an immediate referral to the Cochlear Implant Clinic for an assessment, particularly for her left ear which had recorded the most dramatic change. Some children are only implanted in the worse ear and wear a hearing aid on the better side.

Amelia's level of deafness, which until this point had positioned her on the cliff-face between hearing aids and cochlear implant candidacy, now plunged her over the edge into a wholly unfamiliar world. We were definitely not in Kansas anymore.

I remember I had this stupid, polite smile on my face while our audiologists spoke about the assessment program, like they were telling me a story about the weather or the traffic. I would have slapped my own face if I'd been able to see it.

But if I had spoken too much or allowed the dread inside me to leach into my features, I would not have made it through the next five

Amelia has grown to love her hearing aids

minutes, or the drive home, without totally losing it. And Amelia, as usual so blissfully unaware of the catastrophes befalling her, did not deserve to be confronted by my tears, my pain.

The experience took me back to the ground zero of our original diagnosis day and it felt nearly as horrifying, but I had good company there.

I found out later that week that our main audiologist, IS, had carried Amelia's file around with her for days after the appointment and even took it home at night to try and puzzle out the result. To find some other explanation for it other than a permanent one. We shared our mutual sadness and disbelief on the phone and I felt a little better.

So what is it that I feared about a cochlear implant? Why was I so resistant (as I still am) to the idea of it? It is indeed a wonderful technological development and has transformed the lives of many deaf children and adults. That is something I would never dispute.

But contrary to popular opinion, it's not the deaf person's equivalent of winning the lottery or finding one of Willy Wonka's golden tickets. We did not hope that our child would one day be 'lucky' enough to need a cochlear implant.

Yes, we are fortunate to live at a time when this technology exists and in a part of the world where it is available to us. But finding out Amelia had apparently lost a significant amount of her remaining hearing could never be a cause for celebration.

Cochlear implant surgery is relatively routine and low risk. But that doesn't mean that it isn't invasive, and that agreeing to it for your four-year-old isn't a gut-wrenching decision.

An incision will be made into your child's head and part of their skull excavated to accommodate the internal receiver. Once the implant is in, it's inside them for life.

Cochlear implants are not a 'cure' for deafness. When the external processing hardware is removed for sleep or bath time, an implanted child is still deaf, just as Amelia is at night when her hearing aids come off.

And in most cases, implantation will cause ALL of a person's residual hearing to be destroyed.

Surgery is only part of the story. A cochlear implant turns sound into electric signals, where a hearing aid works to make sound louder. One simulates where the other amplifies.

It takes a lot of programming, effort, and long-term commitment to help a child to interpret these electric signals through the implant. It involves learning an entirely new way of hearing.

If we were running out of time to find the right intervention for Amelia, an implant did not promise a quick fix. It guaranteed a much harder path than the one we were already on.

Whatever the circumstances, the benefits, or the urgency, you do not rush into a decision like that.

My husband and I agreed that if the clinic could show beyond any shadow of a doubt that Amelia's progress and development would not continue to flourish with hearing aids, then we couldn't in all good conscience deny her a cochlear implant. But we had to know for sure.

The assessment process is long and arduous, as it must be. No-one at the clinic wants to implant a child unless it can be proven that they will benefit from one.

From November 2012 to the end of February 2016 Amelia endured rigorous testing and re-testing of her hearing and her communication skills – there's a multitude of appointments to attend with Ear, Nose and Throat specialists, speech pathologists, audiologists, and so on.

I have written before about how Amelia finds tests difficult to navigate sometimes, so every appointment presented itself like a stressful obstacle to the completion of the assessment process.

It was an intense and often nerve-wracking program akin to being on a rollercoaster. The initial hearing tests in December and January conducted at the clinic confirmed the poor October results. We resigned ourselves to agreeing to an implant in at least Amelia's left ear.

She went to hospital for MRI and CT scans to examine her cochlea, auditory nerve and brain, to make sure implantation would be risk-free and achievable in her case (some children are born without a cochlea or auditory nerve making surgery impossible).

Amelia's not a massive fan of hospitals or keeping still for doctors, so I had to pin her to my body with the help of two attendants while they put her to sleep, containing the rising sob in my throat as her flailing body slowly gave up the fight.

But it wasn't all doom and gloom – the rollercoaster transported us up as often as it took us down.

Amelia's communication tests showed that her speech and language was around a year off the pace, but for a child only aided for two out of her four years on Earth, that showed an astonishing rate of development.

And just as we were getting close to hearing the Clinic's final recommendation, Amelia's hearing tests shifted back to their original levels – to the blessed 'moderate-severe/profound'. No-one could explain why the previous tests had been so dramatically different. Fluctuations are not uncommon, and for us it didn't really matter.

These hearing tests along with the MRI/CT scans (which identified no internal problems that might cause further hearing loss) and the positive assessment of Amelia's communication skills combined to give us a stay of implantation. After months of uncertainty it was a huge relief.

The final report said that Amelia is not a candidate for a cochlear implant right now, but if in six months her speech and language development has stalled, then we'll be back in the courtyard wrestling with ghosts and one of the toughest decisions of our lives.

Amelia is only four years old. It doesn't sit well with me to let doctors take a drill to her head without her permission or knowledge and potentially take something precious from her like the rest of her hearing, unless it is absolutely neccssary. Not until all other avenues have been tried, tested and shown to be useless.

I think she deserves at least six months to progress and prove what she has been showing us all along – that she is an amazing little girl with more guts and determination than anyone I've ever met.

I know we might yet again have to weigh up the benefits of a cochlear implant, the evidence of which surrounds Amelia every week in her deaf kinder class, but thankfully for now we are free of this particular 'sea of troubles', as Hamlet himself might have put it.*

Wherever we are headed next, I will put my hopes somewhere safe – with my daughter Amelia – who doesn't know what a cochlear implant is, but she can tell me she loves me and hear me when I say it back, and that's all the armour I'll ever need.

* *As of March 2017, Amelia's residual hearing appears to have permanently declined (severe-to-profound). We're now considering the cochlear implant option again, but this time I feel like we are better prepared to face the challenges ahead.*

The strange tale of the doorway and the evil Swiss ball

28 June, 2013

John Ford's 1956 masterpiece *The Searchers*, is a Western bookended by two famous shots looking out from the doorways of connected family homes, nestled in the wilds of West Texas.

In the film, these shots and the points of view they frame represent many things. The opening doorway view captures the staggering scale of a remote frontier land that dominates the family home perched so precariously there.

For the arrival of the film's central protagonist, Ethan Edwards (brilliantly played by John Wayne), the framing signals his status as an outsider – he emerges from the wild 'out there' and is more at home in its harsh environs than the domestic spaces he visits.

In the end, after returning the once lost Debbie to what is left of her family, Ethan stands tentatively within Ford's final doorway frame, but we understand he cannot join the others inside.

Some doorways can't be entered again, not after so many lines have been crossed to get there. For Ethan, there's nothing to stay for – Debbie is rescued and Martha (his love) is gone.

In my home, the doorway to my bedroom has for the last few months been a barrier to Amelia, who has positioned herself as the Ethan to our Aaron and Martha (do yourself a favour and watch it). Her comfort zone is the outer limits of the hallway, not the warmth of her parents' cosy bedroom.

In the early hours of the morning, Amelia will come and visit us for a short, iPad-induced stay, but during the day she will stand nervously on the threshold and never enter our room.

I didn't really notice the demarcation at first, except to remark that it was a welcome thing that one room in our house was free from the onslaught of toys and the relentless prying of small hands.

The objects within our room remain safe; precious possessions do not need to be hidden or squirrelled away. I can actually go and get dressed or tidy up without Amelia's 'helpful' assistance.

A small victory, yes, but she's running the rest of the show, so I'll take all the privacy I can get.

Lately Amelia has become strangely agitated by our doorway – it looks pretty non-threatening to me, but for her it clearly looms up and signals something fearful beyond its perimeter. I have puzzled over it for weeks.

If she is the director of her own story – and she most definitely is – then the open space of our bedroom doorway is certainly not the frame Amelia would choose to make romantic or mythical points about belonging and unrequited love.

No sirree. From the moment we break ranks with sleep in the morning, she starts barking orders at me in a dictatorial tone I'm sure Ford would have used with his film crew: "Shut the door!! Shut the door!!!!"

And what do I do? I shut the damn door and I keep it shut. All day.

One day I absentmindedly opened it while I was on the phone. I forgot to close it on my way out and walked into the kitchen, still talking to the person on the end of the line.

The next thing I knew, Amelia was sitting on the floor in front of me in tears of distress as she began hitting herself on the head with the flat palm of her hand while yelling, "Shut the door, shut the door!!"

Okay, I thought, this door business has got to stop. I tried talking to her about it, asking her what she was afraid of or didn't like about the interior of our room during the daylight hours. But she wouldn't tell me or didn't know how.

Then I remembered something from her younger days, when I used to use a Swiss ball to do some crazy home exercise program. She really hated that ball, and it now resides permanently in the corner of my bedroom.

I wondered, 'is it the Swiss ball, so innocuous to me (and a reminder of a long-abandoned fitness regime) that she fears so much? Is that ball like a sleeping giant to her, ready to pounce unless the door is closed?'

I'm not above pondering the evil properties of a Swiss ball if it helps to calm down my agitated child.

So on Tuesday this week I experimented with a little acting of my own. I took the dust-covered ball and brought it out into the lounge room.

Amelia bolted like Lord Voldemort himself had swept through the door (actually she would have liked that a lot more). I discovered her cowering in the toilet. My instinct about her terror of the ball had been on the money.

Then I commenced my pre-meditated pantomime of hunting down that poor unsuspecting Swiss ball and committing cold-blooded murder. In the kitchen. With my foot.

Yes, with my sock-covered foot I did slay that good-for-nothing ball. I took out its pin stopper and invited Amelia to peek out from her toilet hidey-hole to witness its painful demise.

To hasten the death throes of the ball, I pushed my foot down repeatedly onto its once shiny, silver skin. I watched Amelia's eyes widen in awe at her mother's unbelievable bravery as the life-giving air hissed out of the Swiss ball's body for the last time.

That ball now knows never to mess with a red-haired woman with murder on her mind.

The sordid affair ended with the ceremonial carriage of the deflated ball-corpse from our house to the garage.

I shouted "Be gone, foul beast!" (or something to that embarrassing effect) into the suburban air, to mark the end of a once mighty (cough) foe.

But did my theatre of the absurd exorcise imaginary demons and convince Amelia to stop being so frightened of our doorway and the bedroom space behind it?

Well, so far, so good. In the mornings since my crime, she has looked anxiously at the door and asked me the vital question with her eyes, 'is it okay?' Yes, dear one, that big, nasty ball is gone and the room is 'good' now. You have nothing to fear.

She now performs my act of brutality for anyone who asks about the story of the doorway and the evil Swiss ball. "Go away big ball! Mummy's room good now." She signs 'good' with a generous thumbs-up.

Her gleeful rendering of my ridiculously overacted (think Ward Bond) stomping makes me laugh and laugh every time I see it. But she is deadly serious when she acts it and tells it, just as she was serious about never coming into our room while the ball 'lay in wait' for her.

While she remains somewhat wary of coming into our bedroom during the day, that's fine with me. I was running out of places in the house to safely hide a stash of chocolate or presents bought for her birthday.

But the incessant yelling and anxiety about shutting the door has ceased for now. Calm has been restored, at least on that score.

I'm no superhero – I can only slay the fears that are identifiable, that I can see. Some Amelia will have to fight on her own, like the loner Ethan Edwards, out in the wilds of West Texas and beyond.

Choose your own experience

3 July, 2013

It's not often Amelia will see her specific life experience as a deaf child reflected sensitively in the media, in books, on television or in movies. She could count the instances to date on one small hand.

Of course there is more to my girl than her deafness and I hope like me she will one day fall in love with wonderful real and imaginary hearing characters like Elizabeth Bennett, T.E. Lawrence, Sam Spade and Angel (the vampire with a soul) regardless of how far their lives diverge from her own.

It's called having an imagination, and we think Amelia has a vivid one.

But let's face it, there is a dearth of representation in popular culture of deaf people and their experiences, from the historical to the contemporary or the entirely fictional. If you take Helen Keller and Marlee Matlin out of the mix, it's slim pickings indeed.

I never realised how 'cutting-edge' *Four Weddings and a Funeral* was to feature a young signing deaf man called David (played by deaf actor David Bower), who is more than incidental to the plot, until I grasped how rarely this happens in mainstream cinema.

Ever on the search for positive examples like this one to show Amelia, I was excited to come across a company called Experience Books, which sells texts for deaf children and children with autism.

But they're not just selling books, ready-made in the hope that they *might* mirror something about your child's journey, they are (and the clue's in the title) offering a rewarding experience that is both interactive and tailored to tell their unique story through words and pictures.

So, a few weeks ago Amelia and I sat down to personalise a book about her deafness and what it means in her life right now. It's a three-step process: you build the main character (hint: she's a rambunctious, blonde four-year-old), choose the text and create the book. Too easy.

First we selected the book's theme, which for us was deafness (rather than autism or, say, a book for siblings). Then Amelia was able to choose how she wanted her 'avatar' to appear, so that in the finished product she would recognise herself in the blonde hair, pale skin, dark eyes and most importantly, silver hearing aids of the main character 'Amelia'.

Then, the website provided us with an opportunity to drill down into greater detail about the kind of hearing loss Amelia has and the type of equipment she uses to access the world of sound.

A free-text section prompted us to talk about what she wanted to say about herself – who her family is, who her friends are and the activities she loves. The nature of Amelia's 'self' is somewhat enigmatic so I welcomed the chance to test how far she could talk about small things that make up her identity.

Amelia with the book written just for her

Amelia was so excited by my questions and our enterprise that she kept throwing names at me for inclusion, like all of her cousins and almost all of the kids from her deaf kinder-garten class (which, in most cases, I had no idea how to spell). It was intoxicating.

We ran out of text space, but we filled in more than a few gaps about what is important to her, about what ticks the workings of her innermost clock.

Another key section of the book is on communication, and it's great for parents who want to share some crucial aspects about what makes things difficult for their deaf child (loud noise, people talking at the same time), or how people can help (use sign language, get their attention first before speaking).

And finally, the website asked us to enter more detail about Amelia's favourite things. So, it's not simply about her deafness and describing what that's like for her, it's also about Amelia the girl who likes painting and dancing and signing with her friends.

After we finished entering all of Amelia's characteristics and clicked 'send', it occurred to me that I didn't really care what the book ending up looking like.

The experience of sitting with my daughter, jostling for space in front of the laptop as we chatted loudly about the big ticket items in her life ("we can't fit any more names, Amelia!"), is one of my favourite moments as a parent.

Because I'm still working out the best way to be with her or how to reach her, and the opportunity to sit and talk and learn together in a relaxed way does not present itself that often.

Happily, for the purposes of this story, Amelia's enjoyment and my bank account, the book is a winner. It's not long and there is a typo where I managed to misspell Grandpa (Granpa is still phonetically correct, right?) but it does everything I hoped it would and more.

It offers that rare thing – a deaf character who also wears hearing aids and does kooky, fun things like most four year olds. She lives hard and she plays hard. And has four million friends.

But it's not just any child's story, or an approximation of Amelia's, it is precisely HERS, with the right language to define her deafness, the colour of her aids worn in both ears and some of the things I want people to understand about her deafness before she can grasp them herself.

I don't expect this degree of looking-glass reflection every time Amelia opens a book or switches on the television. If you constantly search for yourself in the stories chosen by a media beyond your control you will inevitably be disappointed.

Deafness and the lives of deaf people are a marginal interest in that mainstream world, so you have to grab every representation you can find and shine a big light on it.

Like this book called *All About Amelia*, which for other families is just a mouse-click away from telling the story of their deaf child in bold colours and important words to cherish for a lifetime.

What happens at the park, stays at the park

8 July, 2013

Having a child who is deaf has mostly hardened me to the questions (well-meant and not so much) that people tend to ask in shopping centres, waiting rooms, and other public spaces when the topic comes up in passing conversation.

Since Amelia's diagnosis, I think I have developed a second, tougher skin that has helped to guard me against genuine offence or my own hyper-sensitive reactions.

Two years down the track from the moment we emerged from the chrysalis of one life pre-diagnosis and emerged somewhat bruised into another, I have developed ways to evade questioners when I'm not in the mood, and found better ways to answer them when I am.

It really all depends on the day, which way the wind is blowing, and the nature of the approach. If a person is having a good old Aussie crack at trying to understand something new, then clumsiness is certainly not a sign of bad intentions. It just means they have minimal exposure to the intricacies involved.

The keys to 'getting it right' are the demonstration of qualities like restraint, thoughtfulness and compassion from the questioner. Questions themselves are not the enemy – a communication started with care, that is watchful of the signs about how the questions are being received, is less likely to tread on vulnerable toes.

I'm not hanging around waiting for people to 'get it wrong' so I can rain blows of righteousness down on their heads. Well, I used to be, but now I'm more interested in solitude on those days when Amelia and I can just *be*, without questions, tests, diagnoses and labels disturbing the peace. Yes, solitude or privacy or anonymity, even when we're in public.

So I'm not exactly sure why I was *so* bothered by the woman – a fellow mother – I encountered last week at the park where Amelia and I went for a run in the winter sun. But there was something different about the way she came at us, with her machine-gun mouth, poised to fire as many questions at me as she could muster before it was time to re-load.

It was, on reflection, a combination of the level of her intrusion into our hard-won solitude, her condescending tone, her incessant questions and her lack of reading my mood – in my eyes, my voice, my body – that made me feel that enough was enough.

I'll try to keep it short, but here's how our meeting played out.

I was signing something to Amelia as we walked over to the swings and this woman, also with her kids at the swings, said to me, "Oh it's really great that's you're teaching sign to her."

It's not unusual for people to remark on our use of Auslan – I understand that it is a novel sight, and to many a beautiful language to behold, so I don't mind being asked about it.

Usually once people have chatted with me about the topic and some related things for a few minutes, they move on to the busy job of watching their own children navigate the pitfalls of the playground.

And then Amelia and I are free to return to our blissful solitude.

To this woman's opening question, I replied, "Yes, it's really important for us to sign with her."

My response seemed to confuse her for a second, but I wasn't sure why. Then her tongue tripped awkwardly over the words, "Oh right, does she have some kind of disability or difficulty…or something?"

"Um, yeah, she's deaf, so she is bilingual – she speaks and signs."

"Oh, right, ok, wow."

"Yeah, I wouldn't choose to sign with her unless it was a necessary part of her life."

It dawned on me that she had not been asking me about sign language because she immediately associated it with deafness – as the language of the Deaf. No, she was congratulating me because there are people out there for whom teaching 'Baby Sign Language' (not Auslan) to their infants is an optional luxury, not a necessity or a defining part of their child's identity as it is for us.

That's a new one, I thought. This was the first person not to assume Amelia was deaf after they saw her signing. It was an odd start and it went downhill from there.

The woman then began peppering me with a barrage of questions over the next fifteen minutes about the diagnosis, my feelings, behavioural problems, hearing aids, deaf primary schools, and on and on. It was more interrogation than conversation.

There were no queries about my daughter's age, name, habits (standard park chatter), just an endless quiz about her deafness. I tried in vain to steer her away from the topic, to avoid her, but it's a small park and there was nowhere to hide.

She also ventured a number of uninvited statements about how she imagined Amelia's deafness had affected me, such as, "Ohhh, how *heartbreaking* for you", or "You *poor, poor* thing". I don't think I cut a particularly forlorn figure at the park, but what do I know?

It all went way past my personal mark of 'too much'. It's an invisible line, sure, but most people seem to know where it is.

My answers became increasingly brief, curt, I turned my back, anything to send the signal that the subject was closed, but she wasn't reading me and I didn't want to have to be more explicit. I just didn't feel like expending the energy.

When she wasn't speaking directly to me she was in the background loudly telling her kids all about Amelia, the deaf girl. She adopted an affected teacherly-tone to say things like, "Honey, do you know what DEAF is?" Then she reminded them about a story featuring a deaf turtle from a book they had at home. It was excruciating.

I just kept thinking, dear god, please make this woman go away.

Thankfully, a parent we know through Amelia's childcare came over and started talking to me about ordinary things, which broke the park-hold the woman had on us until then. She drifted off and our privacy was restored.

I didn't want to have to fire up and be rude by saying to her "Please don't take this the wrong way, but we just came here to enjoy ourselves, not answer question after question about deafness and listen to you 'educate' your kids about my daughter like she's some kind of 'special' case."

And anyway, I don't believe the onus was on me to point out how far she was pushing the boundaries of decent behaviour and I've come too far to let people like her bring out the worst in me. When I cross that line myself, it comes at a cost – giving in to anger is usually more upsetting than whatever I'm reacting to.

Throughout the conversation it seemed as though the woman was trying to prove just how 'right on' she was about the difference we introduced to the park when we stepped onto the tanbark that morning. 'Look how tolerant I am with all of my probing questions, I'm not shy about disability!'

Unfortunately, her tactless, dog-with-a-bone approach had the opposite effect, making me feel harassed and uncomfortable. I wasn't upset as I might have been a few years ago but the unrelenting tentacles of irritation curled around my mind and stayed there all day (I wrote an excoriating blog post when I came home but it was not fit for print).

I had gone out with small intentions, which included Amelia and I maintaining our status as the unexceptional mother and daughter at the park, but the woman was determined to mark us out as something else; something reduced within the limits of her too-bold attitude to the private lives of strangers.

It's possible I'm being too harsh, but in life you have to be guided by your own thoughts, feelings and responses. It is not for me to re-cast the interaction as something other than what it was – an unwelcome disturbance to the peace of holiday solitude.

I'm glad to say this type of negative encounter doesn't happen too often, if at all. Most people understand how to balance their curiosity against the need for discretion.

The 'rules' aren't obvious to everyone, and I understand how tricky it can be, but it's not that hard, is it? Just imagine how you would like to be asked about deeply personal, complex things (cautiously) and have your life commented on by someone you have never met (sensitively) and then, simply do the same for everyone you meet. Provided your baseline is a kind-hearted one, I suppose.

And always look for signs of discomfort or unease, and when in doubt, begin by saying, "Do you mind if I ask you about…?" before you go hurling question Frisbees across the park when no-one asked to play.

What is it that shines in the night sky?

15 July, 2013

It's the moon, isn't it? Or maybe it's the stars. It's not clear from the question, but it could be either.

Most of us instantly understand what is being asked here and can readily name at least one heavenly body we expect to see gleaming in the sky at night.

But what for us might seem like a simple question was, for Amelia, a challenging hurdle in an obstacle course of tests conducted by her psychologist, MC, over the last two Sundays to assess her for suspected autism.

Some tests, like naming random objects in pictures, assembling puzzle shapes and reasoning out visual sequences presented no problems to her at all – she sailed high over these hurdles as far as her abilities could carry her.

When her focus could be captured and held tightly before it evaporated, the alertness of her mind and her desire to learn and share lit up her face like a beacon. Like that round, shining moon in the night sky.

Other tasks frustrated her or downright eluded her grasp; more complex puzzles, increasingly abstract questions and images, or the replication of assembled blocks 'just like' MC had done before her were abandoned in quick time.

For the most part, Amelia's behaviour imposed its mighty will on the proceedings. Her strategies for defending herself against the 'tyranny' of testing were devastatingly effective and impossible to countermand.

From the moment we walked into MC's large and clutter-free office space, Amelia clicked into her manic mode of being. There was no shaky start leading to a calm middle with a fiery end. It was game on from the get-go.

MC had arranged a table with small chairs where she intended to sit across from my girl and enter into some controlled back and forth for her assessment. We were to sit at a larger, parallel table and stay very much in the background.

Predictably, Amelia had other ideas. There were so many examples of her need to assert complete control over this new environment (and person).

First, she selected one of the 'adult' chairs and moved it to the smaller table. Then, she rearranged the rest of the furniture to suit her purposes. It was the feng shui of a defiant child who will sit wherever and in whatever chair she damn well chooses.

As for our location, well, Amelia was having none of this stuff about parents playing a two-hour game of 'keepings off'. She dragged our chairs close to hers and MC, like us every single day of our lives, just had to go with it.

The psychologist was forced to conduct her tests on the table, under it, on the floor, everywhere except where she had intended. MC quickly worked out that it's Amelia's world and we're just in it.

The rules that govern this kind of assessment are highly strict. Parents are not allowed to verbally intervene or help unless under specific instruction. Questions are defined by a tightly-crafted script, designed to give the least information or hints, hoping to draw out responses that identify understanding without aid.

Sign language and gestures are also not permitted in this context so could not be used to help Amelia comprehend what was being asked of her. Nor were there attempts to use touch to catch or regain her attention, even when it was such a struggle to hold.

While I understand that cognitive testing needs to be conducted consistently (and without undue influence), I have been wondering and worrying about the efficacy of a purely verbal process like this for a bilingual deaf child with a speech delay.

It was very difficult for me to literally sit on my hands and keep my mouth shut when certain questions – things I am sure Amelia knows – were posed to her while her face was averted, in a soft voice, using a lexicon that she would not recognise.

Allow me to interpret an instruction such as 'Amelia, build the blocks like I have done' and I could construct meaning with key words and the accompanying sign of 'same' along with a strong voice and clear gestures and I am certain she would know what to do.

But there's a big difference between knowing what to do and being prepared to do it. The very real disadvantage of a speech-only approach explains part – but not all – of her refusal to participate in the tasks set for her that first day.

I could see a little switch flick inside her as soon as a question had genuinely taken her outside her field of knowledge. Once that little circuit breaker had been ignited, Amelia escaped to a small, empty cupboard.

That's not a metaphor; it was literally, an empty cupboard near the door that seemed to appeal immensely to her. It was safe, dark and she had already begun storing objects from the room inside it. It was the quickest creation of a makeshift comfort zone I have ever seen.

It clearly fit the security bill for her, because she spent about ten minutes of each appointment inside it. At the beginning of the second session, she walked straight into MC's room and set up the cupboard space in preparation for its imminent use as a recovery bolt-hole.

As a place to regroup, I wish I could have climbed in too. Because it's a weird feeling to be in an appointment where you so want your child to 'do well' but at the same time you want the specialist to see all of the strange and difficult behaviours that have led you to be there in the first place.

Okay, so there were plenty of low lights and we spent a lot of the time sitting awkwardly, unsure what our role was or wishing we could take a more active one, but there were some sweet moments in the mix that made me smile.

The majority of the second appointment was taken up with 'free play', where MC placed lots of toys around the room to watch Amelia's activity, how she played and for how long. Then MC engaged in some one-on-one play with her to see how well she related to someone other than us.

Out of her enormous bag of tricks, MC produced a *Finding Nemo* bubble blowing machine and cranked it up for Amelia. It released a multitude of tiny bubbles, sending them high into the air before they popped   on their way to the floor.

I watched Amelia hold her beautiful face up in welcome supplication to the generous cascade of bubbles as they dropped onto her cheeks, nose and mouth. The pleasure in her features, now open and receptive, was so powerful I just stared and drank it in. I took every last drop of her joy to sustain me for the rest of the session.

In that same appointment, she took three chairs and lined them up in a row in the window corner of the room. She ordered me and her Dad to sit while MC sat behind taking copious notes.

Then Amelia 'took to the stage' before us and grinned, a signal of something exciting about to commence, and belted out a heartbreaking rendition of *Twinkle, Twinkle, Little Star.*

She was so proud, so delighted with her performance – this child who would not sit or comply or do anything other than what she wanted – and I had to bite down hard on my bottom lip to stop myself from crying.

My husband and I are taking a great leap of faith here, placing the hopes and fears of our family in the hands of a stranger in yet another clinical setting but we have no other options available to us. We simply have to keep our minds open to the possible benefits and the answers MC might provide.

But it's a hard road. In the end, it doesn't matter if Amelia sang about stars 'up above the world so high' – there are no points for effort or heart on a standard IQ scale.

And she didn't know the answer to the question about what shines in the night sky. I don't think she knows what 'shine' is and there weren't enough key words or signs to help her decide which celestial object to name.

But last night, while I was driving Amelia home from visiting her grandparents, she craned her neck to look out of the car window to tell me excitedly and repeatedly all about that big, glittering moon she knows so well.

Yes, she knows about night and the sky and what a moon is, just not in the right order and not always at the right time.

Going the whole hog

17 July, 2013

Just a girl and her novelty hog

For a four-year-old with a lust for life, it was love at first sight the moment Amelia clapped her eyes on the bright pink hog mascot who was working the room at her cousin's birthday party.

She spotted his towering porcine frame from across the restaurant, and a feverish light went on in her eyes as though candle-lit from the inside.

To me, this novelty hog looked like a reject from the puppet cast of Sesame Street – a little too grotesque, too cut-price, to ever really make it 'where the air is free'.

But who cares what I thought of his polyester charms? Not my daughter.

Amelia careened across the room to meet him and gazed up at his curved, white tusks and incongruous sunglasses (I mean, indoors, I ask you).

She didn't wait for a sign or a green light, she just leapt into his furry arms and held on tight. It was the embrace of long-lost love, of the hog you've waited for your whole life but never dared dream you'd meet on a Sunday night at Highpoint Shopping Centre.

Possessed by her need to keep him close, Amelia placed his arm over her little shoulders and they took a turn around the restaurant like a King and Queen greeting their subjects with restrained magnanimity.

The hog-King (in reality a jester) was clearly on an hourly retainer to bust some sweet dance moves for the receptive child diners. Amelia joined hands with him and twirled, moonwalked and swivelled her tiny hips in perfect time, a graceful partner in this modern ham-hock jive.

When it was time for the hog's smoko break, my girl was bereft and sat in the hallway near the kitchen awaiting his eventual return.

I had to find a way to prevent her from searching for him in the off-restaurant space behind the 'do not enter' sign. So, I broke that covenanted rule about not telling a lie, either white or black, to your child and said, "Amelia, your friend's gone to the toilet but he'll be back soon so please come and sit down with us at the table".

For a moment, I thought I had broken through her Pepé Le Pew-style pursuit of the party mascot until she signed to me that she would also like to go to the toilet.

I gave Amelia the benefit of the doubt and escorted her into the cubicles. But I had been hoodwinked by a master because she dashed ahead of me and started beating on the closed toilet doors, looking for her true pig-love, and calling, "Hello? Hello?"

Good one, Mum. Lord knows what the women in the locked cubicles made of it.

I dragged her outside and explained the truth that this time she just had to wait it out. The poor hog was tired from all of his grooving and greeting and needed a well-earned breather.

This story she was prepared to accept but her eyes never left the kitchen corridor, willing him with all her steely might to return.

When the novelty hog finally reappeared, Amelia ran to him for another long hug and bless that person behind the fluffy pink costume, he did not break free until she was done.

And then they danced once more and paused to capture the moment on film, to freeze in time some joy amidst the evening chaos.

The hog lifted his thumb in mute approval and Amelia did the same – they were at one in this as they were on the dance floor, and for a moment her little girl's heart was filled to the brim with love for a hog with no name.

A scar is born

22 July, 2013

I have this tiny scar on my face, just under my lip where Amelia accidentally hurled an iPad in my direction during our last summer holiday in a lakeside town.

I was half asleep, lying on the bed, so I wasn't ready for the force of the blow; I could not defend myself as the sharp corner of the device crashed into my face, leaving a deep hole in its wake.

My hands flew up to my chin in shock, and when I removed them I saw the unmistakable red of my own blood, pouring from the wound onto my fingers, and marring the whitest of white sheets (not my own). My god there was a lot of it.

I screamed. Amelia ran.

Frantic, I ran my finger inside my mouth to make sure that my teeth were intact. My nails sought confirmation of structural safety as they travelled gingerly along my gums.

My choppers were okay; my gums were torn but I did not lose any teeth that day.

The women in the local chemist looked dubious at my claims of a close encounter with an iPad of the flying kind. Unbelievably, it was a first for them in the town. How very modern and high tech of me to present with a wound attained in such a way.

They took one look at me and sized up my predicament – band aids and steri-strips would not suffice here, only stitches would do. I was packed off to an ancient GP practicing at the medical centre around the corner.

I was seen to immediately and I thought, *Oh no, what is this decrepit man with the shaky hands going to do to my face? I'll walk out of here looking like Frankenstein's monster.* So vain, so very vain.

But he was in fact a master surgeon in pensioner's clothing. As I lay on the exam bed in his office, I glanced up to survey the official-looking papers framed there, a lifelong testament to his expertise in greater things than minor cuts and abrasions.

Three stitches later, his exceptional needle work was done. My face was swollen and numb from the solution used to dull the pain of the stitching, but at last the bleeding had abated. Outside the cool, sea- breeze was a gentle salve to my traumatised face.

Amelia didn't make eye contact with me for twenty-four hours after her mighty swinging action set the events of the morning in motion. Shame and fear drove her from me.

But slowly she made her way back, drawn to the black stitches protruding from below my lip, fascinated by the sharp feel of them. I let her touch them and talked to her softly about what they were.

Emboldened by my sweet reception, she began play-acting the fateful moment that the iPad left her hands and slammed into my prone head.

As though it had happened to some other mother and daughter, Amelia mimed the story with great excitement and swashbuckling verve. The magnificent Jean-Louis Barrault would have applauded her artistry.

For me, the healing was better and more rapid than I had anticipated. With care, my gums, mouth tissue and skin repaired quickly and well. In time, Amelia stopped mentioning or performing the accident and I was not one to remind her.

The summer holiday rolled on and I got over it, in body and spirit. But I have this little souvenir – my tiny trail of a scar – to ponder some-times in the mirror or when my hand strays to feel the slight indentation under my lip.

I really thought I would mind that mark, that I would resent the imperfection, but I have grown to appreciate its presence on the left side of my face.

It reminds me that in some ways my life is not what I thought or hoped that it would be. That things have happened to my family we did not foresee and we have had to try and accept them.

But like all scars, mine is unique and has its own peculiar beauty, as do those spidery blemishes that seem to enhance the visage of that unfor-gettable Nordic heroine, Saga Norén from *The Bridge*. Her scars are like a question with no answer; they foreshadow a depth of experience, but they in no way detract.

Now that it has healed, my small scar sits in harmony alongside the other features on my face, none of which are perfect or conventional in any case. It belongs to me and it is permanent, like so many of the things that have happened to my family, to my daughter.

And yet it is not a cross to bear, just a sign that at times I have known temporary pain and suffered wounds that felt so raw in the beginning that I thought they would never heal.

As sure as the mark on my face that no-one can really see but me, I know that new injuries will also settle and be reconciled with the rest of my life and recede in their importance.

They will become a natural part of the everyday, these scars worn with secret pride in the overcoming and acceptance of a fate very much out of my hands.

Guess who's coming to tea?

27 July, 2013

Amelia, tea party enthusiast

At Amelia's kindergarten, the teachers collect pictures and videos to document each child's progress from term to term.

They're candid observations about things like social interactions, learning skills and styles of play.

This week Amelia's teacher showed me a video of an outdoor scene featuring my little girl and her classmates.

We had been talking about how she socialises with the other kids, particularly how she finds it difficult to join other children at play, and the teacher wanted to show me an example.

In the clip, it's free playtime in the afternoon sun, and Amelia's classmates are all engrossed in one activity or another.

Some are riding little bikes around a bricked path, others are messing about in the sand pit. A gang of three girls has set up an impromptu tea party under the dappled shade of a gum tree.

Most are playing in pairs, or at least displaying some sort of 'togetherness' or common aim, even when side-by-side.

And where is my Amelia? In this scene she is playing the lone wolf. A wolf in a red hat who is running around and around in wide, continuous circles.

There didn't seem to be any rhyme or reason to her running at first. She's just running, well, to run.

Her slightly awkward running style (with a little bit of Kerry Saxby-Junna in the shuffle of her feet) and steadfastly upright gait made me smile as I watched.

Then it became clear that Amelia's initially aimless path had shifted to track the direction of the bike riding boys.

She was trailing their course, dogging their journey, and running faster and faster to catch up. They were not aware of her at all.

Amelia had 'joined in' their game as a tail-ender, playing with them in her singular way, maybe the only way she knows how – just slightly behind, out of shot, waiting to see what the reception to her involvement would be.

Her impassive face briefly lit up with the thrill of the chase, the way we see it come to life at home when she's playing the Cave Troll to my Frodo Baggins (about to be skewered *again*), or when she's diving under pillows to evade her 'terrifying' Dad-turned-monster.

As she sprinted on, my eye caught a subtle move of her head and the flick of her eyes towards the tea party corner. Amelia had clocked them, this solid clique of three, but she didn't seem to know how to approach, let alone breach their imaginary game.

So she kept on moving away from them, but her progress had slowed with the hesitation of someone wondering what to do next. Stay the course or stop to take tea under the tree?

The video clip gave no clues as it came to an abrupt end.

It was the briefest of snapshots of Amelia at play, but it spoke volumes to me about my sweet girl, who is so often happy in her own company but also desperate (and painfully unsure how) to interact with other children.

Amelia's teacher continued the rest of the story that wasn't captured on film that day; about how she finally willed herself to break into the circle of that exclusive tea party.

She 'sharked' the girls for a bit, testing the water for signs of risk and making sure not to draw attention to herself.

I see her go through this same routine on kinder mornings when she is sometimes at war with herself about whether to sit in with the bus kids gathered for breakfast. On those occasions I am there to ask her what she wants, to encourage and guide her to a place at the table.

This time there was no one to smooth the way but she took the plunge and sat herself quietly down, making no fuss and speaking not a sound.

Thankfully, the girls were untroubled by her late decision to attend without an invitation. Amelia was a tea- party-crasher, yes. But she was a polite and deferential guest and so she was welcome to stay.

I see it as a triumph of her spirit, this small story about how a girl who hasn't begun to understand the rules of social engagement punched through her fear to join in with such a tight group of strong personalities.

And even though Amelia is light years away from being ready to ask to join in and participate on an equal social footing with her peers, I am filled with hope that without me she will eventually find her way.

To my eyes, she cut a wistful figure in that playground, running and running to show movement and activity (and because running is just something she loves) but I could sense that she was also looking, searching for a place to fit in.

Then I was shown one more clip that pointed to an alternative Amelia, one with the potential to be the confident leader of the pack.

She was up on the playground rise, near the fence line and had marshalled that same gang of three plus one to follow her in some invented game with undeclared rules.

It seemed to have only one premise: that all should join her in a conga-line of expressive marching along the fence line for as long as playtime allowed.

Amelia didn't speak but her hands showed, nay commanded, the way; 'Come on, come on', they seemed to say as she urged them on. And follow they did, every last one.

Not drowning, waving

29 July, 2013

Last night I dreamt that Amelia was running ahead of me near a water's edge I did not recognise. I was sprinting to stop her but she was too quick for me.

She was laughing, her head thrown back in a pose of delight as she looked back in my direction. Amelia was having the time of her life; the dream version of me did not agree.

I saw it all in hazy point-of-view shots. My hand as it reached out and missed her as she leapt into the air, pink backpack and all, and jumped into the water feet first; the surface of the water as I dove right in after her, face forward, frantically searching the murky depths below for a sign of her.

The topmost handle of Amelia's backpack – the one with the mermaids – the weight of which had pulled her down fast, so fast she was almost gone.

And there was my hand again, elongated in supernatural elasticity, stretching out to grab that handle and then, 'Got it!' I had it in my grasp and I pulled my little girl up with all the strength I could muster.

I pushed her onto the bank and my husband was there to hold her, to roll her over while she coughed unwanted liquid from her lungs. I ripped the backpack off her shoulders…

It was over and I woke with a start.

Sleep was hard to find again after that – the fear and anxiety of my dream all too familiar.

Amelia is so determined to go her own way in the world that I often feel no more than a powerless onlooker. As a parent, so much seems (and is) beyond my control. Her deafness, her now-confirmed diagnosis of autism.

But I was forgetting about the hope the real-world Amelia brings to my daylight hours. In the morning she came to my bedside and reached out for my hand and I pulled her up into the safety of our bed.

I put my head on her shoulder and felt consoled by the sight of her, the feel of her warm body next to me, the smell of her hair.

Amelia saved *me* this time, from the dark thoughts that visit me at night, that haunt me even when I am asleep. And she reminded me that nothing, no pain or problem, is ever as bad as our nightmares make them out to be.

On being brave like Coraline

"Being brave doesn't mean you aren't scared. Being brave means you are scared, really scared, badly scared, and you do the right thing anyway."[3]

"I've started running into women who tell me that Coraline got them through hard times in their lives. That when they were scared they thought of Coraline, and they did the right thing anyway."[4]

— Neil Gaiman, on *Coraline*

6 August, 2013

Neil Gaiman's book, *Coraline*, tells the story of the eponymous girl-heroine who goes through a mysterious door at home and finds a parallel-but-more-than-slightly-off version of her family life.

At first the door opens onto a bricked-up wall – a barrier between the here and there – but for Coraline it later reveals a once-hidden corridor to a place where her parents have buttons for eyes and everything is a little too perfect for comfort.

Like Pandora and Alice before her, Coraline's curiosity (and profound boredom) compels her to open the door and enter without thinking first

---

3   Gaiman, Neil, Coraline (electronic edition), London: Bloomsbury, 2012, p.15.
4   Ibid.

about the risks. Her mantra is and remains, "I'm an explorer", and because her parents are too wrapped up in work to notice her departure, she takes advantage of the free rein.

In the breathtakingly spooky stop-motion animated version of the book made by Henry Selick in 2009, the door is a tiny cut-out set low to the floor. It has been papered over but its outline and keyhole are still visible and the old key still works in the lock. It's a door that just begs to be opened.

Once unlocked, it exposes a magical, blue-lit worm tunnel that seems to shudder and move like it's alive; I don't think it's a stretch to see it as a fantasy birth canal, delivering Coraline into the place beyond the door.

Searching for fun, adventure and nourishment, our girl finds her Other Mother and Other Father waiting on the other side to 'love' and 'entertain' her.

They are creepy renditions of her real parents, like the doll she is given that bears a resemblance to her but loses something vital in translation from fabric to girl.

But Coraline is smart and she instinctively reads a warning in the outer signs of this same-but-different world, like the horrifying, black buttons everyone has instead of eyes. There's something so shiny yet dead about them – no smile will ever be reflected there, nor anything natural or good.

Though filled with freedoms and delights unavailable to Coraline 'back home', this 'other' place is really an elaborate trap. It's a web dressed up to look like her heart's desire by a very cunning spider (the Other Mother), who aims to catch, keep and devour her.

The request to have her own eyes sown with buttons by the Other Mother is a bit of deal-breaker for Coraline, as you can well imagine. The last time she goes through the door, it's to rescue her real parents who have been captured by the Other Mother to draw Coraline back to her.

The courageous girl confronts many fears in her fight against the will of the spider-in-Mother's-clothing; hideous things like dog-bats, a slug in an egg-case "as if two Plasticine people had been warmed and rolled together, squashed and pressed into one thing", and a shapeless grub, with twig-like hands lunging at her in a dark basement.

Despite this catalogue of horrors, Coraline tells herself that she's not frightened "and as she thought it she knew that it was true". One can only marvel at her bravery, at her brilliant use of positive self-talk.

Gaiman's wonderful, terrifying story and its film adaptation struck a huge chord in me. Aside from the delicious thrill of the tale as I tucked my feet under my body (lest a spidery hand should grab me from under the couch), the idea of being caught in one world while longing for another was painfully familiar.

Most of us live with disappointments and frustrations in the 'real' world and perhaps fantasise about an 'other' world, where the colours are so vivid and the experiences so rich we don't have to confront hard things.

Coraline imagined a world where her parents would be different, remoulded into people who cook her appetising meals and exist solely to amuse her, and so she was offered a brief glimpse of what that life might be like.

It is a credit to her that she rejects that life as a lie, even if her real existence is less than ideal.

For me, an 'other' world would be a place where I have no big-ticket worries. In it, the Other Amelia, the facsimile of my daughter, is not deaf. She can hear everything and anything and she can speak fluently and tell me her mind. And she definitely does NOT have buttons for eyes.

The Other Amelia is a child without autism. The words disorder and delay are unknown to her, to me. There is no sensory chaos and making friends is easy. Anger, rage and hyperactivity belong to another hemisphere of experience. To another child.

We walk together slowly and she holds my hand, never running away. And we sleep for a very long time.

But if I take these things away from her, who is the child left over? Is it still Amelia? Or, a distilled version of her, a person negated? Does she become like one of those husks left behind when the Other Mother is finished feasting on little souls?

She would be different, yes, and maybe her life (and ours) would be easier, I am not afraid to admit that I do wish it sometimes.

But she would not be my Amelia. To excise one element would be to ruin the whole, to make her less than she should be and much less than her strong personality makes her.

I myself have opened many doors containing fearful things since that first one, when I gave birth to my girl, and there is nothing scarier than suddenly becoming responsible for a tiny, vulnerable human being.

I didn't know for instance that deafness was behind another secret door in the house of my family. I only knew that there was some dark problem lurking there and it had to be unlocked, no matter how afraid we were.

As for autism, perhaps my greatest fear of all, well, that one has whispered to me through keyholes from the beginning, and over time it has become a shrill and insistent voice, demanding to be heard. Okay, I surrender; we have opened that door now and let the truth of it in.

Like calling out the bogeyman who lives under your bed (or Bob from Twin Peaks who crouched under mine for all of my adolescence and part of my adulthood), the most dreaded thing is never as daunting when you drag it out into the light.

I love Amelia more than I love my own life or anyone else's. She isn't defined by her challenges but they are part of what is shaping her, in the mix with her character, her brain, and her heart. So we must embrace it ALL if we are to keep her happy and safe on this side of the door with us.

But my anxiety about further unknowns surrounds me always, crowding me for space and air, and I can't just hide from it in some fantasy world.

Because like Coraline, who my own gutsy daughter adores for her blue hair (and insists her own hair be styled to match), I have to do the right thing and face up to what scares me and keep telling myself, "I will be brave. No, I am brave."

Senses working overtime

12 August, 2013

Finding out that your child has autism is a bit like reading the last page first in an Agatha Christie murder-mystery.

Through the big reveal, you might learn 'who dunnit' from Hercule Poirot or Miss Marple, but you can only guess at the what, how, or why of the events leading up to that moment.

By this, I'm not referring to the missing pages of cause and effect that remain hidden behind my daughter Amelia's latest diagnosis. To me, the pursuit of causation seems like a completely fruitless and time-wasting preoccupation when emotional and intellectual energies need to be spent in much more constructive (and urgent) ways.

Searching for some random reason to explain what caused Amelia to be born with a disorder that some refer to as 'atypical' neurology, is about as helpful as locating a needle in a haystack only to find that the eye has rusted over and you have no cotton to thread anyway. And you really hate sewing.

What I mean is that we have an answer to one big question (is it autism?), but we are no closer to understanding the associated behaviours, to knowing why our daughter finds aspects of her life so difficult, or how we can help to ease her passage through it.

The bigger mystery than autism, which was not really an unexpected narrative twist for us (though no less painful), is the triggers for the autistic *behaviours*, like her meltdowns and hyperactivity.

But there are clues. You don't have to be as clever as Poirot (or have such an impressive moustache) to read signs of significance in the way

Amelia acts in certain situations and not in others, to begin to draw some amateur-sleuth conclusions.

Take, for example, her almost textbook behaviour as the 'compliant child' when she attends kindergarten across three days of the week. She is able to follow routines, generally does what is asked of her without complaint, actively participates in activities set up for her, and does not act out at all.

Amelia the kinder-goer is the very model of a cooperative, well-behaved and calm child. That is not to say her personality is subsumed by this conformist way of being. She's not a robot; her independent spirit is detectable beneath the surface, but it seldom comes out to disrupt play.

It is simply that she is working very hard to observe and puzzle out the rules of the kinder game. I think there is security for her in knowing what to expect of this environment and what kind of behaviours are expected of her. Following an explicit routine and the lead of others provides her with a perfect map for fitting in.

Sometimes Amelia's teachers spot her in a corner, silently acting out play she has seen performed by other children, or she signs conversations to herself. It's like a dress rehearsal before she decides to step onto the real-life stage of social interaction.

This mostly compliant version of Amelia is not, however, the child that I take charge of at the end of her kinder days. The moment I pick her up she switches gear into full-throttle girl, almost like the sight of me or the touch of my hand releases a pressure-valve inside of her.

She throws off her cloak of flexibility, of quiet observance and obedience and lets her wild hair down in the carpark.

It's a battle to get her to notice, let alone watch out for the buses, cars and people as she dashes ahead of me, heading for the two giant volcanic rocks that reside in the garden near the carpark. Her hometime ritual – and it is the same every time – sees her scale each one and leap to the ground before we make it to the car.

More than half the time, our journey home will be punctuated by an epic screaming fit in the back of the car. On the surface, the spark that lights these fiery outbursts is my failing to 'get right' something that Amelia wants to tell or ask me, like naming an object for her that she can see (but I can't), interpreting a hard-to-understand question or retrieving a toy that has fallen beyond her reach (I prefer a 'two-hands-on- the-wheel' approach to driving as I don't want us to die).

It's a miracle we haven't crashed many times over, but I've become quite skilled at blocking out the resultant shouting and flailing from the backseat and dodging the toy missiles aimed at me. Amelia is a Jonty Rhodes in the making… you know, if the wicket is my head.

Sometimes the afternoon will continue in this upsetting vein, as her rage spills from the car and into the house until we're both emotionally spent.

But what's really going on here? I used to think the X-factor was all me, the 'bad' mother. I knew how well- behaved and engaged Amelia could be when I was absent, so naturally I associated her meltdowns with my way of parenting her.

Now, I'm beginning to see things differently. Ellen Notbohm (mother of sons with autism and ADHD) writes that for many children with autism, sensory perceptions are disordered and can become overstimulated in certain situations. [5]

These children can be deeply sensitive to the ordinary sights, sounds and sensations of daily life and feel under siege in environments where their senses are likely to become overloaded.

Bright lights, loud music, pungent smells, certain textures on the skin, all can combine to push the autistic child over the edge; it's just too much sensory stimulation for their brains to sort and filter.

Imagine the impact of this often stressful way of receiving signals from the world, and then picture Amelia at kinder, a setting filled with competing stimuli and demands, where she spends between six to eight hours at a stretch.

It is remarkable to me that she is able to cope so well with these days, to try and understand what the rules are, figure out how to behave and to remain composed while her senses are working overtime.

Amelia's paediatrician, KS, offered further insights into just how great a feat it is for her not to unravel during the kinder day. Because she is deaf, Amelia's brain is already highly taxed by the effort to listen, hear and translate the sounds coming at her through her hearing aids. Despite her deafness, she seems peculiarly, but not uncommonly sensitive to certain loud sounds. Amelia has started to say "too loud" and hold her hands over her ears when music blasts out of the PA at kinder.

Our one disastrous attempt to take her to a cinema had to be abandoned quickly. The music was so intensely loud and she couldn't stand it, tearing her hearing aids out to find some relief. That'll teach me.

It pays not to assume that a deaf child cannot be hypersensitive to sounds of a certain pitch or frequency, especially if autism is in the neurological mix.

With these new ways of understanding just how difficult everyday life can be for Amelia, it is no wonder that when she is released from her kinder day and the pressure to comply and cope with the situation, that a meltdown is so often the result.

It's like that feeling you get when you come home from work and you close the door behind you, kick your shoes off and expel the effort of the day from your lungs. Home is a sanctuary, and you don't have to pretend to be polite or obliging or anything other than your true self.

Again, our paediatrician gave us some reassuring advice on this score. She told us that it is precisely because Amelia feels so safe with us, so loved and protected, that she can exhibit her most challenging behaviours without fear of the consequences.

We provide the sanctuary for her to kick her heavy shoes off, and hopefully duck at the right moment should they fly towards our heads.

Now we understand a little bit more about the potential impact of specific situations on Amelia's behaviour; it is important to be mindful about just how intensely she's working to defend herself – either through detachment or anger – against a sensory chaos that is beyond her control.

The mystery might be incomplete, but we take this emerging knowledge about our daughter as a reminder to be ever-compassionate for her struggles, even on the toughest day in the hardest week.

Because the tiniest hint or evidence of Amelia's need and love for us, even when her hands and voice seem to push us away, is greater than any big reveal delivered to us on the final page.

The symbiosis of moon and moth

14th August, 2013

I n the phase of this burdened moon I see myself
Peering up with weary eyes at her, seeking respite
From her flight across endless night skies

She's part moth –
An insect I fear like the blackness of death
Come to catch me when I least suspect

But her wings are soft as downy velvet
Soft as those deep brown eyes that watch
And regard the dark with melancholic grace

And though her small body brings much weight To my
rounded back and the orb of my face
It is the moth's rightful place to take rest on me

On this moon, with its life-giving light

Because in the loving curl of her tiny hand
And the upward bend of her too-pale legs
I feel her need for the shielding form of the moon

So when the stars blur her eyes to the path ahead
Or the fatigue in her delicate wings and her mind
Makes it unbearable to keep soaring on alone

The moon will always be there to guide the way
From its predictable station in the heavens above
And onwards, to the tender space of home.

Rock and roll hearing test

26 August, 2013

*It's alright, she was born in
a cross-fire hurricane*

Just when I think I have this parenting game sussed and my daughter Amelia all worked out, something remarkable happens to surprise me and put me back in my assumptive box.

Every eight weeks or so, Amelia has to have her hearing tested to make sure her loss is stable, that her ears are healthy and her aids are in tip-top shape.

Over the last few years since her deafness was diagnosed, she has had so many hearing tests and her tolerance for them has waxed and waned like the phases of the moon.

Sometimes she's raring to go and happy to play most of the games set up to drill her into a cooperative subject who can provide accurate responses. I can see that her understanding of the testing and what is required of her is developing all the time.

Yet there are still parts of these appointments that Amelia is unlikely to submit to willingly, if at all.

I can't remember her ever allowing the bone conduction headphones (for testing the sensitivity of the cochlea via a small vibrator on the mastoid bone behind the ear) to be put onto her head.

And it's been a really long time since she was prepared to sit and have her ears examined for wax, fluid or any other obstructive nasties.

This resistance makes it hard for her two audiologists, IS and LB, to complete and verify their tests, but you can't force a bucking bronco to hold her head still if she doesn't want to. And mostly, she really doesn't want to.

Each time we try a little more, testing the waters with tentative hands, waiting for the right temperature and Amelia's attitude to improve, which it has to a large extent in two and a half years.

It is now pretty common to see my girl sitting for twenty or so minutes wearing her favoured big, soft headphones, happily completing her hearing assignment.

It's just all of that 'other' stuff where the examination gets a bit more up close and personal that she struggles to comply.

So last week we dutifully trudged along to our local Australian Hearing office, Amelia with her pink bag filled with 'special' objects, and me clutching realistic expectations about what we would achieve that day.

I even took my mum with me like some kind of talismanic good luck charm (she's a little bit Irish, optimistic and pint-sized so there's a whiff of the Leprechaun about her...).

My handy motto for these outings goes something like: never go into a hearing test with inflated hopes because you will get BURNED. Cheery, isn't it?

I needn't have worried.

Amelia strode into the testing booth, and if she could have, she would have said, "Pipe down everyone, it's BUSINESS TIME," because that child as good as rolled up her sleeves and bashed out the best damned hearing test I have ever seen.

She was a like a surgeon in there, asking for the requisite implements to get the job done right. Without hesitation, she took off her aids and handed them to the trusted IS for safekeeping.

Got my headphones? Check. Marble game ready? Then let's do this thing.

LB was our booth DJ, running the sound mix for Amelia to hear (or not). I wore headphones too (as did my lucky charm) so I couldn't hear anything but I sat at the little table and watched every movement as Amelia slotted marbles home when she had registered a sound.

I was utterly spellbound as I observed her on this day because she was so very serious, so determined to get the job of testing done well. Her sweet, round face took on a pose of solemn concentration, even disdain, as she selected each marble with careful consideration and calmly waited to slot it into the box hole.

There was something so intense and wonderful about it, as though Amelia had morphed into a mini- Kasparov playing a high-stakes game of chess on the world stage.

That's how it seemed to me, like she'd been in training for this big day and she was ready to give it her all. No interruptions, please.

Amelia's powerhouse performance of total focus was inadvertently hilarious too – little people taking themselves seriously so often are. Many times IS and I had to stifle our giggles in case our facial expressions distracted her from the end game. But she never flinched from the process, not once.

When the main test was over, the audiologists (emboldened by Amelia's newfound patience), decided to have a go at using the dreaded bone conduction headphones. The never-before-worn ones. Those.

My eyes opened wide in shock as I saw her dip her head in deference to them, her great testing foe, allowing IS to fit and re-fit them when they needed an adjustment. Unbelievable.

Who the hell is this child? I tell you my skin was buzzing from the excitement of it all. I wanted to sit on my hands to hide from Amelia my desire to start madly applauding her efforts. I thought, she'll see the pleasure on my face and fling those hateful headphones at the wall.

But no. The test went on and on. Anxiety-inducing ear check-up, you say? No problemo. She smashed it out of the park. Even when IS had to swap fittings on the tympanometry machine or in any way pause during the exam (which usually means DEATH to all who come at her), Amelia just sat quietly and *allowed* it all to happen to her.

The most inflexible child in the world, with a mother prone to over-statement (tick), just sat like a total BOSS. It was one of the happiest afternoons of my life, I am not ashamed to say.

It means so much to see Amelia getting better at tackling the little hurdles she will have to scale for the rest of her life. Part of what has helped is the visits Australian Hearing make regularly to her deaf kindergarten.

She gets to see other children having the same examinations and the habitual check-ups are serving to desensitise her to the endless ear prodding. And Amelia's getting older so she's learning how to cope with certain situations as she grows into herself.

We don't get to do a lot of 'normal' family things with great ease, like go to the movies, the zoo, for long walks, have coffee or dinner out and so on. That's okay, we are finding other ways to work some fun and release in amongst the grind of daily life.

But in our world, where tests are at least as common as park outings, it's important to feel as though they are a success, or there is at least progress towards improvement each time.

So when you witness a five-star, rock and roll triumph like I did on Friday, you can sit on your hands and stifle giggles, but you won't be able to hide the joy shining from your eyes. Nor should you ever try.

Kindergarten klepto

2 September, 2013

One of my favourite movies of all time is David Lean's masterful version of the literary classic, *Oliver Twist*, one of two brilliant Dickens adaptations made by the director in the 1940s (the other being *Great Expectations*).

Lean manages to bring Dickens' colourful world to life in shades of black and white; from the pitch-perfect performances (Alec Guinness's unparalleled Fagin) to the way he renders the horror of Nancy's murder by showing only the distress of Bull's-Eye the dog, frantic to escape the room and all of that screaming.

But it's the pickpockets I love the most, led so ably, so charismatically, by Anthony Newley's splendid Artful Dodger. If you're going to be poor and homeless in 19th century London, you might as well do it in *style*.

Little did I know as I watched this film in my childhood, transfixed by the characters on screen, that I would one day grow up to raise an artful little Dodger of my own.

Because my daughter Amelia is a bit of a kindergarten kleptomaniac, prone to cunning sleights of hand that end with her pocketing classroom objects in the 'secret' spaces of her kinder bag.

It started with a tiny fish of the plastic variety. It appeared one day in the side pocket of her backpack and I thought, *Oh, maybe it just fell in there by mistake*. You know, the way inanimate fish can sometimes jump into zip-locked pouches.

I quickly learned there *were* no mistakes, only carefully-squirrelled triumphs prized by this wily klepto-in-the-making.

And Amelia is quite the crafty customer. She has learned how to purloin a special item during the day and, undetected by adult eyes, find a quiet moment to hide it in her bag for later.

Patience is not a virtue common to Amelia's waking hours, but when it comes to executing petty acts of larceny, she has more of it than any Saint could claim.

It took me a little while to work out precisely what she was doing – what her racket was – but one day on the way home from a kinder pick-up, I looked over my shoulder at her in the backseat to find her searching her bag for something. It was the loot of the day as it turns out and she held it aloft to me with barely contained glee.

Amelia takes small things like play-dough, toy cars, pencils, marbles – I don't think she's that discerning or even interested in the things themselves. Maybe it's the success of a carefully planned five-finger discount that really excites her.

My (boring) role is to play the anti-Fagin as I collect up all of the stolen artefacts for return to their rightful place.

I had to rat her out to her kinder teachers too. They now know to conduct a little frisk of Amelia's bag at the end of the day, running a quick hand scan for pilfered products pocketed by my cheeky child.

The teacher holds them up to me one by one through the glass of the kinder door (carefully out of Amelia's sight) and I nod or shake my head, confirming or denying if she is the legal owner.

In these moments, I wonder at the twists and turns of Amelia's behaviour and I also recognise the humour she brings home with her too, alongside the pocketed stuff.

The other morning, one of the teachers said to me, "Do these bangles belong to Amelia? They were left behind last night." I replied, "Well no, but check her bag at the end of the day and ask me that question again!" We couldn't stop laughing.

We chuckled because we adore Amelia, our kindergarten klepto, even if we're not really sure why she does it. It has to be connected in some way to her need for hoarding and the obsessive-compulsive collecting of arbitrary things that are important to her in some way.

Apparently, she's just got to pick a pocket or two. Or three.

Amelia does the same thing with DVDs, which she loves to watch but equally gets a kick out of gathering into groups and hiding under her bed covers. I never know what I'm going to find when I make the bed each morning.

It's just another example of the slightly strange acts that pop up in our family soup from time to time and then fade when Amelia doesn't need to do them anymore. She's not hurting anyone and the things she 'steals' do not belong to other children (thank god).

So while I'm not about to reward or reinforce the dodgy side of her artfulness, I think I can gently guide her to some kind of understanding or awareness without stifling her, well, individuality.

We talk to her about what she's doing, and then we give the little bits and bobs back each week (when we can find them or separate them out from her own junk).

Once Amelia has developed an obsession with an object or an activity it is very hard to convince her to change course in any way.

Like the orange and black Matchbox car that keeps reappearing in her bag, no matter how many times I restore it to its kindergarten home.

It has struck Amelia's magpie-fancy for some reason, so I guess I'll just continue taking it back in this endless loop of secure-steal-stow-re-veal-return until she is ready to find a different way of expressing the innermost parts of her self.

Benevolence worked for Oliver Twist, so why shouldn't it do the trick for Amelia? His time as a nascent thief was short-lived so I'm hoping my resident pickpocket will soon turn over a new leaf instead of hiding it in her bag.

Acting out a mellow-drama

6 September, 2013

I was talking to the mother of one of Amelia's kinder mates the other day. Her little girl, like mine, was born with a hearing loss and has additional needs. She was telling me about how her daughter had started ballet this year and how transformative the classes had been, how happy they had made her.

The impetus for enrolling her in ballet came partly from her child's interest but also from the family's need to do something 'normal' outside of all the therapy and medical appointments that populate their days.

Just one day, a single hour, a few stolen moments, where her daughter is merely a girl who likes to wear a tutu, stand in first position and have a go at a plié.

As Hooper says to Quint when they famously compare battle scars in *Jaws*, "I got that beat".

Meaning, I know what it feels like to long for normality in the midst of intense times punctuated by diagnoses and treatments that stretch out before us like a highway with no end.

Our weekly escape isn't ballet though, it's Drama Play, which is held every Friday in a small church hall on the other side of the city. The program is run by a youth theatre company and a finer group of creative adults working with children you could not hope to meet.

It's not that I think Amelia is a budding thespian or the next Jackie Coogan (pre-Uncle Fester), even if she does seem to have a flair for mock-pathos. The point of going is partly about tapping into a stress-free activity that might help to build her confidence and her understanding of social situations.

But the main reason is far less didactic – I'm just looking for a safe place outside of home and kinder where Amelia can simply be herself. No needles, no tests, no judgements, just fun if and when she chooses to participate.

Each session is loosely structured around a wonderful children's story told in various modes: verbally, visually and through play. A hand-drawn map of the morning's activities (courtesy of the gifted HL) shows us where we are and also where we're headed.

Over a child-friendly forty-five minutes, the little troupe aged between three and five are led by three awesome pied pipers whose intuitive approach to the creative needs of their charges has been inspiring to watch.

To commence, we sit on colourful cushions for the welcome song (accompanied by animated gestures) then we do some mad cavorting as we 'sign' our names with our bodies.

Time is set aside for some free-form dance where every child has a turn to express their individuality and lead the group with their own special moves. No-one directs or pushes. The adults are there to guide and encourage, or step back if that is the appropriate response.

Amelia still talks to me excitedly about a session from a number of weeks ago when the theme tune from the *Harry Potter* movies was the soundtrack to her turn at the helm of the dance parade.

Back then it didn't seem as though she was super aware that the spotlight was on her for her two minutes of fame, but these happy recollections tell a different story.

There is a clue in this for me that involves not worrying too much about what Amelia *appears* to be feeling or experiencing in the moment because looks can be deceiving about just how deep her engagement with the world really is.

Story time is conducted by the dynamic AW who reads to us enchantingly from a carefully chosen book, like *Where the Wild Things Are*, by Maurice Sendak. Then this narrative world is opened out to include the children and the scope of their imaginations.

The little actors are helped to set up key parts of the story with props, often tactile objects like furry carpets or textured grass-like mats. Then they become 'Max', playing the role of the little boy from Sendak's tale – untamed things on the hunt for an adventure of their own making.

There are no passengers on this journey of self-discovery; parents can't opt out for fear of embarrassment. We are drawn into the performance fray as much as the little ones and for me it's actually incredibly freeing to run and jump and sing and harness my 'child within'.

A final map-check tells us it's time to go home, so we belt out the closing number and say our goodbyes. The time really flies when you are laughing and soaking up the kids' joyful antics.

I like the sessions because they are so visual and full of non-verbal communication. I'm also a huge fan of the way they follow a familiar pattern every time but allow for loads of flexibility and inventiveness. You won't find a more go-with-the-flow space to be with small children.

For a bilingual deaf girl with autism who is often rigid, sometimes anxious and always into routine, Drama Play is a match made in heaven. And there is so much ROOM to play or not play, whatever her mood is on a given day.

Sometimes, she takes twenty minutes to warm up but no-one fusses over her. If she prefers to lie on a cushion or draw, then there is freedom for her to do that. When she wants to keep holding onto a torch prop long after they are in use, honestly, no-one gives a damn.

But they never stop encouraging. The fabulous artistic director, SA, is always at ground level asking Amelia to engage and then backing right off if the response in speech or emphatic head shake translates to a resounding NO.

And when Amelia is ready, the team embrace her involvement with warmth and positive energy to burn. I don't really have to do anything, except model what 'joining in' looks like, provide some Auslan interpretation and assist with the gentle coaxing.

Last week provided something new: a whole session where Amelia was on board from the start of the map, not somewhere down the track after she'd walked her own road for a while.

It may have been because her dad came with us that morning and Amelia was excited to show him this special place where we go most Fridays.

Or it could also have been because there was only one other little girl there that day who was keen to share in all the drama with her. The girl took her cushion for story time and positioned another one next to her for Amelia to occupy.

Usually, Amelia does not connect with the book reading part of the session or with the other children but on this occasion she sat next to her fellow thespians and really *listened*.

A ham off the ol' block

After a few moments she went back to sit with her dad, her parental anchor in the circle. But her new friend looked around for her and tapped the cushion as though to say, "Come back, this is your place, next to me".

It was a sweet gesture of inclusion and after a brief hesitation Amelia did go back and take her place next to that girl who I wanted to hug for simply looking back and asking my daughter to join her. To belong.

It's a blackboard jungle out there

"Nobody ever thinks that you're going to send your child to a special school. You know, you don't wake up and think to yourself, I really hope my child gets into a special school. That's just not how we are is it? I think I've changed." [6]

— Sara James, foreign correspondent,
author and commentator

13 September, 2013

I recently watched this episode of *Australian Story* and the above quote from Sara James, mother of a young daughter with a disability, stopped me dead in my viewing tracks. Because a variation on her words could so easily have been spoken by me about my own little girl, Amelia, who will begin her primary school years at a school for deaf children.

We certainly didn't think we would end up sending her to anything other than a mainstream school. Going to any other kind of school wasn't on the list of hopes we had for her before she was born, but like Sara James, I have changed my mind about how I feel about this too.

---

6 "A Place for Us", *Australian Story*, ABC, 12 August, 2013. Television.

You see, Amelia's deafness and autism (and their impact on her development) make it impossible for us to plan her school years more than six to twelve months ahead. Right now, we know where she'll be next year but after that, it's hard to be more definite.

The pre-birth notion of mapping out an arrow-straight educational course for her, from attendance at the small local kindergarten in the church hall a few streets away, to the nearby primary school we liked because of its bright, new buildings and wide open spaces is now just a fanciful set of ideas turned to dust.

Thankfully, we didn't have enough time to really take those places to heart before we understood that for us, and for Amelia, the path of life would never be so clear-cut or sure. We have also worked out that institutional structures won't always be central to our truest, deepest wishes for her.

What do we care about brand new buildings now, or the 'best' scholastic reputations or keeping up with the expectations of others? Not a goddamn thing, because when the goal posts move to the margins, you have to start playing a different game – the long game.

It's funny how far my attitude to this situation of uncertainty has evolved in a period of just two years, as we have adapted to two life-altering diagnoses before Amelia is five years old.

I will never forget the first question that popped into my head when the audiologist at Melbourne's Royal Children's Hospital opened the floor to me after we found out that Amelia was deaf: "Will she be able to go to a normal school?"

Normal. I would cringe at that word now, but back then, I seized on it without thinking twice. But in that room, 'normal' was just a code for the life I had imagined for Amelia while it slipped through my hands in a matter of minutes.

What I really wanted to know was, "Will she be able to live the life I expected her to have, just like everyone else? Do I dare to hope that despite her deafness (her difference) that her life will be easy enough to navigate? Please, will she be okay?"

I admit it was a desperate grab for a slice of optimism about the future. I'm sure my questions, both articulated and unsaid, are not uncommon to those parents who have found themselves in a similarly dramatic position.

My panicked mind flew years ahead to school because it was an obvious point on our family timeline where I imagined the normality of our lives would truly be tested. Before then, the outcomes for pre-school aged children are much more private and far less scrutinised.

If school age represented a big fork in the road, I didn't want us to take a hard left while everyone else got to turn right. We're most of us pack animals at heart, and never more so when trying to slot our children into the 'safety' of the herd.

The audiologist reassured me, "Yes, with lots of work on her speech and language, Amelia will catch up by the time she is six or seven. She will be able to go to a mainstream school." At the time, there was no reason to think otherwise.

So, I clung to that small promise for the next two years. I had to believe that if we just did the tough yards of early intervention and speech therapy and everything else, we would emerge from this temporary blackout and resume normal programming.

But something happens to you over the years of taking your child to appointments and tests and scary places you never thought you'd be. You grow into it, you stop resisting and you begin to accept this life as the real one, the one you were meant to have.

It started in no small way with Amelia's time at her three-year-old bilingual kindergarten run by the Aurora School's early intervention service. It gave me a chance to see first-hand the benefits of a bilingual learning environment tailored for deaf kids.

Far from emphasising difference, this program offered its charges the security of shared experience. It gave them multiple ways to communicate (sign, speech, gesture), exposure to a wonderful Deaf role model and the freedom to develop at their own pace.

I watched Amelia embrace the visual communication that helped connect her to people, places and things. That kinder year laid some important foundations for her when she needed it most.

By the time she was four, it was clear Amelia still needed a lot of support to develop her speech, language, and social skills. There seemed little point throwing her into the deep end of a mainstream kindergarten three days a week just so I could walk her there and console myself about 'normality'.

We chose the bilingual kindergarten for deaf children on our side of the city because it is a twenty minute drive away, and is part of a primary school for the deaf so there's lots of expertise and support available.

Three of Amelia's classmates from Aurora joined her there this year, so she's been able to follow a group of friends through the early stages of school life. In this, we count ourselves very lucky indeed.

Seeing my daughter's growth in stature and self in this class has filled me with a happiness I did not dare wish for at the start of the year. It is so clear to me that she has found a soft, enriching place to land while being challenged to learn and play in novel and stimulating ways.

At this school, deafness is the baseline, the common denominator. It defines what is the *same* about her peers, not what is different. It requires no explanation; it is simply understood and catered for in every possible way.

Hands up who's ready for school

Amelia is talking and signing so much more every day and is fast outstripping her mother's knowledge of Auslan. She's even started correcting me when I try to copy a new sign she brings home with her at night. Cheeky little blighter.

My girl will turn five in January 2014 and I did not think that she would be ready for school – any school – by this age. The recent diagnosis of autism didn't knock us off a straight line because we've never known one. It merely confirmed to us that there is still much work to be done.

I thought perhaps Amelia would repeat another year of kinder, play it safe for a bit and see what the following year might bring. Being a January baby I could have reassured myself that she was entitled to an extra twelve months of development under her belt.

But her marvellous kinder teachers were having none of this overly cautious, pessimistic stuff. It is their strong belief, and I do have faith in their opinion, that Amelia *is* ready to make the leap to the big kids' part of school.

It helps that our paediatrician and child psychologist support this assessment and agree that a bilingual school for deaf children is the best place to 'super-charge' her progress.

Although this decision made me a little nervous, I couldn't feel more supported by all of the people who count. I soon realised how low-risk our choice was while paving the way for so many benefits and rewards.

I took a tour of the primary school and current Prep class last week and discovered it has four children with the teaching shared by two people (one deaf, one hearing). Not fourteen kids or ten. FOUR.

I had heard the numbers were small but I had no idea just how optimally low they would be. The numbers are capped at eight, but five is usually the highest number. Now that's a teacher-pupil ratio we can all live with.

The school already has a number of children who are both deaf and autistic so there is plenty of built-in specialist support on the spot and ready to go.

The primary school children have weekly speech therapy sessions and start to learn more formally about deafness and Deaf Culture among the other programs like art and sport and music that make up the curriculum.

What this unique context means for Amelia is that despite her less-than-perfect start to life, at five she will be able to go to school with a handful of friends, one of whom she has known since she was three. They are a tightly bonded group and it's thrilling to see them advance together.

Money can't buy the kind of confidence and self-esteem that comes from progressing with your peers from one milestone to the next, no matter what your individual challenges might be.

In a specialised setting like this, every child gets a chance to grow and move on and up.

If the next twelve months are principally about taking stress *off* Amelia's shoulders and helping her to realise her potential, then I couldn't really think of a more suitable place for her to be.

No mainstream school with all the best intentions, good will and deaf-friendly technology can give her the same guarantees of security and personalised support, particularly at this most crucial time.

I do not see this choice of a school for the deaf as a compromise or as something below par, as I might have two years ago. We are choosing the right school at the right time for our daughter and her needs. Our family feels incredibly fortunate to be able send Amelia there.

If you'd asked me back in 2011 if Amelia would be starting school in 2014 and where she would be going, I would have answered, "I just don't know." But here we are, with our collective bags packed with books and excitement, ready for school next year. Prep is a happening thing.

So, I've opened my mind and my heart a little bit more, just a touch, to let in the dreams that Amelia's ascension will bring. She will stand on our porch in her red and blue school uniform and have her photo taken and maybe I'll surprise myself and be one of those mums who cries on her first day.

Or maybe not. But who even cares? Because my beautiful girl's going to school, and baby that is a wonderful thing.

Waiting for God knows

18 September, 2013

Waiting rooms. For any parent, they're the lowest rung on the ladder straight to hell, aren't they? If you want to replicate purgatory on earth, go ahead and turn up the volume on an episode of *Ellen* on the medical clinic television, especially the bit where she *dances*. Kill. Me. Now.

I'm a bit of a veteran of medical waiting rooms, cubicles, and hallways as I have dragged Amelia across town to see the specialists and therapists we consult about her deafness and autism.

If she has nightmares, then I suspect they are set in a dark, cold ante-room embedded in a doctor's surgery where there are no doors or windows and everybody has dead, staring eyes filled with condemnation.

Or maybe that's just me.

Because I loathe them so passionately, so completely, I begin to dread them hours before we've been formally introduced.

The awful ones we must return to regularly loom in my mind like a familiar foe, and not in a cool way like Moriarty (as interpreted by Andrew Scott in the British TV series *Sherlock*).

A quick recce of the set-up in one of these places and you just know how far into the mouth of hell you are going to fall.

Common to the worst examples are big, echoing rooms, with no warmth, colour or anything resembling child-friendly comforts except a monolithic, flat screen TV perched aggressively on the wall. With the sound cranked up to eleven and it always seems to be Dr Phil o'clock.

I tend to think if a big chunk of your clientele is small children, there's no excuse for only having a few weather-beaten Little Golden Books and two mangy looking toys slung in a corner to divert the attention of sick, anxious and/or bored kids.

The better waiting rooms on our roster have managed to create a discrete waiting area within the main one that is targeted at its paediatric patients. The best ones will have dedicated a whole room to this purpose.

It doesn't take a lot of money or architectural redesign to cordon off a little space, make it bright and engaging and fill it with second-hand books and games to distract children from the typically long wait to see a busy doctor.

Without the promise of something, *anything*, to help divert Amelia's attention from the loud noise, hostile atmosphere and the stressful examination waiting for her, I know I'm on a hiding-to-nothing. There will be one or more of screams, meltdowns, tears, frantic escape attempts, disapproving looks (from Amelia and the adults around me), and often the whole shebang.

In short, there will be blood and most of it mine sweated through pores or springing from cuts sustained trying to put my darling child-genie back in the bottle.

As parents, we're not asking for the world, just some safe territory – an island if you will – that signals the welcoming support of the people and places we invest so much time, hope and money in.

But in the mix with the dreadful, the so-so, and the pretty good I have discovered the gold standard, the Ferrari of all waiting rooms, and it's inside our new Occupational Therapy (OT) clinic.

Of course it makes sense that a place like this one, which specialises in helping children like Amelia who are dealing with serious challenges, would take extra care in the design of its interior spaces.

But this waiting room benchmark honestly took my breath away. Set apart from the front reception area, it is situated around the corner, occupying its own quiet, judgement-free space.

In fact it is made up of two areas, the first being a corridor with bookshelves and chairs for the parents. Then, nestled into the t-section of the hall lives the WAITING ROOM TO BEAT ALL WAITING ROOMS.

It's dark and quiet and it has a pirate tent in it. That already puts it in Amelia's top five spaces to love list. Need more? How about huge, billowing cushions and pillows of vivid colours not seen since Gene Wilder so dazzled film audiences as Willy Wonka (please don't mention Johnny Depp's Wonka to me. Ever).

Two large, wicker boxes hold further curios and delights, like torches to light the way into the pirate den or soft fabrics and toys for the more tactile child customer. There's also an egg-shaped chair that swivels and has a cloth lid that pulls down to obscure the seated party.

Things to touch and places to disappear – Amelia took one look and fell head over heels. Then in true hoarding style, she dragged most of the contents of the room into the tent and I didn't see or hear her again until it was time to see our OT.

The space made her feel instantly secure and it kept her busy exploring and hiding for as long as was needed. I'd call that mission accomplished.

The therapists at this clinic don't seem to keep people waiting more than ten minutes but somehow they've already made waiting the best part of the appointment, not the worst.

Best waiting room ever

It's fanciful and unrealistic to expect other places to have such purpose-built waiting rooms for kids, but if I walk in and see that your centre hasn't thought about children at all then I'll just assume you don't care. About me, or my child.

Think about how that makes people feel and then maybe try for an upgrade. It doesn't have to be as stylish and flashy as a Ferrari, but there are plenty of good, second-hand cars on the market that will take its passengers to the same welcome destination.

Then we'll really know we're in safe hands.

It's a small world after all

27 September, 2013

When I had a baby, one of the things I expected was that my world would contract while our little girl, Amelia, worked out how to live outside of the tightly confined space of my body after nine long months.

Nothing can really prepare you for the intensity of that newly-contracted space as the changed dynamic of a family of two adults adjusts to life as three, including one small person who is completely defenceless and totally needy.

But the thing that got me through the life-changing chaos of those early days was the promise of growth, of progress – of the eventual expansion of that changed world we now occupied. Its limits would open to include old experiences temporarily shelved, or new ones we had yet to discover.

Expansion could mean anything, like us being ready to go outside and take a walk with our baby in the pram. Or feeling able to sit down at a café and order a coffee while (fingers crossed) she slept. Just ten minutes, not long, to feel like moments of the old life could be incorporated into the new.

During the first year, progress included things like visiting people or taking short trips together. Our first holiday was a driving expedition across the state for two fabulous weeks. Amelia was seven months old and apart from the logistical challenges and the cold weather, we created some of our best family memories on the road.

The world of our family grew at about the pace you would expect – just fast enough to adapt to the challenges of each main stage. We imagined that this expansion would just go on and on. And hopefully, it would bring more SLEEP (it didn't).

Our ambitions for growth extended to things like going to the zoo, the circus, the movies, or that brilliant outdoor production of *The Wind in the Willows* performed in the Royal Botanic Gardens every summer. Amelia would join other children and follow Toad, Rat and Mole down the River Thames.

Silly things, I guess, but they're the stuff that parental dreams are made of, at least for us. You picture sharing magical new events with your child and it's only a matter of time before you get there.

But it's not. Not for us, anyway. Before Amelia turned three, I thought for sure we were on track to growth and progress but since then (and with the escalation of her autistic behaviours) our world has been steadily contracting again, even where seemingly trivial things are concerned.

It's not exactly like the first few months of Amelia's life, that almost suffocating isolation of early parenthood, but some days it's not far off.

Even 'easy' activities like going for walks to the park, or actually *being at the park* have become fraught with danger and the promise of failure.

Last weekend the sun greeted us upon waking so we thought, 'why not try for a walk outside and see how we go?' We jumped into the car and headed to a lake area with a lovely walking track and playgrounds at either end.

But we didn't get too far. About one hundred metres actually, in about forty minutes of movement in large, frantic semi-circles punctuated with frequent tantrums while fellow families streamed serenely past on bikes, scooters or just on foot, ever moving forward while we stayed in one place.

The ease of their walking and forward progress, this evidence of how different their lives are to ours, made me feel desperately alone.

If I do manage to get Amelia to a playground (usually by car for sanity's sake), she will invariably become anxious or angry about some indefinable thing and so we have to leave. It's like she's suddenly forgotten how to just *be* at a park, how to play on the swings and slides and enjoy herself.

The zoo (like any busy, public place) is a nightmare venue to take Amelia and I have tried it several times. She doesn't really understand how she's meant to behave or what she's supposed to be looking at. Such a shame for a girl who loves animals so much.

The sights and sounds seem to overwhelm her auditory and visual senses so we cover little ground before another meltdown kicks in and our departure becomes long overdue.

I used to visit my Mum frequently to break up the stress of the days spent at home, and Amelia always enjoyed this time with her beloved Nan. Now she becomes highly fearful and angry at the mere suggestion of going there so I've had to cross that safe house off our list for the time being.

If I manage to convince her to go there, Amelia will begin insisting that we leave as soon as we have arrived and repeat this request incessantly into my face or by urgently curling my hand into the Auslan sign for home until I acquiesce. You can see it's hardly worth the stress.

So, for the most part, the world has contracted once again to the boundaries, nay the limits, of our family home. The walls have closed in and sometimes it's hard to breathe. Sure, we can enjoy the garden together, the lovely outdoor spaces when the weather allows, but some days that doesn't feel like enough.

It's school holidays right now and those weeks are by far the worst. Not for reasons you might expect – I love to have Amelia with me and to slow our routine down to a lazy jog rather than the frenetic sprint it usually feels like to get to kinder and the like. We make our own fun with paint, play dough, cooking and silly games.

No, what makes me feel so bereft at these times of the year is the painful exposure of just how small our world is, how limited the opportunities are for being out and about together.

Lots of other families get to plan things like long trips or day excursions, or even just walks to the park. They say they're going to do it and they just *go and do it*. Idea becomes reality; the run-of-the-mill activity or the special childhood dream event happens and the photos are added to the scrapbook.

The novelty of this is like a curio I'm peering at through a glass cabinet – I can see it but I can never reach out and touch it for myself. I'm told that things will get better and our world will expand once again but I can't afford to create more fantasies that are beyond the capabilities of my daughter to fulfil.

It's not fair on her and it just breaks my heart.

Mermaids for merit

9 October, 2013

At the end of one particularly challenging day with Amelia, in what sometimes feels more like a warzone than family home, my husband turned to me and in true deadpan style said, "they're going to give us a Victoria Cross (VC) for this." Not for valour perhaps, but for stamina definitely. Or maybe survival.

Just who might award us the prestigious Victoria Cross for parenting in said domestic warzone, well, I'm not really sure. And I don't think the Jacka Boulevard in St. Kilda is in any actual danger of being re-named in our honour, but at that moment a VC seemed like the least "they" could give us.

Decorations, awards or prizes, either real or imagined, are important I think. For me, the reward is being married to someone with a whip-smart sense of humour who can cut through my darkest moods and elicit laughter instead of tears.

For Amelia, coping with deafness and autism in a world that's not exactly fit for purpose, the opportunities for prizes are slim. Simply making it through the difficult day, the stressful hour, usually takes more than mere gallantry on her part.

Some days I want to pin a medal on her just for making it over new hurdles and managing to be such a wild and wonderful human being into the bargain. Other days, there are no deeds to be rewarded, no behaviours to be mentioned in dispatches. I close the blinds and wait for the dusk and hope for a better one tomorrow.

But you have to keep a sense of perspective about things like this. I would, for instance, give Amelia a thousand dollars if she would sleep past 7am. Just once. Perspective's a very individual thing.

I have actually assembled a box of 'treasures' (read = toys that cost no more than $2 at K-Mart) that she can dip into if she makes it to 6am each morning without appearing by our bedside. I'm sad to say the box is still filled to the brim with handpicked delights.

Clearly, the lack of treats is not harming our daughter's psyche too much. One recent morning, when Amelia trotted into our bedroom at her customary wake-up time of 5am, she smiled, stretched like an evil cat and said "Oh well, no present!" It was the four-year-old's version of 'C'est la vie!'

In our situation, I think there is a need to sometimes reward behaviours that come quite easily to other children. We're not dealing with an ordinary person who acts in a predictable way most of the time, so there are occasions when special rewards are bestowed with good reason.

Two weeks ago, Amelia and I went to her regular speech therapy appointment. Suffice to say it was an unmitigated disaster. My daughter did her best impression of Linda Blair from *The Exorcist* as I, Ellen Burstyn, cowered in a corner to avoid the torrent of screams and kicks aimed in my direction.

There was no pea-coloured vomit and I didn't see her head spin all the way around, but she hit some serious Mercedes McCambridge high notes in her demonic performance.

Mermaids for merit and every one earned

On Tuesday we returned, and I admit to being nervous about how the session would go. Amelia assured me she would not be angry or scream or try to hurt me, but inside that room I knew she would have little control over these things if the environmental patterns didn't align the way she needed them to.

Yet align they must have, because for forty minutes her angelic face matched the serenity of her demeanour and despite tiny ripples in the pool of her mind, Amelia played well and learnt well too. It was fantastic.

Like me, our speech therapist, PP, understood how impressive Amelia's calm and cooperative effort that morning was so she decided to give her a merit award. It was only a rudimentary certificate with mermaids on it, but my girl was transfixed, her eyes shining with delight.

PP spoke out loud as she wrote Amelia's name on the paper and outlined the reasons for her award, namely, for "playing and for being a good girl".

It doesn't sound like much, but when PP handed it over, my dear girl accepted that certificate and pressed it to her little chest with pride.

Because it meant something to her to have her good behaviour acknowledged and enshrined on a personalised artefact that was hers to keep.

I could see it on her face – that happiness as her eyes closed for a second to pause on just how good it felt to win something.

And it was a win. Every time Amelia is able to sit for a while longer and learn a little more, not just about speech and language, but also how to observe the tricky rules of play, she is gaining more of the social skills she needs to cope in the world.

For the rest of the day she showed every man, Nan and her dogs that merit award and it made it onto the fridge next to her animal magnets and her cow drawing with the fur appliqué.

I sent a photo of Amelia holding it to her dad because I needed to share it with him as much as he needed to see it. Small things, tiny rewards, are enormously significant to us all these days.

Although, I still wouldn't say no to a VC. Or a thousand dollars. Or even just one decent night's sleep.

Now, hearing

24 October, 2014

Before bedtime last night, Amelia was doing her usual interpretive dance routine and entertaining us with her best jazz hands followed by the deepest of bows and an enchanting flourish of her hand from brow to floor to signal its choreographic end.

Her avant-garde performance, matched only in its breathtaking awkwardness by Marty, the Dude's 'artistic' landlord in *The Big Lebowski*, was accompanied by music she had chosen herself. Born Ruffians, if you're asking.

It's music she couldn't really hear as she doesn't wear her aids at night after her bath. However, like many things in her life, Amelia digs the need for tunes to complete the picture, the context for a show. People dance to music, and so does she, whether she can fully appreciate it or not.

It certainly doesn't affect her enjoyment of dancing and she knows music, rejoices in it when aided, so her imagination and failsafe memory lend her the rhythms (well, motions) where her hearing cannot.

After about five encores, met with raucous laughter and hearty applause from the couch seats in-the-round, our exhausted tiny dancer opted for a story break to catch her breath.

Amelia picked up her big, interactive book, *Peppa Pig on Pirate Island*, with its picture buttons to be pressed for character sounds and music that children can play as the story unfolds. You know, Peppa giggles on cue, there's a jaunty pirate theme and on it goes.

Then something happened that we did not expect, that we had not seen or heard before. After a few seconds of pressing the sound buttons, our girl spoke and signed, 'Need hearing aids. Can't hear it.' She was not annoyed, it was simply a matter of practicality.

We just sat in stunned, wowed silence for a second, because this was the very first time Amelia has ever asked for her aids and explained why. That she needs them to hear.

She knows what they are and doesn't like to be parted from them but I've been waiting to see when she would become aware of just what her aids are for. What they mean beyond mere objects we put in her ears every morning.

Last night was the night for a revelation of that anticipated cognisance of *necessity*.

Her dad rushed off to get them as I sat, spellbound by my daughter's sudden self-realisation – this emerging understanding of being without hearing; of the connection between her aids and sound. Of being deaf.

As an audience, we could not have been more gripped by the scene playing out before us. She'd trumped herself in the post-dance segment of the evening's activities.

Well, it is Peppa Pig

Amelia nodded approvingly as the aids were finally inserted and switched on. Then she sat down again and pushed another Peppa-related button. Her voice was clear and true as she announced, "Now, hearing!" Yes, my beautiful girl. Now hearing.

What a moment this was for us and for her. I wonder all the time about when Amelia will begin to understand that she is deaf and what this means to her life and her identity.

There are many more layers of this process to come for her and I have a feeling none will be as matter of fact as this one.

So last night represented an important first – the first time Amelia seemed to know that her ears do not operate the way ours do and that she would need something extra to let the world of sound in.

She's so used to enjoying books, movies, music without the aural reach provided by her aids but this time, it wasn't enough.

Amelia may have chosen to dance as usual to music mostly lost on her ears but she'd have her Peppa Pig pirate tale *with* the sound, thanks very much.

Accentuate the visual

"I need to see something to learn it, because spoken words are like steam to me; they evaporate in an instant, before I have a chance to make sense of them.

Without [visuals], I live the constant frustration of knowing that I'm missing big blocks of information and expectations, and am helpless to do anything about it."[7]

7 November, 2013

It sounds pretty simple, doesn't it? When I first read these words by Ellen Notbohm about the visual orientation of children with autism, it made perfect sense. But until it was pointed out so clearly, so definitively in print, I was exhaling a lot of steam in Amelia's direction.

Useless, evaporating steam, disappearing over her head along with my parental confidence.

It's a revelation to discover that you have been using the 'wrong' language to reach your child; that mere words weighted with serious intent were never going to do. It doesn't matter how much you want to

---

7   Notbohm, p. 23.

be heard, if your choice of communication is off-target you might as well shout into the wind.

Of course, an inadequate method of communication is nothing new to our household. When we found out that Amelia was deaf, it was painfully clear that our spoken words had fallen on ears ill-equipped to decipher our meaning. So, we had to learn sign language – Auslan – to finally get through to her.

We also learned to accentuate the visual as much as possible, to provide images as shorthand for directions, rules, new frontiers, but we were still using lots and lots of words. Enough steam to power the Puffing Billy train I suspect.

It is a hard habit to break because we rely so much on words and unconsciously expect others, even our own child, to do the same.

With the diagnosis of Amelia's autism has come an increased focus on just how important visuals are to her understanding of the world. We are also realising that it's not really enough to introduce non-verbal cues without a concrete strategy; a clear purpose for using them.

What are we trying to teach Amelia? How will these pictures tell her a story she will grasp and absorb? Will they help her to learn?

For us, they have to be embedded within the routines we are trying to create for her, where life is safe and there are few unplanned surprises. Visuals are becoming like tiny building blocks within a larger structure – the fabric of our daily lives.

Thankfully we have lots of help and support to make this happen. Our occupational therapist, clinical psychologist and speech pathologist (it takes a small village) provide a lot of practical ideas and coach us through trial runs at home.

One great recent example of how we are using visuals to guide Amelia through a typical day is an iPhone application called a Visual Timer that we use to smooth out daily transitions. Honestly it is the simplest and most successful idea (courtesy of our OT) that we have tried to date.

One of Amelia's biggest struggles has always been transitioning from one activity or place to the next. Our days would grind to a (literally) screaming halt over and over again, each time she was told that it was time to shift focus or location.

No matter how much verbal preparation I used to give her beforehand, saying "Five minutes until it's time to go" was like a red rag to a determined blonde bull.

Now I only need to take out my phone and open the bright clock face on which I can set any length of time I want from a single minute to multiple hours. Instead of *telling* Amelia how much time is left I can *show* her. And it's visual information that *can stay in front of her for as long as she needs it.*

The proof is in Amelia's total acceptance of the timer into her day. When it is close to bed time and we are talking or signing about what's coming, she now says, "Show me timer" and will check it from minute to minute to see how much time is left before she dutifully heads under the covers.

If she becomes anxious about when her dad will be home from work, even if it is hours away, I can calm her down by showing her the pie wedge of time on my phone and leave it in front of her like a visual anchor. It keeps her feet on the ground so she can focus on other things.

Her favourite thing about the clock is the colours. It has a blue shade for timeframes over an hour and pink for anything under that mark. But when it nears the end (less than one minute) it switches to bright green and Amelia waits excitedly as the timer clicks down to zero.

On the clock face, green means that time is up but it also signals something else to me about moving on and forward. The time passes and Amelia understands what is expected of her. She is happier and more willing to bend with the world instead of fighting against its demands.

Beyond the confusion of words there is very real comfort for Amelia in visual cues, and something approaching certainty, in minutes and hours, for us too.

To infinity and beyond

18 November, 2013

What's that famous tagline from Ridley Scott's movie, Alien? 'In space no-one can hear you scream'.

It somehow came to mind last week in the lead up to the music concert, 'A Trip to Space', staged by my daughter Amelia's school for the deaf.

I hadn't been paying proper attention to the school newsletter updates about the concert. I sort of knew it was happening and my husband and I had sold wads of raffle tickets to raise money for the music program, but I had assumed it was only for the older kids at the school.

Phew, I thought. No need to get all stressed out about a new social event with its terror-inducing unknowns for a family that really hates, well, unknowns.

Then it dawned on me a few days from the big rocket launch. Amelia, along with all the other kids from the school's Early Learning Centre, was expected to attend. And participate. And *perform*. And we, her fellow rookie astronauts, were to accompany her and watch either a spectacular lunar lift-off or a fiery re- entry to Earth.

Regardless, it was to be our maiden voyage into the unchartered world of child pageantry and by Monday I was reaching for my inner sick-bag. I've seen *Gravity*, so I know that space is not for the faint-hearted. There's a lot of debris out there. And occasionally Sandra Bullock. Who knew if we would make it out alive?

Little notes and pictures started arriving home in Amelia's kinder bag with instructions about her costume for the night – black clothes from head to toe. Although I was still undecided about whether I would even let her go, I dutifully went out and found the garments she would need. The Right Stuff, as it were.

Then her space training went into over-drive. There was a mid-week rehearsal at the concert venue, a local school hall, and Amelia came home to me pumped to the eyeballs with the mysteries of the world beyond Earth's atmosphere.

She began humming odd tunes around the house that I'd never heard before. New signs to describe the upcoming event suddenly appeared in her Auslan vocabulary. Her imagination was captured by the importance of her special voyage ahead.

Who was I to stand in her way? When I discovered that all but two of her fellow classmates would be on stage with her, I had to take the plunge. Into that black hole where new experiences lurk with the promise of success and the portent of failure.

I talked it over on the morning of the concert with our family psychologist, JM, who supports us with Amelia's autism. I confessed my nervousness about the night and she simply asked me: What's the worst that could happen?

I guess I had visions of my girl struggling to cope and turning on a mighty meltdown within the first two minutes and we – her dad and I – would tread those familiar boards of embarrassment as we beat a hasty retreat to our car with a screaming banshee in our arms.

People would look at us and judge us to be bad parents of an uncontrollable child. JM reassured me that these negative thoughts were far from the reality of what those families – all with special needs children – would think. The most important thing was to offer Amelia the chance to be a part of something nurturing and above all, fun.

I am ashamed of my pessimism, of how far I underestimated my daughter, but it is a cold, hard fact of my time as a parent that many family missions are aborted shortly after take-off and there's no amount of planning you can implement to avoid metaphorical meteor showers.

Pessimism is terribly corrosive because it holds me back from being open to the *possibility* of change and growth but it is also my friend, ready and on guard to protect me from the risk of heart-break.

But negative feelings are there to be conquered and, like all good colonialists, my husband and I took a collective breath and made the journey anyway. Win or lose, we had to try and we had to hope, which is far better than hiding from your own life. Or, far more deplorably, denying your only child a wondrous space adventure.

And it is no exaggeration to say that the concert was close to the best night of our lives. From the moment we stepped out of the car and Amelia ran to join her friends and run with them on the school oval, the planets that had scattered within our orbit suddenly aligned.

The kinder group was scooped up and marshalled expertly by one of their incredible teachers, RS, and before we knew it, our girl was led away from us to get ready and we were free to sit. Just sit. And watch the wonderful performance unfold before us.

We did not need to mitigate or negotiate. I kept waiting for the BAD THING to happen but it never did.

The school had Amelia in its care and, as it has so often this year, it enveloped her in its safe embrace and she was happy to be separate from us. To belong to another group of trusted adults and children. To belong to herself.

Of the eighteen numbers performed in Auslan, voice, instrument and dance on the night, Amelia appeared in four magical moments. As debuts go, I put it in the class of say, Barbra Streisand's captivating introduction to film goers in *Funny Girl*. Although there's an outside chance I could be displaying some parental bias.

In any case, my little one took it up to Babs in the show-off stakes and no mistake.

She was a shocking lair up on stage. Whether she was hamming it up with her space walk, her scene-stealing turn on the bongos, or vividly signing the 'I've Got a Grumpy Face' song, Amelia was lit from within by one sight – her audience. And we couldn't tear our eyes from her.

After the opening act set to Strauss's *Also sprach Zarathustra* (what else?), she bowed deeply, repeated it with her patented Pimpernel hand flourish, then strutted along the stage line and did a few jazzy hand wiggles at her face before standing at the top of the stairs and offering a sombre salute. A salute.

The spotlight was hers to own and she was loving every second of it.

My husband and I have never laughed so hard or been so proud of a single person or event in our lives. Our hearts were fit to burst from the sight of Amelia's confidence, her *presence* in the moment. For a deaf girl with autism that is no mean feat, in space or otherwise.

I'd always watched sappy American sitcom renditions of school concerts with a mixture of cynicism and scorn. But that was before our own journey into that world, where our daughter showed us that she is already light years ahead of where we sometimes imagine she is, emotionally and socially.

Amelia spent an hour and half going on stage and off and staying patiently with her merry band of space cadets. There was no crying or screaming or running away. She knew where we were and felt secure enough not to keep seeking us out.

And when she returned to us she looked different to my eyes and it wasn't just the addition of the silver jetpack to her shoulders or the bright star now stuck to her chest.

Because when I looked at her this time I saw only possibilities. The dark matter that often weighs

A winner in every way

heavily on my mind turned to moon dust for an evening and was replaced by a feeling so radiant it would have outshone the sun.

And that was all before Amelia won the raffle prize – a chocolate hamper fit for an overacting astronaut on her first flight into the beyond. (To be strictly accurate, my husband's name was on the ticket, but who could deny Amelia another victory on such a glorious occasion?)

At night's end, we walked to the car with the other families calmly exiting the building. Just plain old walking with laughter and excitement as our soundtrack. Our feet were on the ground but for the next few hours my heart remained in space, and my eyes stayed firmly on the stars.

In safe hands we trust

12 December, 2013

A few months ago, Amelia fell over at kindergarten and hurt herself pretty badly.

It appears that she had been playing on a boat-like structure in the playground and tumbled somehow, her face taking the brunt of the collision with whatever hard surface met her fall.

No-one's really sure, because the fall itself wasn't witnessed by her carers.

Amelia was found sitting quietly to the side of the play area with her hands covering her face. She wasn't crying. She wasn't making a sound.

The first adult to approach her saw a dark red substance pooling under her hands and onto the bridge of her nose. "Amelia, have you got paint on your face?" No, turns out it was blood and a fair bit of it too.

In vain, her lovely carers tried to offer her help, to clean her wound, to see if she had broken her nose, to apply a cold compress – to help their little charge. But Amelia wasn't having a bar of it.

By the time I reached the centre, she was clutching a dirty, blood-stained tissue to her face and would not remove it. On seeing me, I watched her face change a little, registering some kind of release. Her lips quivered and her eyes filled with tears.

Amelia was obviously relieved to be taken into my care and the momentary warmth of my embrace, but she never lost control. She held onto herself and the pain and let me take her home.

I've wondered a lot about this incident since. It's not that my daughter doesn't feel pain, not at all. But the cost of showing that she is hurt is that people will come at her with their unwelcome hands and heightened emotions.

So, Amelia would prefer to sit quietly and take the pain than risk the unwanted attention of pesky Good Samaritans. Imagine the self-possession of someone like that. The will it takes not to cry, despite great pain, at four years of age.

It makes me worry for her, because as much as I want to respect her limits – those defensive walls she needs to erect between herself and the world – everyone needs a little nurturing some of the time. Noses need to be checked for breaks and blood has to be washed clean.

But how do we make Amelia feel safe enough to let us parent her? How can we help to soften her tough-guy 'Popeye' Doyle exterior enough to be comforted?

I was at a bit of a loss with all of this until September this year when we started working with our occupational therapist, MM. Her intuitive, hands-on treatment program has created some space for Amelia to let her guard down a touch and open herself to new guiding hands.

For a child like mine with autism, OT sessions serve multiple functions. They are designed to be open and flexible so Amelia doesn't feel overwhelmed or pressured.

Through this loose structure, MM is building trust, but there are rules too. If we start a new game or activity, the old one has to be cleaned up and packed away.

If Amelia kicks up a fuss about having to conform to these rules, we do not bend or back away. We just wait until she is calm enough to play again.

The effect is to create a safe environment where Amelia feels a degree of control and a lot of security at the same time as her social skills are being tested and developed.

Amelia's face, as usual, says it all

She is being taught how to wait, how to negotiate, how to live in a world governed by rules and the needs of others.

Gradually, I have watched my tough, inflexible girl change from someone who was frequently intolerant of the (not unreasonable) demands MM places upon her in each session, to a mostly willing and enthusiastic participant.

Amelia is beginning to shed a layer of deeply engrained fear and anxiety and is more ready to be guided, touched and taught than ever before.

Some appointments are held entirely in a brilliant sensory room filled with cushions, mats, swings and slides. In this room, we are testing the types of activities and sensations that work best to calm Amelia, regulate her often haywire senses and give her lots of stimulation without triggering meltdowns.

There's a large swing in the centre of this space that requires a lot of balance to stand or lie on it. At first, Amelia was reluctant to try it. But very quickly she became keen to jump on board, with me as her initial passenger. Then she graduated to swinging solo, knowing that if she fell there were mats underneath to break her fall.

In essence, that's what these sessions are all about: providing a safe platform for risk-taking and bravery. For going beyond the limits of Amelia's slowly expanding comfort zone.

These days she is like a Cirque du Solei *trapéziste* in training while looking unquestioningly to her coach, MM, for encouragement. Lying on her stomach, Amelia is encouraged to pull herself forward holding ropes or MM's hands, locking eyes with her in total trust.

Not so afraid of the Swiss ball now

I will never tire of seeing her face like that – so alive with the happiness of letting herself go, of flying without fear when there is a safety net ready to catch her no matter how high or fast she might go.

The swing involves tough core work, the kind that would challenge the most avid gym junkie, and it is teaching Amelia to push herself beyond the point of frustration to greater strength and confidence. She is now more aware of her body and what it can do. And it can do so much.

There are of course rewards for this level of commitment. The other day, after the tiring physical activity of the session was complete, MM invited Amelia to lie on the floor as the 'meat' in a cushioned 'hamburger'. One thick mat was placed on the floor and without hesitation my girl lay face down on it, waiting excitedly for the next fun thing.

The therapist then grabbed a second mat and pressed it onto Amelia's back, applying deep pressure to her small body.

After the exertion of the physical work, this pressure clearly had an instant soothing effect, bringing her sensory levels down to a calm place where balance was restored.

Then, MM took a small Swiss ball and moved it over Amelia's body in circular motions, applying more pressure to her prone figure. I have never seen her so still, so content. So *relaxed*.

Her eyes rolled back in her head and she closed them for a time, simply enjoying the bliss of the deep massage.

In this pose I could see her register, perhaps for the first time, that touch does not have to be feared or rejected and it can offer so much more than mere hands or bodies making incidental contact.

In her OT sessions, Amelia is stretching herself to new physical heights and we are all learning how long it takes to exhaust the seemingly boundless energy that burns inside her. Her social skills are improving and she is beginning to appreciate the benefits of contact tailored to suit her needs.

I am discovering there are many more ways to reach my daughter than I ever thought possible. MM has helped me to understand and accept that when Amelia hurts herself or is in need of comfort, it is not a rejection of me if she cannot tolerate my arms around her for more than a second.

She may never let me hold her the way I still long to but Amelia *does* need the security of contact and care, just not in the way most people expect of a child.

So, I will be more than happy to let the cushions, mats and balls we have acquired for our home therapy program be an extension of my mother's arms – reaching out to be close to her, offering protection, relief and all the love I can give.

Piano palmistry

4 February, 2014

The graduate

At the end of 2013, Amelia graduated from her kindergarten class. As seems to be the custom these days, even for children so young, her school fashioned junior mortarboards out of black cardboard and printed special certificates to mark the occasion.

The mini graduands even had a small stage upon which to stand as they received their laminated diplomas.

The use of academic paraphernalia to honour pre-school achievements had seemed a little over the top to me.

That was until I saw Amelia and her friends take it in turns to leap from the stage-end with unrestrained glee.

I watched them clutching their flowers and personalised documents with raw delight. Check your cynicism at the door, woman, because it is not welcome here.

This group, which had become so close during the year, really seemed to cherish their final minutes together. They hugged each other tightly and we, the parents, held onto the sight of them gathered for the last time.

To cap off this momentous day, the school's art teacher came to collect some children to be part of a special project.

The school had been chosen to decorate one of the small street pianos to appear in the Melbourne arts precinct over the summer as part of the 'Play Me, I'm Yours' community art installation.

Did we want Amelia to come and put her handprint on the piano in black paint? You bet your sweet Steinways we did.

The teacher led our girl into the art room where a small upright piano stood front and centre. It had been painted with bright, vertical stripes of red, blue, green, yellow and orange. To complete the design, little hand prints were gradually being placed across the surface of the instrument.

Amelia's palm was dipped in paint and she knelt under the keys to carefully press it onto a section of blue stripe. I looked in fear at that black hand and her clean, yellow dress, but the teacher was like a magician. Now you see a paint-spattered hand, now you don't.

Making her mark

The generous teacher then mentioned something to us about where the piano would be located in January but we were too caught up in the events of the morning to commit it to memory. It was enough that Amelia, who had come so far in a year, would be moving on from kindergarten to the big leagues of school. Leaving her mark in indelible black paint seemed like the most apt way to end things.

Almost a month later, Amelia's dad and I were walking near the back of Melbourne's Arts Centre. We had tickets to see a famous (and as it turns out not very funny) British comedian, so we were killing time in one of our favourite parts of the city. Yeah, that Jimmy Carr is a must see for anyone with a love of finely- crafted one-liners about disabilities and kids with special needs.

As we rounded a bend on the terrace I saw it: the stripy piano with its distinctive hand prints made by the students of Furlong Park School for Deaf Children.

I couldn't help myself, I jumped into the air and exclaimed loudly, giving my husband a start. It was the unmistakable sound of happiness. Of joy.

A piano with a view

Because I'd forgotten all about that piano and Amelia's palm print so carefully planted there. But seeing it out in public, seeing people playing it for the free enjoyment of others, I felt an overwhelming sense of pride.

The piano was decorated as a gift to the community and finding it by accident on that warm, summer evening felt like a gift to us too. No-one needed to know the identity of the little artist who'd given her right hand print for the sake of art.

But we did. The secret was ours to share and we couldn't stop smiling. Well, at least until the 'comedy' show started.

Good vibrations

12 February, 2014

Parenting and privacy are about as compatible as warring armies facing off in the heat of battle. Or Russell Crowe 'singing' show tunes in the film adaptation of *Les Misérables*.

Doors blissfully closed, toilet breaks taken in peace, showers enjoyed in quiet solitude: all these taken-for- granted 'you' spaces are rapidly and irrevocably invaded by 'them'.

The boundaryless child, whose chief aim as they grow and increase their gross and fine motor abilities is to keep you in full view and on tap *at all times*, cares nothing for the selfishness of time spent alone.

This process took a while to take root in our home. For her first few years of life, Amelia was very slow to crawl, to walk, to really care that much where her parents were at any given time.

She was born deaf and no-one knew this until she was two, so I guess Amelia was learning to live inside an impenetrable private space of her own. Our words could not puncture it until her hearing aids switched her on to the sounds of life and her parents reaching in to grab her.

Since this momentous time, our girl has taken great strides to bridge the gaps that existed between us. It's hard to recollect a time before she was forever at my shoulder, by my side or in my bathroom – my constant, wonderful, infuriating companion.

Sometimes I long to just shut the door behind me as I hastily jump into the shower and not hear Amelia calling me, crashing the door open and dragging all of her 'stuff' in to camp out on the floor and harass me with endless questions. So many questions.

But at the same time, those questions are a daily gift, a reminder of just how far she has come in learning to speak, to need and tell us her mind and her heart. To find her way out from dark rooms shaped by deafness and autism.

So the other day when Amelia came to me once more, in our tiny bathroom not fit for swinging cats or wide towels, and asked to join her mum in the shower, I could hardly deny her.

I nodded and in a flash she ripped out her hearing aids and placed them buzzing on the vanity before piling in with me behind the shower curtain with its brightly coloured spots.

Occasionally she likes to sit at the opposite end of the bath to me, letting the water fall onto our legs as we play boats or some silly game. We like to hold our hands under the warm stream from the tap above and enjoy the sensation.

This day, Amelia came and sat in my lap – so close – and lay her small back against my front.

It is truthfully the most happy you will ever find me, with my daughter who dislikes being held, volunteering to lie on me and enjoying the pressure of our skin-on-skin.

She held my hands and pressed her fingers into my face and my legs. And then I started singing, this crazy, high pitched, mock-soprano warbling I have a tendency to unleash in the shower (and all around the house).

I sent a big high note out into the room and the vibration in my chest went through Amelia's back and she paused for a moment before suddenly responding in kind. A big, atonal set of notes flew from her mouth and into the air, soaring high to meet mine as they fell.

And we didn't stop for anything. My beautiful girl, who without aids cannot hear more than fragments of the sound produced from my mouth, was feeling it now through my body and we were locked in a double act for the ages.

My singing was echoed in hers, as was my joy reflected in her beaming expression. Not until my husband was roused from another part of the house and came to see what his mad women of the shower were up to did we break from our performance.

I may not have any privacy to speak of, and there are no doors that stay closed for long in my house, but happily other obstacles continue to shift and open just a little. Just enough to let me hold my sweetheart for five full minutes and reach her through my body and the power of song.

In a garden state

21 February, 2014

If I think back on the last six months, I can honestly say that the turbulence that characterised our family life for close to three years has been replaced by a new and unhoped-for sense of calm.

Things are suddenly more smooth-edged than exhaustingly jagged and uneven.

The colours that surround us are bright and pleasant; flashes of fiery red appear in the corners but they don't seep into the centre.

We are happy.

Since Amelia was diagnosed with autism in 2013, we have taken great steps towards understanding who she is and what she needs to feel less at sea.

We now know she needs lots of intensive, physical activity at frequent intervals throughout the day to reduce the stress on her overloaded senses. Our house can double as a fully-equipped play centre at any given hour for just this purpose.

Physical therapy opens Amelia up to communication, to learning new things or changing long-entrenched, negative behaviours. A child with autism who is under siege is not capable of weighing up the pros and cons of toilet-training or staying in bed – they will dig deeper into a hole of defiance unless you find the right way to tunnel through to the clear air.

It is still early in the journey of course, and each day brings with it challenging variables in behaviour, in mood. What worked yesterday might need a tweak tomorrow but the basic set of strategies is usually the same. It may sound like an overstatement but it has been revolutionary to find a few really good ideas that work after throwing thousands at the wall with most missing their intended mark.

The proof is not just in how much calmer Amelia is than the child who used to scream for hours on end, or how much easier it is to help her when she is anxious, angry or scared. It's also in how much better prepared we are when the delicate balance we try to maintain everyday goes awry. We are reminded that control is never a sure thing; no child (especially Amelia) is predictable and we are in a much better place to weather a sudden, isolated storm.

Take last month for example, when we ventured out to meet family at the Royal Botanic Gardens for an early morning walk. We've enjoyed the best of times and worst of times with Amelia in these gardens but we always love taking her there.

It was a beautiful summer's morning but the café area where we parked ourselves was surprisingly quiet.

We were sitting enjoying some coffee and scones and Amelia had grown bored of the adult conversation and was skipping happily around the concrete space close to the lake. Then, as luck would have it, she ran too fast for her feet to keep up with and came crashing down, tearing her pants and skinning her knee.

While Amelia hates being helped or touched when she hurts herself, she has been getting better at letting us near her without flying off the handle.

Sadly, this was not one of those days. Her dad jumped up and moved slowly towards her. He knows not to be too forceful or crowd Amelia with lots of talking or touching if she is hurt. His voice was gentle as he sat beside her, "Are you okay?"

But it didn't make any difference. She was about to disappear into the red haze of a full-blown public meltdown and no amount of sensitivity would bring her back.

It's a bit like watching a seesaw hovering on it axis for a moment and waiting to see which way it will fall. On one side, Amelia might not react to the sudden shock of pain at all. Tilted the other way, the seesaw can fall heavily on the side of panic, anxiety and rage.

Today was an angry seesaw kind of day. I saw her start to wind-up and I instantly went into battle mode. Coffees, plates, scones, swans, company – it all ceased to exist to me as I made my way over to Amelia who had moved rapidly from fight (screaming, crying) to flight (running for the lake's edge).

She was inconsolable. I could see that her knee was very badly grazed and bleeding but I knew she wouldn't let me look at it, let alone tend to it. My first job was to physically restrain her as she tried to escape by jumping into the water

Our daughter had become a mini tornado and she was chewing up the garden scenery as her meltdown spun further out of control.

Of course people stared, I'm sure I would have. Amelia was quite a sight (and sound) to behold. But as opposed to previous years where my primary worry was what strangers were thinking about me and my child, I discovered in this moment that I didn't care about them or their thoughts at all.

My husband and I were like a united SWAT team of two. We didn't turn on each other (another thing common to the past) but we were blunt and to the point. In the maelstrom there's no time or place for politeness.

I barked, "We have to get her away from the water and to a quiet place so we can help her." Amelia was not happy when her dad lifted her then, so she started pummelling him, scratching and tearing at him as we pushed our way to the safe haven we sought, nestled on a hill with hedges for cover.

Once we made it to that space we were stuck there for the next thirty minutes while our poor, distressed child screamed and wailed and tried to gather herself. Our role was just to sit with her, talk calmly, and wait. Just wait. There's really nothing else you can do.

Amelia desperately wanted a band aid to cover the sight of the wound on her knee. She's had this visual aversion to physical injuries since she was very small. A bad toe cut was covered by her with a sock that had to be worn in the bath every night for over a week.

On the shoulders of a parental giant

But I had chosen this day to be unprepared with the most basic of first aid remedies. So instead we practiced taking deep breaths together. I would show her a big inhalation and ask her to try and copy what I was doing.

I watched Amelia valiantly draw a lungful of air into her little chest and then another as her lips quivered from crying, and I have never loved her more. For a moment these breathing exercises seemed to work their magic on her and her expression would relax, soften just a little.

Then her face would crumble again and the distress would return. We sat there for ages just taking deep breaths, holding Amelia's hand, comforting her as far as she would allow, and protecting her from the harm she might do to herself (and us).

In that secluded section of the gardens we had managed to throw a blanket over us, underneath which nothing else mattered except making sure our girl felt safe while the storm passed. No stares from strangers can penetrate that.

Sometimes, being in a family like ours, you can feel like you exist in some alternate, surreal reality to other people, and this day was no exception. Would enlarged photos of the park that day even show we were there at all, like in Antonioni's *Blow-Up*?

It's hard to say, though I suspect an audio recording would have picked up our presence pretty well.

After what seemed like an eternity, Amelia regained enough composure to leave the gardens, but only if she could ride on her dad's shoulders.

It was a long trek back to the car and that poor man's back was close to breaking point by the end. I valued every step they took together knowing we were closer to making it out and home.

Yes, our outing was most definitely ruined, cut off before it had really begun. We have spent many days like this one and they used to crush me and fill me with despair. But on this occasion I felt curiously content. Maybe it's because we understand more about what tips the scales for Amelia and sends her into an epic meltdown like this one.

We appreciate better than ever before that she can't help it. She is not being naughty or deliberately wilful or trying to hurt us. And she is suffering, so our job is to be there to do whatever she needs us to do. If that's sit in a park for thirty minutes practicing deep breathing until the panic and distress subsides, then that is what we will do.

As my knowledge about Amelia's autism has grown, so my compassion for her has deepened. When I was sitting on the grass holding her hand I wasn't feeling sorry for myself because it had all gone wrong. I only felt sorry for my little girl and the weight of what she has to endure.

I didn't indulge in self-pity, because even though we sounded and looked like a mess of a family, with all of the screaming and scratching and weird breathing, we were a total boss of a team out there.

Nobody sold anybody out on the green and no-one was left behind. We arrived together and sure, we left as a much less merry band of three and my husband was temporarily crippled, but we made it home together and that's all that counts in the end.

The ABCs of number ones and twos

11 March, 2014

Toilet training is one of those mountainous milestones that looms for many parents like some evil lava-spewing edifice from *The Lord of the Rings.*

And the burning eye glowering above it is the collective judgmental stare of the people who are sure they know better than you about how to make it to the top.

Let me clue you in on a little secret that isn't written in Elvish nor does it require fire to bring out its one true message. THEY DON'T.

Our personal story about this much-discussed but frequently misunderstood subject has all the hallmarks of an epic quest. Intrepid (read defiant) protagonist? Check. Seemingly insurmountable mission? Yep. Many years in the making and way over budget? Even Peter Jackson's accountant would have blanched at the nappy spend.

Amelia just turned five and she has only been what you could officially term 'toilet trained' for about ten weeks. We got a certificate for her birth. Something like an Oscar might have been appropriate for this milestone.

It has been a very long road marked by potholes, rugged terrain and a lot of frustration; until Christmas time just past I honestly never thought we would reach the end.

At about two years of age, when some people begin to encourage their toddlers to go the toilet (the phrase 'go potty' will not be in use during this chapter, we found we had bigger problems on our hands.

Amelia had no speech except for a few broken sounds. Her deafness meant that language had failed to penetrate her ears and her mind in any meaningful way. She was now in a state of delay, so soon it seemed after her momentous arrival.

And my god was she angry about it.

As you can imagine, toilet training was not very high on my list of parenting priorities at this time. If I had a list at all, regular items of childhood development were on the back of the page under the heading, 'I'll get to it when I can breathe, when this freefall ends. When I don't feel like I'm drowning'.

The urgent need to get hearing aids fitted for Amelia, to help her to listen, to speak and sign, all outweighed something as inconsequential as her toileting habits or how long she would wear nappies.

That didn't stop the helpful suggestions from a small but insistent peanut gallery that 'we really *should* (a hateful word in the wrong hands) start trying to train Amelia to use the toilet'.

It was like being stopped mid-spin in the centre of a tornado and scolded about not making the beds before I left. I bet Dorothy Gale didn't have to put up with that kind of nonsense.

No amount of explanation from me about the futility of training an enraged and anxious child with almost no language how to do *anything* at this stage seemed to dissuade the toiletariat from their superior view.

So we agreed to fervently disagree.

The next year was spent in the haze of medical appointments, meetings with social workers, teachers of the deaf and sign language tutors, as we grappled with this new world we had arrived in.

I did try to put Amelia on a potty and dress her in underwear but she was as far from being ready for toilet training as Neptune is from the Sun.

I didn't worry about it too much, unless the gallery popped up to remind me about it. You know, just in case I wasn't tied up in enough knots worrying about my daughter's progress and behaviour. Her future.

As a family, we preferred to celebrate genuine triumphs, like the first Christmas after Amelia received her hearing aids and she proudly sang a lullaby at the dinner table. Or any new word or sign she learned to repeat and understand.

Or how diligent she was at wearing her aids all day, every day, giving herself the strongest chance to make up for lost time. She was tough on us about everything else, but about her aids Amelia has never been anything but wonderfully compliant. And of course, she was never at risk of throwing them in the toilet.

Besides, she slept well through these years and usually ate everything on her plate as though it was her last meal on earth. We thought we were doing pretty well as parents, all things considered.

But the spectre of toilet training lies in wait in the back of a dark cupboard somewhere, knocking like hell to get out. You've squashed it in there behind the musty old linen you need to throw out and the clothes you can't wear anymore, but you know it's there. There's simply no forgetting it.

That's what really gets to me about the people who feel the need to keep telling you should 'do something about it'. Like you aren't already lashing yourself with a thousand bloody cuts of self-doubt that your approach is wrong or isn't working and will this blessed thing ever happen?

It's the same with crawling and walking, all the key milestones (are you sure they don't mean millstones?). There are always children who will reach them first and super early. Good on them. But equally there will be others who take longer, in some cases years longer, to hit their straps.

You need those polar extremes to form a broad spectrum of normal development. But it can be hard to feel relaxed about this when you're flailing around at the deep end calling for a lifeguard and there's only some preachy old washed-up surfer standing above you waxing lyrical about the tides.

As Amelia grew older and was able to communicate better and understand more, we tried many strategies to encourage her to shed the nappies for good.

Confiscation of pull-ups, reward charts, bribery, visual aids, watching her cousins 'do it', showing her books about characters going to the toilet, asking her childcare centre to encourage her (sometimes neutral but trusted adults have initial success over parents), anything we thought might work.

But she hated the idea of it all so much I had to keep abandoning it, lest we killed each other in a violent battle of wills. The mere mention of the word 'toilet' would send her into incredible paroxysms of rage, which in the confined space of our tiny bathroom was a combustible scenario.

I admit I would sometimes lose my temper and try to hold her onto a potty or toilet but this was an utterly ridiculous and upsetting tactic.

You can't physically force anyone to go to the toilet if they don't want to, and Amelia REALLY didn't want to.

I would watch her stand in fear on those occasions when her nappy was removed, and if she had an accident she would shake with revulsion at the sensation on her body and scream and cry like she was being tortured. It was awful.

Of course, I didn't know then that she had undiagnosed autism – that had to wait until she was about four and a half – but I know my mind flitted over the possibility more than once during this time.

Amelia's extraordinary defiance, her anxieties, obsessive compulsive tendencies and curious sensory needs and responses were a deadly combination when it came to achieving 'timely' toilet training.

But linking these traits to her autism mid-way through last year helped me to understand more than ever that you just have to wait until your child, whatever their personality, is truly ready to make developmental leaps. They WILL get there.

And there are positive signs of progress; it's just hard to see them when children younger than your own seem to be somersaulting through hoops to use a potty without much fuss.

It was progress when Amelia relaxed enough to wear underpants during the day all of last year to kindergarten. And though I worried about her little kidneys, it was progress that she was able to 'hold on' all day until she came home and jumped into her night nappy for bed.

Her readiness was a long, slow bow drawn in a wide arc over five tumultuous years but even we got there in the end – and here's the sugary centre to this hitherto sour tale.

It started just before Christmas when we met with Amelia's school and received wise counsel about the process of starting prep in the New Year.

The information night included a gentle but firm note about toilet training and the hope that most of the children would be independent on this score by January. I took a deep, inward breath and steeled myself for the summer holidays ahead. Like every year before this one, I thought "maybe this time…"

I abandoned random 'strategy' and threw off the shackles of good sense. Yes, I did what any decent parent would do when you've reached the end of the line and you need a result: I LIED.

"Amelia, when Father Christmas comes this year, he is going to take your baby nappies away because he said you're a big girl now and it's time for you to go to the toilet."

Her eyes widened at this news. She asked me to repeat it a number of times. I was sure she had taken it in, but would it work?

Christmas Day arrived and Santa was true to his word, swapping out presents for nappies in the most one-sided trade since the Fremantle Dockers decided they could live without 340 games and two Norm Smith Medals from Andrew McLeod.

The day was hectic and at first we hesitated in the execution of our plan. A night nappy was proffered at some stage to get us through events and I thought we might have blown it.

The following day was long and hot and we stayed home in anticipation of either a lot of screaming as nappies were demanded, or maybe, just maybe, a breakthrough.

As is typical of these historic family stories, I was not present to witness the huge moment when my girl finally went to the toilet at home for the first time in her life. I was in another room when I heard her calling for Dad. Then I heard him calling me in excited tones.

I ran to the toilet to find Amelia sitting there, a little shocked at herself but mightily pleased. By George she had really done it. And her dad and me stood there and cried behind our hands, in joy and release from the worry that it would never happen. That we would be sending her to high school in adult nappies.

Over the next few days and weeks my hilarious child treated the entire thing like she'd been at it for years.

She would throw a carefree hand over her shoulder and shrug, 'I'm goin' to the toilet, be straight back.' We would fake nonchalance and stare lightning bolts of delight at each other across the room.

It was hard to believe but before the school year was due to commence, Amelia was toilet trained and since that first day she hasn't baulked at it or taken a backward step. Because she was finally ready.

It's amazing to me the amount of energy we have expended in stressing about this particular milestone, in and around the genuinely difficult challenges we have faced in recent years. Enough to power a wind farm or a small helicopter.

Because if it doesn't come quickly or easily to your child it seems to be the one area where the greatest amount of judgement is served up to parents who are already doing their best. If that doesn't add to existing stress levels then I don't know what will.

Even after we hit pay dirt with Amelia and anticipated some praise for her or at least shared excitement, our reliable peanut gallery gave us a bit of, "well, I did tell you it was a good idea to train her but I guess you had other things on."

Other things on. Yeah, you could say that.

As domestic battles go, toilet training was hard fought and we sustained more than a few casualties of confidence. But it's not Agincourt, is it? It's not life-threatening and it's far from central to the wellbeing of a deaf child with autism. Or any child for that matter.

Yet we filled the problem of toilet training up with concrete and made a hideous skyscraper out of it; a massive grey bogey man to haunt us when we had already confronted far scarier things in the daylight.

Thank goodness Santa was around to turn him into rubble or I don't know what I would have done. And Amelia still asks me to tell her the story about how dear old Father Christmas came and took her nappies away in the night, 'Because I'm a big girl now'.

I only see spiders

2 April, 2014

When I first met Amelia's occupational therapist, we spent some time mapping Amelia's sensory challenges such as how she processes certain tactile, auditory and visual stimuli and the impact these have on her behaviour at different times.

Then MM supplied me with a valuable analogy to help me understand what it can be like to be on the autism spectrum and have your senses under constant attack from assailants invisible to the untrained eye (or ear).*

For instance, if I detect a sudden movement – something small and black perhaps – out of the corner of my eye, my heart rate might increase suddenly and my body tense as my brain calculates the risk and makes the initial assumption of 'spider!'

But if I turn to look more closely at the object and see that it is only a piece of dark paper, disturbed by a gust of wind from the window, my body will relax. My heart will return to its normal resting rate. The panic will have proved to be momentary only and I will quickly discard this memory as inconsequential.

For most people, this minor example of 'fight or flight' is one in a series of challenges to our senses we instinctively meet, manage and shrug off throughout the day.

The process is more-or-less unconscious, so that our responses to harsh sounds, bright lights and sudden contact do not spin us out of control. We may experience spikes of panic or confusion, but once we understand there is no genuine threat to our person, we can usually go about our business.

For a person who lives with autism, this process is no less subterranean but is it far from instinctively navigated. The black paper 'spider' could be among a cluster of sensory events with the potential to build to a screaming crescendo on any given day.

Or not. It need not be so obvious a threat as a creepy, crawly insect (or a moth – now that would be BAD). Amelia might detect danger in a sudden piercing noise or too many people talking loudly at once (often already stress-inducing for a deaf child), the scratchy sensation on her skin from a coarse shirt tag or a knock to her elbow from a fall.

I may not even realise that each of these things has happened to her; Amelia doesn't always show outward signs when something is bothering her. But internally, her 'fight or flight' instinct is most certainly in overdrive and her panic-ometer has spiked into the red zone.

The final straw could be something equally trivial, like a prized object moved 'out of place' from its important couch space to the coffee table, but the resulting meltdown is about all of the mini-sensory events that led up to it.

MM's analogy about autism and the senses taught me to appreciate how differently Amelia's brain functions to other people. I only wish that I knew how to anticipate or identify the trigger points to her more distressing outbursts. But at age five, with deafness and a speech and language delay thrown into the mix, Amelia is not best placed to tell us a lot about how she sees, hears and feels the world. I barely know if she has ever had a nightmare or if she is afraid of the dark. Barbie dolls freak her out though – that much I know for sure.

So for now all we can do is try to read the signs, on Amelia's face or in her behaviour, that there is trouble brewing inside her mind and body. We can't control her environment all the time but we can start to teach her how to find tiny ounces of perspective in amongst the chaos.

Or how to breathe when she feels so scared and anxious that she sees danger in every dark cloud, even when the sun is just overhead.

While there are commonalities, not all children on the autism spectrum have the same sensory processing profile. This chapter relates to the individual features of Amelia's Sensory Processing Disorder as identified by her OT.

Out with the mould, in with the new

25 April, 2014

When Amelia was nearly two and a half, we had her first appointment to be fitted for hearing aids. It's a big milestone day that one, making the cutting of teeth and other family firsts seem trivial by comparison.

This event was the start of something scary and new, from which there was no turning back. In the two months prior to her deafness being diagnosed, we'd floated anxiously in the no-man's-land between knowledge and action. We knew Amelia was deaf but nothing else changed in the weeks that followed. The news just didn't feel real until the post-diagnosis machinery cranked into gear and Amelia received her hearing aids.

I remember the trepidation I felt, the anxiety that hovered behind me during all of those initial 'big' appointments like a dark shadow. How would we get Amelia to sit still for the mould impressions to be taken? Would we remember all of the instructions given to us?

Thankfully, everything went smoothly and our girl sat statue-like while a strange green substance was squirted into her ear, forming the individual shape of the moulds that would hold her new aids in place.

The audiologist started talking to us about the aids themselves, how they worked, how to put them in and so on. They were a lot smaller than I thought they would be, which I remember brought a feeling of relief. At the time it seemed important that the physical load Amelia would bear on her tiny ears be as light as possible.

Then the audiologist talked us through the choice of colours for the aids and the moulds. There were aids in purple and electric blue and pink moulds that looked like hard candy. They looked sensational but we were not quite ready to be such exhibitionists on our child's behalf.

On that day, our instinct was to be as conservative as possible, with the standard clear moulds and a discrete silvery colour for the aids chosen for maximum concealment. They would be tasteful, even 'classy', but they would never win any prizes for fun (and neither would we).

Back then we cared a little about just how noticeable Amelia's aids would be to other people. Her 'disability' had no other visual signifier beyond the technology she would have to wear every day for the rest of her life.

So, we chose to be boring, to be safe. In the car showroom we were not the people pressing our faces onto the windows of showy luxury vehicles. Nope, we were wearing sensible, knitted cardigans and talking to the salesperson about 'longevity' and 'practicality'. Eek.

Fast-forward three full years, almost to the day, and I'm glad to say that my daughter, far braver and more interesting than us, has cooler ideas about how to drive her hearing aid choices.

There is a special style of coloured ear mould worn by some of the kids at Amelia's school for the deaf that has not escaped her notice this year. Some kids have a different colour for each ear, while others sport dual-coloured moulds instead, kind of like a Yin Yang pendant. Only, you know, nice.

One of the older boys on her school bus – a unique and beautiful child we are lucky to know – has grey and green moulds that stand out in his ears like sea-coloured whirlpools.

Amelia observed these strikingly individual choices in first term and started reciting the names of the children with different mould colours to me from time to time.

Then one day out of the blue she told me she needed new moulds. Maybe in colour. She was quite coy about her request at this point so I said, "well, we just had new ones made over the summer and they fit just fine, so maybe later in the year."

But Amelia had taken the idea to heart and she wasn't about to give up. New ear moulds. In colour. I gotta get me some of those.

About a week before her latest hearing test appointment, I reminded Amelia that it was coming up. "Don't forget we're going to see your audiologist, IS, next Thursday to play some more listening games."

There was a brief pause before Amelia replied hopefully, "We get the moulds in purple and pink?"

I stopped mid towel-fold (or something) and smiled to myself. "You bet honey, we can ask IS if she has time to do it after the test." Amelia clamped down on my semi-promise like a great white shark on an errant surfer – there would be no other outcome except satisfaction of her deep hunger for coloured moulds.

By the time we (with my mum in tow) were sitting across from IS in her office, Amelia could barely contain her excitement. We tried valiantly to get her to engage in the test but she was too distracted, antsy and generally off her game.

After a frustrating ten or so minutes, she finally turned to me and pulled my shoulder close to her body and whispered into my face, "Ask IS about the new moulds?" Amelia often uses me as her go-between with people but I have rarely felt more urgency than the moment those simple words hit my cheek and revealed the true meaning of her poor showing at the test.

My mum, IS, and I shared a laugh because we knew there would be no point trying to engage her any further that day. If Amelia wanted new mould impressions taken then, by George, she would have them.

My girl sat still, like that child statue of three years past, in anticipation of this self-directed step in her life as a hearing aid wearer. The green gloop was poured into her ear once more and she waited ever-so-patiently for it to set.

IS produced the colour chart for the moulds and Amelia confirmed the decision we already knew – purple and pink – to be made in the half/half style of her sweet friend from the school bus. It would take an agonising two weeks for them to be prepared and then delivered by mail.

It took all of my Auslan skills to explain to Amelia that some man in a back office wouldn't be able to produce the colourful moulds on the spot. She kept saying, "No, we wait." After some wrangling, she reluctantly let go of her heart's desire and went off to school.

It was a rainy, cold day on the school holidays when the magical delivery finally arrived at our house. I secretly retrieved the envelope from the letter box and attached her new moulds to her aids while she was in the bath.

When Amelia was dried and dressed, she waited for me to bring her aids back to her in the bathroom. Barely containing my own excitement,

I carried them in behind my back and asked her to guess which hand held the prize.

Her eyes lit up with instant understanding and delight as she pointed to the left. No, they must be in the right.

I wish it was possible to capture for more than a moment the unbridled joy that shines from a child's eyes when they see something special they've longed to have and hold in their hands. It's a sight that never fails to reach deep into my chest and pull so hard on every heartstring, it's almost painful. Almost.

But the look on her face when she tried on the new moulds for the first time, well, that was an image I wasn't going to lose to fading memory. I snapped some photos as she preened (truly) in front of our bathroom mirror, so very proud of her custom-made bling.

Do you think she's happy with them?

Everywhere we went for the next few weeks Amelia would race up to friends and family to show them. She was busting to get back to school to now be a part of the cool kids group who have cut loose from the clear mould crowd.

We are so lucky to be able to send her to a school with other deaf children like her, who are learning together how to express their identities through things like their hearing aids.

They are not ashamed to wear them or have them noticed. On the contrary, they want to shout at the world in loud colours from rooftops, "look at me!" It's thrilling to see Amelia's personality and independence take shape through the choices she is beginning to make on her own, especially where her deafness is concerned.

At age five, she knows quite a lot about aids, implants, Auslan and even the sign for 'deaf', but she is too young to understand the combined significance of those things in her life. That process is slowly unfolding, inching closer to comprehension every year.

But seeing her assert herself so strongly and positively when it comes to 'owning' her hearing aids makes me worry less about how she will cope with the eventual knowledge of being deaf.

Amelia has a 'come at me' attitude to most things and I suspect on this score she will not waver. Only time will tell. In the meantime, it makes me happy to realise how far we have travelled from our (short-lived) days as conservative parents of a newly-diagnosed deaf child.

I love to pile Amelia's long hair high on her head so that people *will* see her aids. Yes, she is deaf and we are genuinely proud of that part of who she is. And as usual, our daughter is light years ahead, taking us with her to the sky and back on the crest of an exhilarating purple and pink wave that never seems to crash before a new one rises again, brighter than before.

What's love got to do with it?

2 May, 2014

Happiness incarnate

Since becoming a parent, I have received lots of asked-for and unsolicited advice on just about any child-rearing topic you can imagine.

Every parent experiences this at one point or another. When you have a child with special needs there are unlimited opportunities for people to weigh in and give it their best shot.

Many observations are like little gems; I hold them between my hands, turning them over to feel their warmth and absorb the good vibes within. These ones are keepers for sure.

Others, however well-intentioned, delivered by experts or drawn from experience, miss their mark, creating only harsh notes as they glance my shoulder and crash to the ground.

However surplus to requirements these opinions are, I still find myself carefully turning a few of them over in my often stressed-out brain. This isn't always a negative or masochistic process. It can be incredibly empowering to drag up some old advice handed to you about your life and see with increasing clarity just how misplaced it was and remains still.

One special example of this springs to mind, and it seems to grow in meaning to me the more I think about it.

The gap between my experience and this particular (I guess well-meant) remark has stretched so far apart you could fit the Pacific Ocean between the places we're coming from.

It happened during a conversation I had with someone soon after Amelia's autism diagnosis was formally confirmed. We had spent many weekends going back and forth to a clinical psychologist and the results, which surprised no-one, were in.

Mostly what I hoped for from people was a simple acknowledgement of the news, and perhaps in that a sort of agreement would be forged among those closely connected to Amelia that we shared the same aims. To help her. To make things better.

That's my personal definition of support. We confront a problem, give it a name and then we portion it out, dissect it and work out the best way to move forward.

But not everyone approaches life this way. I'd begun saying to this person that I was feeling sad for Amelia about her diagnosis but that I thought we could now help her through treatment, but they stopped me and said, "oh you don't need all of these LABELS, you just need to LOVE HER. That's all she needs."

Just love her. That's all. As though love could ever be enough.

I was a bit shocked at the flippancy of it, at how far the words missed the point, but in that moment I didn't really know what to say. I was trying to stifle tears and I knew that my thoughts wouldn't come out clearly or kindly. So I gulped and pushed my response down until I was in a position to consider the comment properly.

There's something so misguided about saying to a person who has recently received (more) tough news about her child in a family already dealing with so much that she only needs to love her and essentially everything will be fine.

Because everything is not fine. It wasn't fine at the time and it's not fine today. And just saying it's fine doesn't make things better. It just makes me angry, like molten lava could spew out of my eye sockets at the mere mention of the words 'just love'.

If love was enough then I would not have discovered fertility issues in my late twenties and that we needed to undergo IVF in order to conceive a child.

If love was enough, I wouldn't have had to be injected with hormones every morning by my husband for months and months until I was bruised inside and out.

If love was enough, I wouldn't have had to endure the desperate weeks of waiting to discover if the two fertilised eggs placed inside me would make it. One did. That wasn't a miracle of love – it was a victory of science.

If love was enough, I would have been able to have more children instead of finding out that my ovaries had withered on the vine by my 36th birthday. Early menopause is not a gift of love nor is the wall you have to build between yourself and the endless questions about why you haven't had more children.

If love was enough, I would have known instinctively that my cherished only daughter was in fact deaf when I first held her, instead of two long, costly years later. That's not something that can be undone, no matter how hard we might wish for it.

If love was enough, Amelia would not have also been born with what the doctors call a 'complex array of developmental issues', including autism. We don't yet know all of the problems we are dealing with so we just attack them one at a time.

I don't list this roll-call of personal setbacks to suggest I've had it harder than anyone else, or that I sit around every day feeling sorry for myself. Compared to Amelia, who am I to complain?

What I'm saying is that it has been my experience at the sharper end of life that love really *isn't* enough. Interventions, by science and technology, by expert outsiders like audiologists, specialists, psychologists and so on have been unavoidable and necessary realities in the short story of my family.

Love is a fine anchor, a base from which to spring, a strong foundation, an incredible motivator, but on its own I'm afraid it's pointless.

Over the last few years I have learned the hard way that work is the thing that, well, works. IVF works when your body can't do the job on its own. Hormone medication works when you can't sleep because you're sweating six times a night like Albert Brooks in THAT scene from *Broadcast News*.

Rigorous and frequent exercise works when your mind can't take the strain of the things happening to you. Regular tests, therapies and lots of practice work to help Amelia to speak, to be calm, to be well.

Without a doubt, I love Amelia more than I ever thought it possible to love another person. And this never stops, even on the most demanding days when she seems to hate me and the world for dragging her into it without asking.

Love (and Amelia's early-bird body clock) gets us up in the morning for appointment after appointment with speech pathologists, our occupational therapist, a clinical psychologist, paediatrician, GP, even genetics specialists, but it's sheer stamina that keeps us going, ever on to the next thing.

If you know all of these things about me, my life, my child and you can still look me in the eye and say, 'don't worry about all of that stuff, just hug it out when things get tough' then you have failed to really see us and understand what we need.

To me, love is acknowledging our pain and our struggles as well as celebrating the amazing progress and milestones that follow. Anything less is a massive negation of that struggle, of the reality of our daily lives in the trenches.

I need more than whatever love is supposed to do for me. Along with hugs (which are great) I also need time, space, exercise, information, silence, solidarity, respite, contact, friendship, conversation, laughter, truth and action, to name a few key things.

If I 'just' love Amelia, then what else does she miss? It feels like a code for denial to me and I'm not playing that game. No way.

I wake up every day with a limitless base of love for her, but it's the hard work and resolve that's gonna get us over the line. We'll keep our fairy tales for the night-time, when our toil is done and Amelia is happy, safe and well in the strongest arms designed to hold her. Mine.

Look who's (not) talking too

9 May, 2014

"No. More. Talking"

I like to talk. A lot. The vast amount of energy I have in my body often transforms into rapid-fire emissions of endless verbalising, extemporising, riffing, and the expression of random and over-analysed thoughts that ping around my busy head. See, I'm doing it already!

Ask anyone who knows me well, and they'll probably say I remind them of a cross between that manic savant Jordan from *Real Genius* (classic 80s comedy) and the Sally Weaver character from *Seinfeld*. The latter does have red hair and a propensity for high-energy conversation so it's a solid link.

No-one complains when I lose my voice from illness (happens maybe once a year). Indeed non-medical types around me plump for "better not strain your voice, Mel, try being more *silent*." Only yesterday, my friendly local coffee provider recommended I try a decaffeinated beverage to help "dial things down".

Thanks for the suggestion, but I'm either operating at 0 or 11 and there's no dimming of the interior lights when they're burning their brightest.

Unless, of course, you are my controlling, hyper-vigilant five-year-old, Amelia, and you have decided to be the Sheriff of Talk Town. In that case, I have little to no agency, and when her small hand reaches for the 'off' switch, the time for talking is over.

A curious and sometimes frustrating facet of Amelia's autism is her anxiety about people speaking, particularly sudden or raised voices or laughter – anything that signals to her that calm has been disturbed, even if the sounds are essentially happy, at least to our ears.

Amelia is often unable to interpret such sounds as positive ones, and so she becomes highly agitated and on the lookout for ways to lock things down to a neutral (and quiet) zone.

I suspect that her hearing loss plays a role here too, where the increased volume of overlapping speech sounds might come across as distorted and unpleasant, received as they are through hearing aids which can never fully replicate the sophisticated noise filtering of an ear without nerve damage.

I'm also aware how frustrating it must be for Amelia to have to work so hard to listen, hear, and speak so that when other people commence an interaction that is, to her, exclusionary, the sounds might be intolerable.

Whatever the cause, some days are filled with nervous tension as soon as Amelia's dad and I try to have a quick conversation, share a laugh or shout to each other from one room to the next; all ordinary sounds of life in a communal household, but to Amelia, they're like alarm bells heralding something disquieting that needs to be warded off.

She used to shout at us to stop talking or put her body between us to cut things off mid-stream. For a long time we would just wait until she went to bed at night to try and resume a story begun many hours before. We're often awake in the wee small hours of the morning, whispering our way through a towering stockpile of unfinished chats and exchanges.

On other days when Amelia's anxieties are really out of control, she will run from room to room shrieking, "Are you ok, are you ok, are you ok?!" at me if she has heard me sing or make any kind of sound that is presumably coming at her like fingernails on a blackboard (and my singing's not THAT bad).

She'll yell at us to "stop screaming" even when our voices are low and moderated as we know they need to be so as not to agitate her. But sometimes it's hard to do that when you're having a spontaneous response to something you see on the television or read in the paper.

Or, say, you just like to banter with your life partner.

Amelia's newest strategy has been the most effective and on some level, at least a little amusing, because in our crazy household you gotta laugh. You just have to.

If I come home from somewhere, filled to the brim with anecdotes to be told, funny stories to impart, Amelia is at the ready with her gun hand, poised to take me out of the conversational equation with devastating speed and accuracy.

She will simply climb onto or next to me and place her hand firmly over my mouth. Not in a creepy way like John Huston's giant hand silencing his 'granddaughter' in the final scene of *Chinatown*, but it's not exactly a warm or friendly gesture.

Amelia knows that I will keep trying to talk for as long as I can, underwater, in the shower, wherever I can to feel alive in the world. And she's absolutely jack of it.

Her preference is for me to remain mute until the conversational winds have passed and no-one has the stamina to keep talking anymore. Or that I should only talk to her and answer her relentless questions about where individual characters on the television screen have gone when they're off screen and when they're coming back.

So Amelia employs her patented five-fingered hand clamp on my resistant mouth. She leans in close to my face, lifts a finger to her lips and whispers with some menace, "Shhhh. No. More. Talking."

Yes, my doe-eyed daughter morphs into a ruthless standover merchant and the steel in her eyes and her voice tells me she 'aint messin' around'. I'm only just realising how much ownership Amelia claims over me and my face – she has her hands on my cheeks or my mouth all of the time, pulling me closer to her so she can read my lips or hear me more clearly.

She evens signs words in Auslan on my body as well as hers to make sure she's getting her chosen point across. There's not a lot of scope for free speech or movement in a relationship as full-on as that.

It's not as extreme as this all of the time and Amelia's anxieties peak and trough depending on how calm she's feeling generally, or how under control her senses are on any given day. I suspect her irrational response to our talking has a lot to do with just that – control – the need to dominate us and bend us to her will when so much in her life is far beyond her control.

While we are amused by this 'game' of 'no talking', after a while you realise your child isn't learning at all how to live in a household where sometimes there are people talking around instead of to her and that the sky isn't falling as a result.

If we simply cave in, Amelia will just steam roll over the top of us until no-one is talking, or sleeping, or walking or having showers alone or just getting on with their day without managing the intense needs of the strongest personality to walk the planet since Mohammed Ali.

She has to learn how to compromise and how to WAIT. They're important life and social skills and we're doing Amelia no favours by not pushing back and trying to teach her some behavioural limits.

So when she starts in with the shouting and the mouth-clamping, we have to set a visual timer and tell her that Mummy and Daddy are ok, we're not screaming and that talking is ok. We are going to talk for five minutes and she has to keep playing with her book or game, whatever, until the timer and we are done.

It's a battle that's in its early stages and often five minutes of 'talking' will be peppered with lots of yelling and physical interventions from Amelia, desperate to rest the floor back from us. But you have to persist, if you want to preserve your marriage, your individuality and the relative sanity of your home.

We're nowhere near solving this latest parenting challenge to pop up in our family soup. The minute you think you've covered off one problem, another one pops up ready to confound and frustrate.

For now we'll keep setting timers and having interrupted conversations and hope for the restoration of 'calm' someday soon.

Because noise – jokes, stories, laughter, tales – are the spice of a happy family life, and the best lesson I can teach Amelia is how to recognise the positive notes when she hears them and one day she'll realise that it's safe to join in.

Deaf like me

11 June, 2014

One of the most exhilarating and scary things about being a parent is watching your child grow and begin to understand more and more about who they are and how they fit (or don't) into the world around them.

In the beginning, the concept of 'who they are' is largely defined by parental opinion and self-indulgent projections such as 'oh, she has my eyes', or 'she's strong-willed like her mum'. *She* is in the world but she's not her own person yet.

But at some stage, that child will break the shackles of the prescriptive parental narrator and strike out on their own path, discovering 'who they really are' on their own terms.

For us, that process is made even more complex by the fact that aside from personality traits, quirks and individual preferences, Amelia's life has had some surprise storylines that she is only starting to uncover for herself.

The fact of our daughter's challenges are weighty and have taken us years to deal with and understand. We're far from reconciled to their impact on her life and ours.

For Amelia, the journey to self-discovery is very much at its genesis. About her deafness, she knows that without her hearing aids she can't hear music, television or clear voices.

In this, she has made an important connection between her hearing loss and the technology she uses to access sound and the world around her. Then a few months ago, she referred to a teacher at her school as 'deaf' in speech and sign but when I gently pressed her on what the word meant, she was unable to explain.

No doubt at Amelia's school for the deaf she sees, hears and signs the word deaf quite a lot, but it has understandably remained an abstract concept for her. She uses it as a label for people the way she might say "that man is old", or "my friend is cheeky".

I hold my breath a bit during these interactions with her because each time I'm waiting to see if the penny has truly dropped. You know, the day she finally asks me about *her* deafness, not just some vague, remote concept.

I'm also hyper-conscious about not forcing the realisation onto her before she is ready. It's one thing to learn that your daughter is deaf and to try and assimilate that word and its meaning into your own sense of their identity. But this part of her story is not mine to tell or explain. It's not my right to telegraph such an important fact about who she is. For once, I have to just shut up, listen and wait until Amelia works it out for herself.

Like yesterday, when she came home from school and spotted a picture of a toddler with hearing aids in a newsletter sitting on the kitchen bench. The conversation went like this:

"Mum, the baby has hearing aids like me…"

"Yes, he does have hearing aids," I said.

"Mmmm," Amelia pondered for a second and then said and signed, *"I'm deaf"*.

As usual, I held my breath for a few seconds and then said in a neutral tone, "Are you deaf? Show me the sign again, Amelia?"

She signed 'deaf' once more. I softly asked, "And what is deaf, Amelia?" She didn't say.

Then I asked, "Who else is deaf, Amelia?" to test her understanding and she began to list the names of her classmates, all of whom are deaf.

And then quick as a flash she broke the spell that seemed to hang over our chat for a minute and ran off in pursuit of another game and the brief moment of self-realisation came to an end. I exhaled a long, slow breath and smiled.

I'm not sure how much closer she is to understanding what it means to be deaf but it felt like a big deal to me, the first time my girl said that *she* was deaf. It is no longer an abstract concept that lives outside of her experience or a random label applied to somebody else.

Amelia has begun to comprehend more about who she is, only part of which is being a deaf child. I am sure that once the penny really drops there will be stages when she has different feelings about what deafness (and autism) mean to her identity. To her sense of self.

But whether it's a heads or tails proposition, my only job is to hold her hand as I always have and listen and answer her questions with absolute honesty. Like when she asks me if *I'm* deaf and I have to say no even though I secretly wish I could lie and pretend we are the same.

Five (un)easy pieces

20 June, 2014

Irecently found myself in a situation that reminded me of one of my favourite David Brent moments (and there are many) from *The Office*.

Brent (played by Ricky Gervais with depths of pathos unseen since the days of W.C. Fields) is told by his boss, Jennifer Taylor-Clarke, that Wernham Hogg is under a financial cloud.

Changes to the Slough branch will need to be made in the lead up to an internal merger.

It's serious business, but Brent has his mind on other things – like hiring a new forklift driver and setting Dawn the receptionist up in front of a new co-worker to think she has been fired.

All in a day's work on the best cringe-comedy series ever made.

By episode two, Jennifer is back to find out what changes or cuts Brent has made.

"Can you give me, let's say, five practical changes that you've actually made?" she quite reasonably asks.

The question elicits that now-familiar flicker of panic across Brent's face when under actual work pressure. Then the strategy of the uber-procrastinator: pause, repeat the question back to the person and try to change the rules.

"Five changes? Let me give you three, and then another two if you need 'em….. Efficiency, turnover, profitability…"

Brent's pathetic attempt to offer up 'three things' when only five would do always makes me and my husband laugh so hard. We quote it endlessly and, I'm sure, annoyingly to anyone not familiar with the series.

But some days I feel Brent's obvious pain at being cornered by a question requiring a deeper response, or by an answer that just doesn't come as easily as I would like.

One such occasion struck me a few weeks ago when I was sitting around a table with the other participants in a program called 'Signposts for building better behaviour', designed for parents of children with a disability.

Amelia attends a primary school for the deaf which has organised for a small number of families to access this impressive six-week program.

We are learning more about why our children — all of whom have multiple special needs — behave the way they do, develop better strategies for managing their behaviour and perhaps, fingers and toes tightly crossed until the circulation cuts off, prevent such challenging behaviours down the track.

There's no black magic here. No sacrificial lambs taken out the back and slaughtered at midnight to appease the mighty parenting gods. Nope, it's good old fashioned practical advice backed by sound research.

But that doesn't mean it's short on, dare I say it, Oprah-style light-bulb moments.

Take this exercise as an example. We were sitting around talking about how to describe our child's behaviour. Not just generic terms like 'naughty' but using greater detail such as, "Amelia sat on her dad's lap and repeatedly hit him over the head and scratched his face." You get the Tokyo drift.

We could have riffed all day about the bad stuff, the negative tales, the images of difficulty, the specific definitions of what is hard.

Then, and here comes the Jennifer Taylor-Clarke spinner, write down five things your child has done recently that you LIKE.

Cue crickets.

I was asked to name five things, five easy pieces that Amelia has delighted me with, and for more than a minute I was completely flummoxed.

I have never felt more like quoting David Brent in my life.

We were all in the same, rocky boat, me and the other parents. I looked across the table at one mum whose wonderful son has similar challenges to Amelia and we shared a rueful smile. That we *like*, huh? This was going to be tough.

But in truth, once you switch your mind on to the positives, once you sift out the detritus that sits on the surface all day polluting your thoughts with grim despair, you find that you can't stop accentuating *the things you like.*

My blue pen scratched across my workbook until the words were flying onto the page. What do I like? It turns out I like plenty:

1. Amelia slept until 7am this morning;
2. Amelia gave us a big hug and said 'I love you';
3. Amelia taught me how to sign 'Cinderella';
4. Amelia did not scream when I said no to more breakfast;
5. Amelia played by herself in her trampoline for 20 minutes.

I love the way the program asked us to do this exercise. It had multiple purposes but its real gift to me was the time and space to sit and think about the many things Amelia has done recently that I like, that make me do little fist-pumps of celebration when no-one is looking.

When I look at my list I see how much progress she has made. Living inside the all-encompassing bubble that surrounds families raising a child with special needs, it can be difficult to notice progress and development.

You only feel weight and pressure and, frankly, under-equipped to raise such a complex person who needs so much love and support.

It is unfortunately too easy to forget to celebrate the good things, the small efforts that are a sign of better times to come.

When I went home, my positive reflections travelled with me and they stuck around.

Stronger and more confident everyday

'Signposts' is not offering some kind of silver bullet solution to the ever-vexed experience of parenting *any* child, least of all someone like Amelia – an alpha girl who is both deaf and on the autism spectrum.

Yet it's no less revolutionary in my mind. Now, when I sit down at the end of another long day and I think back on how it all went with Amelia, I'm just as likely to start making a mental note of the things she did that I liked, instead of a black list of 'bad things'.

But more than that, in the moment I am now able to recognise those pleasing things and tell her right then how helpful she is, how clever, how kind or how funny.

I see the impact of my words on Amelia's shining face; I haven't starved her of positive feedback but her obvious hunger for more has made me rethink what my child needs on a daily basis.

So when Amelia asks me what she is good at or why she won a prize at school for being responsible (last week's massive score), I will never again be lost for words. I'll just take a variation on the Brent route and say, baby, I'll give you three things and then a million more if you want 'em.

Amelia and the magic torch

18 July, 2014

It is a truth universally acknowledged that too many writers use the famous opening line from Austen's *Pride and Prejudice* to kick off their articles.

Yes, it's a brilliantly ironic line (in the true, non-Alanis Morissette sense) from a master writer, but I reckon it's time to branch out and steal from other authors. Dickens does a nice line in, well, opening lines.

It is also a fact that the more Amelia learns to communicate – in both speech and sign language – the more I am beginning to truly know her and understand the cogs that drive her quirky child-machine.

For the last few years it's as though my husband and I have been engaged in an endless game of charades with our girl, or at least some kind of mind-bending puzzle, to try and work out what she wants, what she fears, *who she is.*

We had the picture on the box to guide us, but some key pieces had clearly escaped down the side of the couch.

In the past, if Amelia was unsettled or distressed at night for instance, we never really knew why. Was she sick? Did she have a headache or a sore stomach? Did she fear the dark that enveloped her room after lights out? We didn't know and she couldn't tell us. Her language skills just weren't there yet.

So, we've been miming and prognosticating like crazy, making suggestions to her, offering theories to each other until I'm sure she just wanted to make like Greta Garbo and tell her mad parents she wanted to be alone.

Until recently, we had to rely on more explicit signs of Amelia's preferences in life or trial and error solutions to problems raised by sudden outbursts of screaming or fear.

But I think there's something magical about age five and the first year of school. Amelia has flourished and progressed in ways we never dreamed she would. Especially where her speech and language skills are concerned.

Every day since term one, I have been in a constant state of delighted awe watching my little girl rush from her bus to tell me about the exciting things she has done with her class.

Amelia will dive into her bag to show me the new book she is slowly beginning to read. Or the letters she learned to write that day. Two months ago, she could only write in reverse from the right of the page to the left. Now her writing compass has switched due-East and she is copying whole, legible words with increasing confidence.

But it's the improvements in her speech and language, and with them the expression of her innermost thoughts, that we cherish the most. The other day, my husband heard Amelia talking to herself in her room about writing letters of the alphabet. "Mmm…I can do S, I can't do a K, I can't do E…", and so on went her private recitation.

In this small example what I hear is Amelia's deep interest in learning, her personal reflection on what she is able to do and what she is hoping to work out for herself in time. I can better understand her and I never want it to stop.

Last week, she woke up in the middle of the night, which is generally out of character for her. When this happens we might hear crying or yelling to tip us off that something is amiss. This time though, her voice flew out into the hallway with a single, urgent message: "I'm scared! I'm scared!"

There it was. An answer to a shift in behaviour before a question had been signed or spoken. When I went in to see her she repeated her fears by furiously signing 'scared' on her chest over and over again. Amelia could not have been clearer about her feelings.

We were able to calm her down but it was obvious that we needed to learn more about *what* was frightening her so. The next morning I met her at school for her Monday speech therapy session with the lovely CN.

Partway through the session, the subject of Amelia's early waking came up. Without any probing she said, "I'm scared of my room". I tucked that little clue under my arm and later in the evening I had a chance to probe her about what she feared so much about her room.

I asked, "Amelia, what are you scared of in your room at night?"

She didn't miss a beat, "I'm frightened of the black dark." She emphasised *black dark* with a punctuating rise in volume to make sure we knew just how spooky it was.

I continued, "The black dark? You don't like the dark when the lights go out?"

"No, I don't like it. I'm scared."

Now we knew for sure what was wrong, I said, "Amelia, would you like me to put your red torch on and leave it on your shelf after you go to sleep? It's a special, magic light and it'll keep the black dark away".

I was reaching back into my memory to a cartoon called *Jamie and the Magic Torch*. My brothers and I would re-enact the magical properties of Jamie's torch in my room with a mirror that reflected a circular shape on the wall. I was afraid of the black dark too.

I turned on Amelia's torch to show her how the kaleidoscopic colours would glow warmly in that black dark. She really liked that idea, shouting triumphantly, "go away black dark, go away!" Her hands slashed mightily through the air as she shooed her imaginary terror out of sight.

After Amelia was safely tucked up in her bed and snoring softly, I switched on her magic torch, ready to stand guard over the scary darkness. The night passed without event. There was no screaming from her room, no movement, no sounds of fear or anxiety. The torch won.

In the morning, my daughter who now has whole conversations with me, said, "I like the little dark, not the big dark." Amelia was saying to me that the torch had taken the edge off the dark for her and made it better. She was not feeling so scared anymore.

Some people find Amelia's voice hard to understand and she is shy to share her speech with people outside of school and home. I know people who are surprised when I tell them that she can speak at all.

I also notice that she doesn't sign as much when she is around people she doesn't know very well. Perhaps that is a language she associates more with her deaf school friends, teachers and close family members who share it with her.

But now she's talking and signing like a demon at home, she never, ever stops. Unless she is without her hearing aids when she'll tell me earnestly, "Mum, I can't talk… we need sound." I have a new understanding that Amelia doesn't like to talk a lot without her aids in.

As per our routine, I put them in yesterday morning and she beamed at me and said, "*Now* I can talk! You talk, Mummy. GO!" It was an instruction, not a request. I said, "Hi, baby girl!"

Her answer was short but ever-so-sweet. "You *can* talk, Mummy. You can."

The dad who went up a hill and carried his daughter down a mountain

13 August, 2014

I am only just beginning to understand the pain my husband has carried with him on our path to parenthood. It's a subterranean heartache but I can feel it beating beneath the surface of our lives, growing louder when times are hardest.

In his eyes I can see the cost of past experiences that have made him yearn for deeper bonds with people. Friendships are deeply important to him, as is that reciprocal give-and-take of a connection truly shared.

When it came time to start a family of our own, I know he (like myself) hoped to fulfil the dream of having a baby – son, daughter, it didn't matter – who would hold him close in the deepest relationship yet possible. The one with his child.

As a family, we would achieve a grand closeness never before seen in the universe. In short, we would grasp hands and never let each other go.

But try as you might, it is futile to pretend that any of us can control life in this way. Nor is it right to expect that a child should act as some sort of gap-filler for relationships that spun away from us in our childhood.

Together, we have learned this lesson the hard way. Amelia did not receive our exhaustive memos in utero about close companionship or ready compliance. The lists we made detailing the places we would go, the activities we would share, the things we would teach her: all were lost in translation from imagination to stark reality.

Amelia arrived without knowing the great weight of expectation we had heaped on her shoulders. In turn, it took us time to learn that she is deaf and has autism too.

That second, more recently identified fact, struck my husband in the chest like an arrow shot. The wound has not yet healed.

For him, I think it must sometimes feel as though he has been thrust back into the more troubling spaces of his past. Of his longing for companionship and finding only barriers where open arms should have been.

But this is much, much worse, because here we are talking about his beautiful, cherished daughter. The person he most longed to meet and who, when he found out we were expecting, nearly collapsed from paroxysms of joy.

During the worst phases of Amelia's rages, he has woken daily to chaos only to return at day's end to find similar chaos readying itself to greet him once more. I am lucky, because I have been around to witness and enjoy the moments of calm that happen in between.

He has spent endless hours trying to get his daughter to listen to him, to calm down or just sit with him and play. If only for a few moments.

Often the greatest challenge is asking Amelia to leave him alone. She craves closeness too, but filtered through her autism it's all rough physicality and she can't moderate the need in an appropriate way.

So, she presses herself on him, lies on him, punches him and pulls at his face until he often has to abandon her and lock himself away.

But over five years of incredible ups and downs it is possible (read = mandatory) to adjust one's expectations of family life. We have had to put on hold some of the things we hoped to do together. Little things that the majority of people take for granted every day.

We make do with living as a family unit that sometimes needs to split up and create more manageable compartments to survive. It's crucial to recognise which combinations work best for Amelia depending on the situation.

Like going to the football. For as long as I can remember, my husband has dreamed of taking his little girl to see our beloved Bombers play. He would dress her in red and black and talk to her about the rules and the players. We can't control much but Amelia has no say in which team she is required to barrack for. No matter what their recent transgressions, we're an Essendon family through and through.

Sadly for my husband, taking her to games is too high-risk an activity right now. After about the age of two, Amelia has found it impossible to sit down for longer than a few minutes and the combination of crowds and noise makes it too stressful for her.

Very swiftly, Amelia starts to lose control and, as is the ritual, her dad is forced to carry her screaming form out and away from the din, from those screaming just as angrily at the umpires. It's not fair on either of them to pretend the result can be otherwise. At least in the short term.

So we achieve a domestic harmony of sorts by being ultra-sensitive to Amelia's needs and abilities, and by looking out for each other as parents, and as individuals. So when her dad goes to the football it is not with his family but with other dads and their children.

Discovering happiness on the hills of Melbourne

Like a genial uncle, he sits with them and talks to them about the game he loves and wonders at how *still* they are. How *easy* it is to be with them. And he wishes he didn't have to leave his daughter behind.

But just because he sometimes has to be apart from her, as I do, that doesn't mean he hasn't looked for other ways to connect with her. To make himself feel like her father, and she his daughter.

So what do they do? They walk. Most Sundays, Amelia and her dad drive to sundry parks all over Melbourne and beyond and just walk. It's more like ranging really, up hill and down dale, whether it's raining or not.

Amelia is a terrible walking companion. She has no sense of safety, she strays, and runs away and follows other people and animals like a hybrid canine-child catching the scent of something colourful, fun or more interesting *over there*. Always over there.

Last week she spotted a group of horse riders and careened headlong into a valley after them, with no fear of equine retaliation. The riders shouted at her to stop and thankfully she heeded their harsh tones. My husband recalled it to me later, the sense of helplessness as she broke away from him and sprinted towards potential danger.

Clearly rambling with Amelia is absolutely exhausting. But, for all that it is taxing, her dad loves it too. Walking in the outdoors was a treasured part of his upbringing and now it is his gift to her.

Because regardless of the weather or the clouds that pass over her face from time to time, they are together. They're not at the football, or visiting friends. But on the hills of Melbourne they have found each other through walking.

And when they come home to me, their faces flushed from the elements and the joy of adventure I see only closeness. I see the beauty and the depth of their relationship as father and daughter.

The ice girl cometh

18 September, 2014

Warrior girl with water

R ecently I found myself caught up in the wacky Ice Bucket Challenge sweeping Facebook feeds the world over. You might have seen one of these videos, where some poor, charitable soul stands nervously in a suburban backyard, waiting to be drenched with ice-filled water by delighted relatives enjoying their role a little too much.

Yep, that was me a few weeks ago. I was 'tagged' by my good friend CM to take up the challenge and once you're 'it' there's no such thing as 'keepings off' or 'barley'.

So I stumped up and took my freezing cold medicine. For the good of the cause (motor neurone disease) and because I didn't want to be called a wuss. I know, I'm not about to win a humanitarian of the year award.

But I do know someone who would have taken that ice bucket challenge by the horns and never let go. She would have relished it, and asked for more and more buckets until she'd beaten the Guinness Book of Records benchmark that might apply to a weird new age phenomenon such as this.

Who is it, you ask? Some hard-skinned ranger type who feels no pain and crushes all opponents in their wake? No, I'm talking about my five-year-old daughter Amelia, who is wildly passionate about the sensation of very cold water on her skin.

I first noticed this strange sensory trait when she was about two and a half. One afternoon during the winter time, I saw her outside with a bucket of cold water she'd filled when I wasn't looking. She proceeded to fill a smaller bowl with the water and pour it repeatedly over her head and quivering body. It was quivering with the cold no doubt, but also with powerful exhilaration.

Triumph of the will

For a moment I watched at the window, transfixed by the scene. Amelia's beautiful round face was a study in elation, in euphoria. She appeared totally unbothered by the frigid temperature of the water. Instead, it was a delight to her and she welcomed it without fear or hesitation.

I was torn between wanting to leave her be for a while longer to enjoy being at one with the water, and the mothering instincts which compelled me to gate-crash this spontaneous garden party and throw a big towel over it. And her.

Other times I found her in our backyard with no clothes on, holding a gushing hose in the air so the icy plumes of water would fall straight down onto her head. Amelia treated the water with reverence, as something deeply special to her that only she could understand.

It's true that my girl had never enjoyed warm water, especially in the shower. My attempts to add *just a little more* heat to the stream from above were always instantly detected. I couldn't get past my child's incredible sensitivity to the temperature and how it felt on her skin.

For quite a long time this need in her worried me a lot. Every time she'd ask for cold shower water as she sat in a shallow (warm) bath below, we'd wrestle with the taps and I'd think 'I can't let her sit in freezing cold water, can I?' Old sayings about catching one's death hovered close to my ear and increased my anxiety.

Embracing the challenge of cold, cold water

But Amelia doesn't *feel* cold water the same way most people do. You only need to see her at the beach out of season when the water is still too chilly for mere mortals to enter; there she is – my little Tommy Hafey child – striding out determinedly, into the deep folds of all that delicious *cold*.

I think for Amelia, the love of cold water is a combination of the intense feelings she gets from the pressure of the spray and the glacial temperature itself. These elements create a sort of rapturous response in the nerve centre of her body – I can see it in the excited flapping of her arms, the full-body shuddering that makes her squeal likes she's on the joyride of her life.

After years of watching her relationship with cold water unfold, I now understand that it isn't bad for her the way it might be for a different child who could not tolerate the icy temperature at all. Or an adult forced to endure a freezing bucket of water tipped over their head for the sake of charity.

Now most nights, after Amelia has agreed to conduct her clean-up in a 'nice' warm bath, I give her five minutes (give or take) under the arctic torrent from the shower overhead. I peak behind the curtain to steal a glimpse or two of her big, round face, held up in exaltation to the pure thrill of it.

Bath times have been harrowing for us for many years. The allow-ance for icy, cold water when my daughter desires it has made things a lot better. Sometimes it even calms her down, as though the (welcome) shock to her body from the shower helps quieten those other feelings that can send her out of control.

And in relaxing the house 'rules' around water I can also see a little glint of thanks in Amelia's dark eyes. 'Mum is finally working me out', it says. She is giving me freedom to be myself. To take a million ice bucket challenges if I want to.

But it's not a challenge for her at all, it's simply a way of being, a way of life. Trust a child to be so deliberately fearless.

Ogres are like onions

13 October, 2014

In one of my favourite scenes in *Shrek*, the titular Ogre and his Donkey friend are walking and talking about the vagaries of life. Well, at least Shrek is trying to.

He explains to Donkey, "For your information, there's a lot more to Ogres than people think… Ogres are like onions." Not because, as his little hooved compatriot points out, they stink, or make you cry. It's because they have LAYERS.

Shrek is trying to say that he is more than the sum of his parts, more than the brute strength suggested by his enormous, green frame. He is a complex being, with, well, layers.

Donkey's jive-talking wisecrack, "You know not everybody like onions," is followed by a hilarious riff on the deliciousness of parfait more suited to Mary Berry's love of perfect cake 'lairs' than an existential crisis.

I can totally relate to Shrek's onion-based reflections. When we found out about Amelia's diagnoses, my mind reached out for a suitable analogy and came upon the humble onion.

I can remember saying in my flippant-but-painfully-serious manner to our paediatrician, "How many layers does this onion have?" We laughed but neither one of us was taking the news in our stride.

By drawing my own onion parallel with our life, I don't mean that I view my beautiful daughter's struggles as something to be bitter about, though I have cried more tears for her than the most gruelling meal-time chopping session could produce.

I'm trying to find a way to explain how it feels to start out as a family where everything feels certain, solid and whole, for at least a year, and then suddenly important layers start flaking off, one after another, revealing big problems in the rawness underneath.

When I think about the many phases of our life-onion in the nearly six years since Amelia was born, it's hard to believe the number of challenges we've been confronted with.

On one level, it can make you feel dreadfully pessimistic and wary of the *next bad thing* waiting just around the corner. Once the layers start to crumble, it's difficult not to see trouble in every cloud, every rainstorm, or every Bureau of Meteorology forecast annoyingly recited to me by my weather-nerd husband.

But the funny thing about going through massive life upheavals, one after another in a short period of time, is that you exhaust a lot of the energy that would normally be expended worrying about pointless things.

By the time you're standing at the centre of that unstable onion, you have little need to be worrying about the next career move, big promotion, or shiny new car. Your perspective undergoes a radical shift and it will never be the same again. For that, I am extremely thankful.

In a weird twist of fate many years ago now, I was made redundant from what I thought at the time was an important job, the best job I'd ever had. In the blink of an eye it was all gone, the company car, the generous salary, the status symbols of a career I had built over ten years.

I was suddenly jobless, but within three months, we found out that Amelia was deaf and nothing mattered more than being with her and helping her recover lost ground. My life had been stripped back to the bare essentials and I found that I didn't care about anything more than my daughter's happiness. No job can compete with that.

I didn't mourn the sudden loss of my career for too long and I've had a few false job starts since then; it hasn't been possible for me to work for longer than a year or so in the middle of all of the real graft of raising an intense little person with very special needs.

I'm hoping the tide will turn in my favour sometime soon, but I have reserves of patience on that score. Life might not be strictly about me right now, but it will be again one day soon.

Over recent years – and forgive the introduction of a new analogy – life has felt akin to being in quicksand. The harder you try to grab onto the optimism of the proffered branch, the further you sink. And yet you do grow used to the uncertainty of it all. The not-knowing-what's-around-the-corner nature of being in our family.

Maybe we've shed all of the onion layers we're going to and have collected each flaking, brown piece to create a complete picture of our story. I'm not so sure. In fact, I'll never be sure of that, not as long as I'm alive. None of us is in possession of an infallible crystal ball.

In any case, it's a genetic trait in my family to expect bad things to happen to us. We're almost annoyed when things go well because we have to accept that happy outcomes are possible. Good times are not to be trusted. There's a sick kind of glee that makes us jump up and down and say "See, I told you!!" when life delivers us a body blow.

I don't know if that's an Anglo-Protestant thing, a German thing, or just a really weird thing we've developed all by ourselves. But let me tell you, I think this sort of entrenched, biological masochism has set me up for the long haul. I'm not deriving pleasure from it, but it comforts me all the same.

Ogres are like onions and so is my life sometimes. Amelia's catalogue of disabilities too. The general uncertainly of being on the planet and not knowing what the next day will bring. Let the layers fall where they may because I have a thick skin of my own and I'm ready for anything.

Careful she might (not) hear you

28 October, 2014

I'm not sure precisely when I started worrying about the social impact of Amelia's deafness. Maybe it was the day I read too much online about how isolating, confusing and downright exhausting social experiences can be for deaf kids, always up against it in the hearing world.

Daunting words in bold-face leapt out at me from the computer screen. Sharp-edged ones like, depression. Anxiety. Paranoia. And *anger*. That one always seemed to be in italics for maximum impact.

It's not a doom-sayer's checklist – 'nasty things coming your way when you're raising a deaf child' – but it is a set of emotional risk factors that can't be taken lightly.

My aim as a parent is to hopefully reduce their power to hurt my daughter on her path between two contrasting worlds – deaf and hearing.

Amelia is not quite six years old and we have only known about her deafness for a tick under four years. It's not a long time in the grand scheme of things. But already I see just how easy it is for her as a deaf child to be left out or excluded by virtue of her difference to other people.

Let's take birthday parties as a classic example. Oh birthday parties, how I hate thee with a passion. It's unavoidable, but kid's parties are the worst kind of place for a deaf child to feel a part of the natural order of things.

Because they're too loud, too chaotic, too MAD for Amelia to make sense of what is going on around her. Sure, she wears hearing aids but they are next to useless in the face of such an intense racket. Those little devices can't sift the wheat sounds from the cacophonous chaff and so she is mostly lost.

I watch her making her way with excited bewilderment around these parties and I feel like throwing a huge, warm blanket over her. Underneath its soft layers, background noise would be reduced to a gentle hum that would not compete with voices speaking clearly in merry conversation.

In either context Amelia is alone. 'Alone' in the noisy crowd, or by herself beneath the blanket I throw over her every day when we come home and I can set things up exactly as she needs them to be.

It is because of this potential for loneliness that I love being able to send her to a school for deaf children.

When I visit Amelia there and see her with her classroom comrades, it's sometimes hard to see where she starts and they finish.

These six classmates have been together for almost two years now and they are incredibly close. Whether they speak or sign to each other there is something almost organic about how they interact.

It's born of the time they've spent bonding as friends but it is also the result of their shared identities as bilingual deaf kids. Communication between these children operates on a plane of mutual instinct and understanding; touching or tapping to gain attention, waving to be seen or heard, using gesture to add meaning: all form the basis of a code that marks them out as members of a club, a culture.

Within this rarefied environment, Amelia and the knowledge required to be with her and make her feel like an insider are known to everyone. I never need to worry about a scary thing like social isolation.

Seeing how crucial communication is to Amelia and her sense of belonging, it is all the more important for us, her hearing family, to be diligent about always involving her in social activities and conversations.

When we have friends over to visit, she becomes highly agitated and manic when there is a lot of conversation happening across her, between adults engaged with each other rather than with her.

Amelia yells at us over and over again to explain, "What are you talking about? What are you talking about?!" She throws her body into the mix too, placing herself in our eye line so we don't ever forget she's there waiting to be included.

Of course she needs to learn when to wait her turn (good luck) and it is less than socially optimal for us to have to keep stopping and explaining each story to her, but it is her right to be factored into the cut-and-thrust of social chatter.

It is much harder for Amelia to find her way in larger social situations where competing sounds blend into a baffling wall of confusing sounds and she sort of disappears under the radar, unable to get her bearings without a hearing compass to guide her.

This is where our greatest challenge lies, in reminding other people to take a minute to stop and talk to her, lean down close to her face so she can see their lips when they are speaking, use their hands to make the meaning of their words clearer. To see her and invite her in.

In reality, it doesn't take much to make a child like Amelia feel involved AND accepted. I see this every time we spend time with our closest friends, GH and NB and their boys. It's so uncomplicated, the way they ask Amelia how to sign certain words, to share her second language with them.

I watch Amelia's eyes light up with pleasure as she shows them how to sign 'turtle' or 'hippo' in Auslan. They sign the words back to her and, hey presto, she's in their world and they are in hers.

We recently went on holiday together and stayed in the same cottage. At night time as we were getting our kids ready for bed, there was always some story-time happening in the lounge room.

Unprompted on the first night, Amelia grabbed a book and sat next to our friends' youngest boy. She opened the first page and started telling him the story completely in Auslan, with her voice 'switched off'. I've never seen her do that with anyone outside of her family or deaf friends before.

And he loved it, watching her hands describe the flow of river water or the fire expelled by a scary dragon. Amelia repeated this routine each night, and I could tell she felt proud to be like a big sister to her sweet little friend, able to teach him something new. It is lonely to be an only child too.

Sometimes I think it's children who know best how to cut through all of this stuff and find some valuable common ground.

Like the other day when Amelia was with her dad in the park and she ran over to 'talk' to some older boys, aged maybe nine or ten.

Her speech wasn't really up to an in-depth gossip session but she had a mighty crack anyway. In these situations she tends to make a lot of noise, such as loud bird-screeching sounds and flaps her arms around, in her often-strange attempt to say 'hi' and make friends.

One boy saw Amelia's hearing aids and asked her dad if she was deaf, which he confirmed. "Oh, we thought she was disabled or something but then we saw her hearing aids."

The boys then welcomed Amelia into their group and hung out with her. They had zero anxiety about approaching her in the 'wrong' way. They got the hard questions out of the way early and then all there was left to do was play.

And it wasn't that they were tolerating her presence, the boys actively shared their games and conversations with Amelia. They let her hold their hands and there was mutual enjoyment of the time spent together in a small park in the suburbs.

I know that this was a special event because of the way my husband told it to me. He spoke about that main boy reverentially, because for about fifteen minutes he took our daughter into his world and any present worries about her just melted away.

Her isolation, and my husband's, were delayed for an afternoon, halted by the friendliness of those boys and their easy acceptance of Amelia.

And so was mine. Social isolation isn't just a huge risk factor for deaf children, rather it applies to their parents too. Because for every child or adult who 'gets it', there are so many others who don't and that is an alienating fact indeed.

Thankfully at the moment, Amelia isn't really cognisant of the people who accidentally ignore her, nor does she seem to feel the exclusionary effects of situations in which she is a natural outsider. The big job for us as she grows is to try and minimise the impact of this kind of isolation on her generous little heart.

All we can hope for is that there are enough loving family members, cool boys in the park and sweet little friends who enjoy their story time in Auslan to protect her from the feelings of loneliness when they come. And try though we might to stop them, they will come.

L'amour actually

11 November, 2014

First day of school, 2014

Amelia loves school the way Pepé Le Pew had a case of deeply un-PC l'amour for Penelope Pussycat in the old Looney Tunes cartoons.

It's a profound, single-minded passion, and like Pepé, Amelia will brook no barriers (in his case, not even a wrongly identified species) between herself and her love for a paramour called Primary School.

Even on mornings when she has spent an entire vomit-punctuated night on the tiles with her weary head draped over a bucket, Amelia will fight hard for her right to go to school.

As soon as I start to say that we might have to pull the pin on the day's play, she fixes me with a look of desperation, somewhere between sorrow and defiance, and cries, "No, Mum! I WANT TO GO TO SCHOOL!"

I have to sneak into the kitchen and quietly call the office to report her impending absence, all the while aware that my school-obsessed child is in her room struggling manfully into her uniform between bouts of wretching, coughing and sneezing.

I don't know whether to laugh or cry, which just about sums up my experience of parenting such a wild, enigmatic girl.

Eventually Amelia accepts her lot and melds into the couch as she must, but not before many tears have been shed over her tragic separation from the place that gives her so much happiness, so much purpose. So much confidence.

On its own, it's not such a terrible problem to have, is it? A child who will get ready for school in the blink of an eye and stand at attention by the door waiting for her bus ride, a full fifteen minutes before it is due to arrive.

A child who will rush with you from a morning appointment, never tarrying, to make sure she makes it to school before the end of 'brain gym' or to the start of music, dance or Auslan; just a few of the classes that have so inspired her mind this year.

But there is one big drawback to all this school time ardour that has the potential to make life very tricky for me.

Equal to Amelia's adoration of school is her infinite regard for routine. Clearly these loves go hand-in- hand with each other, as school is the central experience in her life that is founded on a strict timetable and the all-important 'knowing what comes next'.

There's nothing that freaks my child out more than not knowing what is coming next. In the next minute, next hour, week, or month.

We spend our lives trying to quell Amelia's anxieties through repeated information about timeframes, plans and some form of schedule, but life beyond school is never as predictable as she would like.

Let me tell you, it is downright exhausting to live with someone who never stops asking, 'and then what? And then what? AND THEN WHAT?!'

So, imagine you are the parent of this rigid, school-loving little person and you realise you have to INTERRUPT THE MONDAY ROUTINE HALF WAY THROUGH SCHOOL TO GO TO AN OCCUPA-TIONAL THERAPY APPOINTMENT EVERY TWO WEEKS.

Sorry to shout, but only caps would do to express my fear of interrupting Amelia's weekly routine – of getting between her and her beloved school – and living to tell the tale.

Amelia has grown used to going to speech therapy sessions and other medical check-ups in the morning and then heading on to school. She doesn't love it, but she'll tolerate the anomaly. It has a sequential flow she can understand. Plus the end destination is school.

This new arrangement was going to involve me attending school on a Monday for our regular on-site speech session with the lovely CN, and then altering the usual pattern of things by taking Amelia to see her OT. By the end there'd be little time to go back to school so it would make sense to go straight home.

Maybe it'll be ok….?, I thought with fake optimism.

But a full week before the first appointment, Amelia turned to me out of the blue and declared, "No OT on Monday, Mum. I don't like it. We do speech then I stay at school. Go home on the bus."

She could not have been clearer about her feelings. I didn't say too much in case I upset her even more, but I had a familiar sinking feeling about how day one of this change in routine was going to pan out.

On the morning of the new Monday world order, all was going well until speech wrapped up and I turned to Amelia and said, "OK, it's time to go and see your OT now, Meels." Yeah, right.

It was like she'd been fired out of a cannon, such was Amelia's sudden and violent desire to escape me and the dreaded idea of leaving school that day. Sling-shot like, she flung her body out of the room and into the school foyer, screaming loud protestations as she went.

I chased after her and CN was hot on my heels. Amelia had sprinted through the foyer and was close to the hallway that led back to her beloved classroom. I did my best to stop her without being overly physical but she was already yelling the school down.

She was NOT going to go gently into that good car park with me, no matter how much I cajoled her or made rash promises of coinage, chocolate cake or park visits on the way home.

Last year, without the insight into the autistic behaviours that drive my child's engine, I might have tried to drag her with me, force the issue, make her do what I wanted until we collapsed in a tear-soaked heap in one of the many public spaces across Melbourne to witness our mutual humiliation.

Now, I am much quicker to accept a situation like this on its immediate merits, and back off if backing off is required. I looked at Amelia's stricken face, her sweaty brow, heard the panic in her screams and summed it all up in a matter of seconds.

Turning to CN, who was a supportive presence by my side (sometimes you want people to flee the scene of a meltdown and leave you, this was not one of those days), I shrugged and said, "It's not going to happen today, is it?" She could only agree.

And though my plans had failed for the moment, CN chimed in straight away with an idea that was brilliant in its simplicity. She would create a tailor-made visual schedule to use on the Mondays when Amelia was due to see her OT.

CN would create one for us to use at home with cards depicting images or photos of things like, 'bus', 'school', 'speech session', 'OT appointment', and so on. She would also keep an identical copy at school and spend time during the week talking it over with Amelia.

Amelia's amazing teacher, PR, was also involved in the planning and offered to discuss the Monday routine with her in class and normalise it as far as possible.

My contribution was to offer to take Amelia back to school after the OT session, even if it was for just an hour, so that she could finish out the day and come home on the bus, restoring some kind of lost balance to her schedule.

It sounds pretty straightforward, but as soon as these strategies were put in place we saw an immediate improvement. With greater visual explanations of what was happening and some time to process the change, Amelia was far more open to leaving the school with me the next time around.

We finished speech, went along to see her OT for a cooperative and happy session and made it back to school for the last activity of the day. The drop off was a bit fraught, but Rome wasn't built in a day and changes to Amelia's routine were not going to be solved overnight.

The next fortnight ticked over and I arrived at Amelia's class to collect her for speech. Her teacher pulled her in close and re-explained what would be happening next. She suggested that this time when I brought her back to school, Amelia might like to walk back from the front office to class by herself, like a big girl. Like she does in the mornings with the class roll. Amelia nodded in silent but relaxed agreement.

Every two weeks, CN, PR and I were like a crack squad, making tiny but crucial refinements to 'Operation: Get Amelia to the OT and Back' and our efforts were paying off. I can't thank them enough for their intuition, care and support.

When I at last took Amelia back to school, she skipped inside without stress or fear. I gave her a soft hug and said, "OK chicken, it's time for you to go back to class now. All by yourself, like a big girl."

She smiled at me and the expression stretched wide across her countenance like the brightest rainbow in the sky. It held all the colours of acceptance and shades of sincere thanks for delivering her back into the warm bosom of school.

Because Amelia loves that place like I love Marlon Brando and potato chips, or indeed like Marlon himself loved potato chips; truly, madly and without regret.

Awake is the new sleep

25 January, 2015

It's dawn, barely a trace of sunshine coming through the windows, and already I can hear her crashing around in her room.

The Kraken, also known as my six-year-old Amelia, has awoken.

I know this because I can hear her clumsy, elephant-like footfalls pounding into the floorboards. Amelia is awake and the whole world must know it.

It would be churlish to complain because she is deaf and so has no earthly idea how loud she is as she moves around gathering her numerous comfort items from the bed for transportation into the lounge room.

This is the routine for her, every day, my girl who hears little of note without hearing aids and is well and truly on the autism spectrum.

Amelia uses various collective nouns to describe her personal treasures. They are her 'things', or sometimes, her 'stuff'.

"Where is my stuff Mummy? I need my THINGS!"

I always know where her stuff is because it is never far from her side. Amelia burrows these objects into her bed covers at night and I have to creep in after lights out to extract pencils from her hair and uncurl sweaty fingers from straws, tape, glue-sticks. The lot.

For a young child with autism, the 'things' have a deep meaning that is mostly beyond our reach. But what we know for sure is that they are absolutely vital to our little magpie's sense of security, her sense of self.

Amelia clings to these things like a lifeline to some magical source of strength and energy known only to her. With them, she is safe.

And so, each morning, this curious set of bits and bobs is dragged from her room and deposited next to her on the couch. Amelia is now ready at 5am, or 6 if we're fortunate, to kick off her day.

It's then that I feel her presence in the doorway to our room. She hovers there uncertainly, watching for movement, for signs of waking life.

I resist for a minute but I can't help but lift my weary arm to offer her a tiny wave – words cannot travel the distance to my beautiful deaf child but one gesture shows her the way is clear to approach.

And with this green light Amelia runs to my bedside, full pelt, to grasp my hand and throw her body across mine.

It's easily my favourite time of day, this part when our bodies are so close and her face turns to my cheek to plant big, passionate smooches there. And if I'm very lucky, she might reach up to softly stroke my face with her hand.

Her sometimes-rough hands become gentle in the morning light.

I am barely awake but the smell of her, the feel of her, is everything to me in that moment.

Amelia is up and now so am I, and no matter what the hour, no matter how sleepless the night, and no matter how many 'things' I'll be carting around for the rest of the day, in this perfect moment my heart is filled only with happiness.

Eyes wide shut

31 January, 2015

When I look at Amelia, I see lots of things. I see a wonderfully healthy, milky-skinned towhead with dark, dark eyes.

My eyes rest on her all-terrain body some days and I conjure up images of her in a field, pausing from her work to glance at the sky, the sun, like a stocky Russian peasant, built to withstand the elements.

Come rain, hail or shine, Amelia was made differently to most people, but man was she made to last.

Through my eyes, the most subjective of prisms, she is the most beautiful child I have ever seen. If I look at her for an hour, a month, a year, there will never be enough time to really see her.

I love to look at Amelia's blonde hair falling in rolling, lazy waves down her back. Tucked behind her ears, some days it's easier to see that she is wearing hearing aids. To see the physical sign of an internal part of her that doesn't work the way it should.

Her autism is not so obvious to the naked eye. It's not etched on her skin or reflected in some mechanical appendage that helps her to think or feel. Amelia doesn't wear a t-shirt reclaiming the word 'Aspie'.

You can't see her autism in obvious ways, but I always know it's there. I see it in her face sometimes, when her gaze drops below mine, and try as I might to regain her attention, she's quietly slipped off to some interior room, far from me and my ever-prying eyes.

No matter what the signs – violent temper, crushing anxiety, rampant hoarding – I see autism but I still see Amelia. I never lose sight of her, working so hard to push her little barrow uphill. I see all that she is and I feel I truly know her. I know her and I understand.

Amelia has many people in her life who look past her 'special needs' and see only what is genuinely special. What is unique about her. The madcap sense of fun, the tenderness, the infectious lust for life.

What they see is mirrored in my own eyes and in my heart. That mirroring gives me strength and so much joy.

Yet now and then in our travels I am forced to view Amelia the way that other people sometimes do and it makes me turn my face away. I can't bear the sting of their unforgiving eyes boring holes of judgement into her. Into me.

When she is suddenly, inexplicably loud or clumsy or different – incongruous – in a public space, I feel strangers' eyes flick up and cast their reductive light over her. Mouths curl up in a mute grimace of distaste. I read their looks and expressions and interpret the words left unsaid.

'Oh, what a *weird* child. Look at the *naughty* child. What on earth is *wrong* with that child?'

And who am I? It's simple: I'm the *bad parent*.

I hate those staring, ignorant eyes because for a second I step outside myself and I judge Amelia too. In that moment I see only her flaws, the things that cannot be contained or controlled. And it hurts my heart.

My inner voice pleads with her, 'Please won't you just be calm? Why can't you walk properly? Stop yelling, just stop it!'

'Why can't you just be *normal*.'

Then there are the people who don't see Amelia at all, who have trained themselves not to see what is different about her and to try to understand. They focus their eyes on the wall above her head or on the easy going child instead.

They ignore her and I despise them, too.

Because they looked at Amelia, but they did not really see her. They saw only gaps and lack and the spaces in-between where a different child might be. And they decided things about her that are only a tiny fraction of who she is. Who she will grow up to be.

I'm not blind to the hardships looming up behind Amelia like a shadow she can't shake. I know she is sometimes rough and strange and hard to take. I know that because I see how being around Amelia makes some people feel: uncomfortable, nervous, frustrated.

It's written in their eyes.

But I can't let those looks and the thoughts that sit behind them slip under my guard too much. They strike me in my nerve centre, and I absorb little shocks and bouts of pain, but they do not defeat me. They could never.

For me, there is always great solace to be found in looking up and seeing Amelia again, maybe running down a path to meet me after time spent apart. She throws her glorious head back and yells my name at the sky and I see only beauty and all that is right.

There are no shadows here, save the ones cast by the sun, warming the head of my sweet peasant girl with her golden hair and those dark, dark, eyes.

Inclusion is an illusion

11 March, 2015

In the wonderfully acerbic political TV series, *The Thick of It*, there's an episode involving a 'Super Schools Bill', which proposes the closure of special needs schools across the UK. The hapless cabinet minister who must argue in favour of this integration agenda is Hugh Abbott (Chris Langham).

In this, Hugh is faced with a moral conundrum. He doesn't agree with the Bill and his senior special advisor, Glenn Cullen (James Smith), has a son who attended a special needs school and flourished there. It's a personal thing.

Glenn's catchphrase to sum it all up is simple: 'Inclusion is an illusion'.

But poor old Hugh doesn't have the luxury of holding to a thing like principles when it comes to matters of state. Instead, he is forced by the government's pitbull-esque director of communications, Malcolm Tucker (Peter Capaldi), to support the Bill.

In doing so, Hugh betrays his own beliefs and sells out Glenn and his son by using their personal story to argue *for* the closure of special needs schools. All in a day's dirty work for the Secretary of State for Social Affairs and Citizenship.

Inclusion is an illusion. I hadn't seen this episode for a while but I was suddenly reminded of Glenn's line last week when I made a foolhardy call to a local activity centre to ask about Amelia joining one of their classes.

Early in the call I volunteered the information, as I always do, that she is deaf and autistic, to be clear about her needs and advance the conversation about how best to include her.

For a minute it all sounded pretty positive. The centre had a separate class for children with attention deficit hyperactivity disorder (ADHD) or autism with an occupational therapist on hand for support. Great, I thought, that might be better for Amelia than the regular classes, at least to begin with.

But I was misguided in that momentary feeling of positivity. Amelia, it turns out, would not be eligible to attend either kind of class. The doors I had hoped to open for her swiftly closed, one after another.

About her deafness, I was asked how far background noise would impact on her ability to hear. This was not so the noise could be controlled or limited in some way. It was to point out how the environment would not be 'appropriate' for my daughter.

I hurriedly explained that while Amelia is deaf, she wears hearing aids, can speak quite well and follow most instructions and that I wasn't expecting anyone to be a fluent Auslan interpreter for her. I just wanted them to know that standing near her and making sure she could see the face and hands of people speaking would help her understanding of any directions in the class.

But her deafness turned out to be a deal-breaker for this centre. They could not be convinced that it wasn't an insurmountable barrier to Amelia's inclusion in the program.

To me, it's simply a fact about her that requires a little effort to understand and accommodate. After that, she'll do the rest because she's tough and ace and super adaptable.

I know people don't often encounter deafness in their day-to-day lives, but there's an unsettling ignorance that surrounds its understanding in the broader community. It's unpleasant to confront this as the parent of a deaf child, but there's a spectrum of misunderstanding that at its lower levels assumes that it is 'too hard' to communicate with a deaf person (so we won't try).

At the extreme end of this spectrum reside the people who mistakenly believe that deaf people are somehow restricted in their intellectual capacity. 'You don't communicate the way I do, so I see you as lesser than me'. Not different, but reduced.

Then I was asked if Amelia attended a mainstream school – the children in the special needs class all do apparently. Well, no, I replied, she goes to a school for deaf children. Then I was asked a theoretical question, about how Amelia might cope in a mainstream school.

How to answer something like that when she has never been schooled in a mainstream environment? That's when my agitation, which had been like a worrisome tickle at the back of my neck from about the four-minute mark of the call, really started to ramp up.

My pulse quickened and a slight tremble rippled across my arms, my back, like a warning on the surface of my skin.

As the call neared its conclusion, I realised it didn't really matter what I said to the person on the end of the line. Every answer I gave presented yet another obstacle to Amelia's inclusion. Another reason to say 'no'.

Instead of answering questions about how they might help, I felt as though I had inadvertently participated in a survey about all of my daughter's faults. It made me feel sick.

This had honestly never happened to me before, so I was more than a little shocked. Most places in my experience will try and meet you and your child somewhere in the middle, somewhere fun and safe where everyone's needs can be met.

The St Martin's Youth Arts Centre invited me to sit down with them for an hour to learn all about Amelia and how their programs could work best to include her fully.

The Northcote Aquatic and Recreation Centre has hired an Auslan interpreter so that deaf kids like mine can access swimming lessons in the only language that's going to cut it in the pool. They also committed to one-on-one teaching when they were informed of Amelia's autism.

Just a few cool examples of how NOT to alienate small children and their families.

The person from this centre gave me nothing, no extension of flexibility or sensitivity, just an empty offer of 'wait-listing'. Our case was lumped casually in the too-hard-basket, and that, as they say, was that. I hung up mid-sentence, mid-sob as the rising lump in my throat betrayed me and echoed its hurt down the line.

But I couldn't just leave it at that. I was still shaking as I sat down to write the centre a message of 'feedback'. I'm not interested in disclosing who they are because I just read Jon Ronson's important book about public shaming and it's an unedifying road that will serve no grander purpose.

I will, however, share my emails (names redacted) here because I think it's vital to show the true cost of these negative interactions, where inclusiveness was hoped for but in reality denied to a child with special needs:

Email # 1

Hi there, I called today to see if my 6–year-old daughter who is deaf and autistic could come and try some [redacted] classes with you. She loves to [redacted] and I thought it would be good for her physical and social development. I was told that she is not eligible for either [redacted] or the [redacted] because of her special needs. It is pretty devastating to have your child turned away from fun activities on the basis of her disabilities. It's great that you have the [redacted] group for kids with ADHD/Autism but apparently my daughter is not eligible because she goes to a special needs school for deaf children. So you cater to special needs kids, just not my kid? I find it hard to understand. Amelia has participated well in programs run by places like St Martin's and they welcomed her with open arms. She is a lovely, bright girl who has challenges but always benefits from new learning environments. I'm really disappointed – you have no idea how awful these kinds of experiences are for parents like me. Thankfully, most places operate in the true spirit of access and equity. Thanks for taking the time to read this feedback. I hope that other kids might benefit from this, even if my daughter is not welcome at [redacted]. Sincerely, Melinda

I did receive a quick response, but it was pretty cold and informal, sticking hard to the company line. In summary, they understood how 'frustrating' it must be for parents like me, but they just couldn't accommodate Amelia right now.

Frustrating? Like when you can't get your car started in the morning or you miss a train? Yeah, I don't think so. That inadequate word inflamed my anger even further, so after a few hours of grumbling around the house and chewing the inside of my mouth to shreds, I emailed them again:

Email # 2

Hi [redacted],

Thanks for responding to my email. I guess I am expressing more than frustration and the reason for that, whatever your company's capacity to deal with different needs in children, is that you wrote off the idea of Amelia joining in on the basis of very little information. I said 'deaf', 'autistic' and 'deaf school' and after that it didn't really matter what that means for Amelia in practice and how far she might be able to participate with only a little bit of prompting.

You concluded that her needs were more severe than is currently accommodated within your programs, and I just can't accept that that's fair. I would have loved it, for instance, if you had suggested that I bring her in to meet someone from [redacted] to get a sense of her, and then decide if she needed to be wait-listed for some other kind of program. The deciding factor of Amelia being in a 'special school' – and I'm not sure that a deaf school fits within that category – is a strange one.

There are plenty of kids with autism who attend mainstream schools but they often need at least some in-class support to do that. Amelia goes to school without the need for any extra help at all. She works on the same curriculum as every other child in the state, the main difference is that she learns bilingually, in Auslan and in speech. To me, it makes more sense, and is far more equitable, to assess the actual needs themselves, not which school system has been chosen by parents as the most appropriate for that child for a whole range of reasons.

Obviously, I wish that you had handled my call with a bit more of an open mind and frankly, a bit less ignorance of how special needs children function inside and outside of mainstream/special schools and programs. I have never been told that Amelia's needs, such as her deafness, make her 'too hard' to deal with, which is the real way of saying 'we can't appropriately cater to her needs'. I mentioned them to you mainly so that her instructor/s would have enough information to be sensitive to those needs in practical ways, like making sure she could see the person speaking, and so on.

You would be surprised just how resilient and adaptable a child like Amelia with her unique set of needs can actually be.

Regards, Melinda

Now I felt better, as though I'd fully advocated for Amelia even if the result was still the same. I might not always be able to knock down the walls that

Signing to her swimming teacher

get in her way, but goddamn it, I will always let people know when their stupidity and heartlessness has let us down.

Soon after, I got a call from the company owner and we actually had a good chat about how to properly include someone like Amelia in their activities. It was the conversation I'd expected to have at the outset.

And this person apologised, saying those magic words, 'I'm sorry that you had such an upsetting experience'. It didn't dissolve my afternoon of distress, but I did appreciate it.

By this stage though, I wasn't looking to convince them to let Amelia join in – I don't want her anywhere near a place that takes such an appalling view of her needs – but I did want the owner to understand what might have worked better in our case. How they might handle future Amelias.

Like, if they had just invited us to come in for a short meeting, we could have had an open and honest discussion about the best kind of class for Amelia. They could have met her rather than judging her abilities over the phone.

Maybe we would have decided mutually to come again at a later time, but really, we're not solving world peace here, are we? We're just talking about letting a little girl try something on for size to see if it might have fit.

Instead, they closed their minds to her sight unseen, which is a great shame. Because Amelia's such a fabulously fun chick, so interesting and full of whimsy. Some people regard her as an asset to their groups, even a leader. This centre will never know her and it's one hundred percent their loss.*

Barriers to access are real and they do hurt. Take note people running programs for kids: pump up your heart valves and have a think about how your special-needs policies impact on people who are already doing it pretty hard.

We're all a part of the same community and when we feel brave enough to step out of our houses to have a go at something new, please hold our hands instead of turning us away.

Inclusion doesn't have to be an illusion, and you might find that instead of a child being 'too hard', they will teach you something priceless about what it means to be alive.

I am happy to report that the centre is now accepting deaf children into its classes. This change was based on the feedback I provided in my correspondence with them.

Sphinx in the sand

17 March, 2015

In her element

She's a 'force of nature' kind of girl. I sometimes can't tell where the waves start and she ends. I try to call out to her and forget she can't hear me. My voice travels in her direction until the wind grabs it and carries it away.

She's not looking at me anyway. It's deliberate, this 'not looking, not looking' game. No one is in charge but her and she'll pay attention when she bloody well likes.

I only want to make sure that she plays in the sand near our feet. Just over there not *all the way away*. So I trudge through tiny shards of shells, slowly broken down from ocean to shore, just to reach her.

I talk to her with my hands. Come closer to Mummy and Daddy. You can play how you like, just stay nearby, okay? My child-Sphinx thinks on that for a second and then nods. It's okay.

She runs behind me to our point on the beach and stays within the invisible flags of our agreement. I watch her, fully-clothed, splashing and laughing in the water, and say to my husband: "She's ours, but she's a stranger too, isn't she? She belongs only to herself."

He can only agree.

Mr Marbles' midnight run

28 April, 2015

There are very few sure things in this life. The rising of the sun in the east. The perfection of Jon Snow's hair, swept back by the wind above the Wall. Death. Taxes. Did I mention Jon Snow?

I would add another certainty to this short list – the inevitable nocturnal stirrings of Amelia.

She has forgotten how to sleep and we can't remember when we ever did.

The pitter-patter of tiny feet long wished for in our pre-parental phase of life has been replaced by a less welcome sound.

That is, the inelegant, stamping footfalls of our daughter, risen from her bed in the darkest hours of the night, running through the house.

Hell-bent on fun and mischief. Foraging for food. Maternal comfort. Her iPad. Anything except blessed *sleep*.

I have heard the chimes at midnight, at 2am, at 4am, and they doth toll for ME.

My husband and I have grown accustomed to sleeping with our eyes barely closed, our ears trained on the corridor space outside our room. Because we know she's coming. It might not be tonight but it will be very soon. Two good nights in a row are a harbinger of a full week of horrifying wakefulness to follow.

It's like that great line from *Platoon*, when King says, "Somewhere out there is a beast and he hungry tonight." I don't mean to compare my first and only child to the Viet Cong, but when we're cowering in our bed/bunker, the helmet would seem to fit.

I have learned from other parents of autistic children that this night waking practice is not uncommon. And it can be long-lasting. One child I know of is twelve and she still wakes constantly through the night, searching for snacks and televisual stimulation.

Twelve? I can't do another six years of this and hold on to my sanity. As it stands, I sometimes can't remember my own name.

But what disturbs Amelia's sleep? Why can't she remain settled, secure inside the soft, thick blankets I wrap around her to keep her warm?

Sometimes I'm certain it's because she is anxious, terrified even. She is deaf and at night I wonder if the shadows don't crowd in on her, and frighten her down to her cotton socks. How would I even know?

One night Amelia told me that her curtains were whispering to her. No, they were singing. When she said that I looked at the gentle, green folds of her drapes and thought, if that's true then I'm out of here too.

Her imagination must be powerful because she can't hear anything remotely like a whisper, or a curtain song.

The night is dark and full of terrors, as Melisandre from *Game of Thrones*, would say. Everybody run.

And yet another part of me suspects that Amelia is foxing. For her the night is merely an extension of the day. Just another moment in time to fit in the things she loves to do. Like eat, draw, create and laugh at her funny little TV shows.

If I didn't know better, I'd suspect she's only pretending to sleep while she waits for us to be out of the picture and she can have her run of the big house for a few hours.

Recently Amelia started hunting for audio-visual devices at night until we locked them all away. We have discovered her sitting up in her bed at midnight, surrounded by a menagerie of toys, drawing items, snacks and her iPad propped happily on her knees.

Her defiant face in response to her dad's appearance in the doorway says, 'What's the problem, mate, I've got this totally sorted. Shut the door on your way out.'

We've taken to calling her 'Mr Marbles'. My husband started it; it's a *Seinfeld* thing. The wonderful 'Chicken Roaster' episode when Jerry has to cohabitate in Kramer's apartment with a creepy (and of course as it belongs to Kramer, this qualifier is redundant) ventriloquist's doll called Mr Marbles.

Jerry becomes certain the doll is going to come to life in the middle of the night and kill him. Despite Kramer's assurances, Jerry sees a doll-shaped shadow move past him on the wall, then hears rapid footsteps.

Holding the blanket up to his chin Jerry whispers in terror, "Hello? Is somebody there? Mr Marbles?"

This is where we're at now. Lying in wait for our very own, albeit much cuter, Mr Marbles to hop out of bed and come running down the hall. We clutch the bed covers in mock horror, but this pantomime belies our true fear – of never having a good night's sleep again.

We amuse ourselves so that we can cope with the regular disruptions, the impact of the deprivation on our lives; the nights when our agreed 'contract' with Amelia is broken yet again and she screams for hours for comfort and attention. It's harrowing.

It's hard to be strong at 3.30am when you've already been awoken at 11.30pm and you're trying to hold firm to the rules about only going in to see her for a short amount of time and then not at all after that.

I have allowed her to have things I shouldn't in those moments. Like access to our bed. Or her iPad, just for a few minutes (in reality hours), so that I can rest my head once more. But she won't learn if we continue to bend to her mighty will. If she has forgotten how to settle herself, how to stay in her room, then we have to remind her. Help her to remember what to do. How to rest.

During the day, when we're all in a reasonable mood, I talk to her about things she can do when she's awake in the night. She can read or draw in her bed. Cuddle her bears. Go to the toilet. Close her door to feel safe. I will come if she needs me but only for ten minutes. After that she is on her own.

Even if she screams and tears the house down and the neighbours wonder whether they need to involve the DHS.

So far we are sticking to our agreement, but it's early days in yet another rebooted strategy and Amelia is always looking for loopholes. A weakness in the plan. In us.

This morning I heard her wake up at 4.30am, earlier than her usual 5am rooster call. She rarely, if ever, has made it past 6am in her life. She knows she is not allowed to get up until 5 and then she can have her run of the house.

Today she worked out how to manually accelerate her alarm clock so that the time was 'just right' in the fairytale parlance of another mischievous blonde. Her dad got up to tell her it was too early and she protested passionately, "No, look!", dragging him to her clock with the revised numbers, the truth written in neon.

We can hardly compete with that, can we?

Post five o'clock, Amelia is all business. She makes her own breakfast: Weet-Bix or porridge in the microwave. I used to cringe into my pillow, worrying about her burning the house down. But no, she remembers what I taught her about the safe number of seconds for cooking and is spot on every time.

She puts on her uniform for school. Her socks and shoes. Brushes her hair. Watches her funny shows and laughs. I hear her singing her school friends' names over and over in the strange circular loop she so often performs.

Sometimes she visits me, signing into my hand, 'Time, time'. It's a question for me: what time are you getting up, Mummy? I sign twenty or ten (minutes). Whatever will buy me more time to SLEEP.

Listening to these morning sounds, the industry of my resourceful daughter starting her day, I lie in my bed and I smile instead of frowning and thinking about an animated ventriloquist's doll out to strangle me in the night.

The night. It *is* dark and full of terrors, for little people and big ones besides. But the day breathes new life into things and it brings hope. We start again with the chime of that microwave as Amelia makes her own breakfast. We are awake together and ready to begin.

Carrying the mother load

7 May, 2015

Amelia running her own show

This week in my house we will celebrate in our own small, quiet way that modern event known as Mother's Day.

For us it still feels like a new tradition and this year will mark the sixth time I will be lucky enough to be in the box seat for a hand-made card from my daughter Amelia, followed by burnt toast served on a large hard-back book (*Bowie: Album by Album*) in bed.

Oh, the luxury.

I get that it's a super commercialised 'holiday' and that the marketing of Mum-gifts is so narrow in its view that it can only imagine one uber-domesticated, goddessy-type mother.

The reality of my childhood is that if you were going to buy power tools for anyone it most likely would have been my mum (sorry, Dad).

I can't get overly energised about public perspectives on what is actually a very private role. It belongs to no-one except the woman who is doing the mothering and the child or children who share that relationship with her.

Mother's Day is about business; but my sense of motherhood is nobody's 'business' but *mine.*

It's such a complex thing to me, being a mother. It has meant so many different things over time, I can hardly begin to unthread one from another. It's a tangle of feelings, thoughts and experiences. And so many ups and downs.

Even before Amelia was born, I felt strangely detached from the idea of motherhood. Her conception occurred in a medical laboratory; her little egg was extracted from my body while I was unconscious, fertilised in a test tube. My husband and I didn't even need to be in the same room for that.

I was technically present, but I felt far, far away from myself, like waving to a familiar shape on the horizon that doesn't see you.

Pregnancy helped to repair that detached part of me, at least back then. It fused splintered bits of myself back onto the bone. Whatever interventions I endured before and after Amelia's birth, carrying her inside me drew me closer to her, to the nurturing experience of almost-motherhood.

My body was not just some broken machine that required drugs and procedures to work like it was meant to. It was life-giving, sustaining another person's growth. Every kick, lurch, forward tumble (what the hell was I growing in there, an acrobat?) inside me was a sign that my body was finally doing its job.

I could pause my lifelong hatred of it and welcome its changes for the first time.

My take on childbirth is mostly a pragmatic one. It's a necessary means to an end. Of course there were more medical interventions, more body-numbing drugs, incisions. I could not escape them, but they did not sever me from the powerful emotions I felt upon seeing Amelia for the first time.

And she was perfect. She really was. My January girl, Amelia Isobel. Named in part for a forgotten woman, my Great-Grandmother, we wanted to remember through the gift of our daughter.

The distance we had travelled to get there, to reach each other, was long and hard. Yet we had made it and contentment washed over me like warm water moving downstream.

It turned out that the perfection we swiftly projected onto Amelia was illusory. Nobody looks at their baby and sees anything other than all that is *right* and *true*.

But there were shadows all around. Third parties. Autism was like another child born alongside Amelia, standing between us. It held out its small hands and shouted, "Stay away from me!" It kicked and railed and screamed and it never let up.

Deafness too. Before we knew it was there, deafness was another character vying for attention in an already confined family space. The cost of not knowing that its presence had stood in Amelia's way for two years, causing us to wonder why our child felt so remote, remains with me.

That grief grows smaller but it never leaves.

Amelia's unique set of challenges have tested to the hilt the ways I see myself as a mother. What it means to love a child who did not hear my voice after she was born and who could not really bear for me to hold her close. Who sometimes seemed to reject my very existence in relation to her.

How can I be a mother if I can't comfort my own child? Show her my love through the warmth of my body, the song in my voice?

The years have been challenging and arduous. I will not deny that for a number of those years I have felt like the living embodiment of *The Wreck of the Hesperus;* a walking tale of woe.

I have been a mother in name, it is true, and I bear the massive responsibility of guiding a very vulnerable person through the mists, onto dry land. But it hasn't really penetrated beneath my skin, my sense of really *being* Amelia's mother.

In our darkest years, mothering her meant learning and then teaching her how to sign before she could talk. I worked hard to give her language and access to the world, painstakingly, word by word.

I watched her tear herself and the house apart in the midst of yet another distressing meltdown. I tried everything and achieved little save hours and hours of sobbing. For us both.

We couldn't go on outings or share in the most basic things like a walk together for the longest time. I would watch 'normal' mothers on the street from my car, talking

My partner in selfie crime

and chatting to their little ones. So effortless, it seemed. I thought my heart might break in two.

For me motherhood exists in those incidental spaces where small exchanges of love seem possible. Long, soft cuddles on the couch, whispered secrets at the park, tears wiped away with the palm of my hand. All are welcome.

They're spontaneous, shared events of connection and they combine to build into a bigger picture of mother-daughter bonding.

It is simply a fact of Amelia's early life and the severity of her challenges then that she couldn't bond with me in traditional ways. I understand now that she did love me and need me, just not in the ways I had expected.

She couldn't show me and I could not see it or feel it, but her love was there, as was mine. It just took us some time to see each other properly.

In my own narrow view of motherhood I had set us both up for failure. I feel very sorry for the pain I inflicted on myself then and the distance that created between she and I. I held her in my mind as though on a string, floating away from me, when I should have tethered her closer still.

Because now she is six and though I feel like I have waited for an eternity, Amelia is really ready to love me, in her own, quirky way. I'm doubling down and keeping her all for myself.

Daily, hourly, she throws herself with gusto into my arms and says earnestly, "I *love* you Mummy, you're my *best friend* in the whole wide world". I am now a mother who feels ten feet tall. A world beater; life conqueror.

I am learning to trust in these moments, rather than unpack them endlessly or worry that my girl is faking it just for me.

On Sunday we ventured out for lunch in a rare attempt at family 'normality' and it was one of our most wonderful days so far. Top five, I reckon. We ate dumplings like Friar Tuck would have if he'd been lucky enough to have a yum cha local to him in Sherwood Forest.

We ate together, we laughed. Amelia sat happily and I actually relaxed. We left and went in search of ice-cream; there was no hurry, we could take our sweet time. Amelia sat patiently on a stool next to me while we waited for her dad to purchase a messy chocolate concoction in a cup.

And then we walked to the lights on the corner to cross to our car. I stopped and leaned against the light pole. In front of me, my dear little person leaned her body back into mine.

It was a subtle movement, but the pressure of Amelia resting on me, the warmth, was a heady mixture. I took a risk then. I reached up my right hand to stroke her beautiful, blonde hair.

She let me, so I grew bolder. I ran my hands through it, letting the strands fall down her back like it was the most glorious silk in the world. As a mother I've only ever wanted to be able to show such tenderness to my child.

She didn't pull away and I didn't breathe.

The extravagance of being able to have this contact without rebuke was everything to me in that moment. I looked up at the people in cars idling on the street and thought "I wonder if they look at me and see a mother?" Because that's how I felt right then. Like a real mother.

It's a new feeling, like a shiny coin I'm turning over and over in my hand, marvelling at the shapes, the grooves I can see in the light. I know I will feel it again and more often and that thought is more exciting than a thousand Christmases at once.

Yesterday, Amelia jumped off the bus from school clutching a plastic bag behind her back. Ah, the Mother's Day stall at school. She'd spent the $5 I gave her that morning and was clearly pumped about her acquisition.

She ran swiftly ahead of me to hide my present under her bed. Last year she would have just shown me, but she's learning how to harbour secrets and cherish surprises.

And I don't care if that bag has a tea cosy in it, a weird tissue box holder, or a garishly decorated mug to add to the 400 others in our cupboard.

It's Mother's Day on Sunday and I want my card, my burnt toast and whatever special prize my beloved daughter thought to choose just for me, her mother and her best friend in the whole wide world.

Thursday afternoon fever

"The main challenge I've had is dealing with society's
belief that since deaf people can't hear, they can't dance.
What people forget or do not yet know is that we all
hear with our bodies before the sound enters our ears.
This is not just through vibration but also through
instinct and impulse."[8]

— Jo Dunbar, deaf choreographer and dancer

8 July, 2015

Who said deaf kids can't dance? Or respond to music, the rhythm in the air, their feet, or in their hearts?

Not me. Not after I saw Amelia and her fellow classmates bring their best jazz hands and a whole lot of funk (is my age showing?) to an afternoon dance concert worth remembering. For like, ever.

We knew Amelia had been working with Jo Dunbar from Deaf Can Dance every week. Some nights she'd come home and try out some sweet new freestyle moves on the lounge room rug and I felt sure she must have been watching repeats of *Breakdance* (no judgement) as part of her training.

8   Edwards, Grace, "Jo Dunbar discusses her journey as a deaf artist", *Dance Informa (Australian Edition)*, 12:2013, accessed 23 November 2016

She's no private dancer. No, she demands a captive parental audience, and as usual when her rockin' recital is done we are instructed to clap as she bows solemnly like the most respectable English gentleman in the county.

We were eager to see how this confident home practice would translate to the bright lights of the school stage. Because every event like this, no matter how small, brings with it a new sense of who our daughter is.

Standing in front of a crowd I see more of Amelia's true self than when she is in repose or playing by herself in the garden. The shifting expression on her face, the way she moves her hands, that tiny twitch of her bottom lip that signals shyness and something else. Something far more determined.

Like sardines, we packed into a small multipurpose room at the school; sweaty parents stacked on top of each other like a human game of Jenga, jostling for the perfect view.

Jo introduced her drumming accompanist, Koffi Toudji – a veritable man-mountain with incredible command of his instrument and the 50-odd children in the room. One wave of his giant hand was enough to magnetically draw the dancers from one side of the stage to the other.

Then we watched, as mini troupes of well-rehearsed kids with painted faces twirled onto the stage, guided by Jo's conducting hands and the deep, resonant boom of Koffi's drum. It was a wonderfully rich sound that seemed like it was emanating from inside the walls.

We felt it reverberate through our own bodies, and saw its impact on the smaller bodies dancing on stage. The beat was powerful and intoxicating, pounding in my chest alongside my heart doing the rest.

If my smile had stretched any wider it might have fallen off my face.

And the dancers. They came in all shapes, sizes and abilities, but they held nothing back. Deafness was no barrier to their instinctive feeling for the music, nor their sense of rhythmic movement in response to it.

Posing post performance

If one performer lost their way, another (or a patient teacher) would quickly gather them back into a carefully choreographed circle or tap them with a reminder of what to do. They danced with passion and with pride, in themselves and each other.

Finally it was Amelia's turn. I couldn't get a clear view of her, but I did see her little hips swinging with great verve and her intense concentration as she executed the steps she'd been practicing for weeks.

Sometimes she would get lost in her search for our faces in the crowd, but the distraction was only fleeting. She quickly got her groove back.

Then it was time for Amelia to bang on her own little bongo and I saw the raw delight on her face when it was time to pause and shout a barbaric yawp at the rafters. She looked like a warrior and she sounded like one too.

My husband and I clutched each other's hands and laughed loudly with pleasure at how free Amelia was, how open and entirely herself. It felt like we were stealing a glimpse of something she didn't mean for us to see.

At the close of her last performance, Amelia stood and did her uniquely refined doff and bow. She held no feathered hat in her hand but her gesture was so expressive I imagined I saw its soft, wide brim brush the floor.

She danced with sheer joy to the thunderous beat of Koffi's drum, and more joyfully still, to the one you can't see; the one that beats inside her, ever constant and true.

On finding solace in the dark

22 July, 2015

People often ask me what autism is, or what it means to have a young child who is on the spectrum.

It's not an easy thing to articulate. All I can reach for are the behaviours that seem to spring from that enigmatic well.

If you asked me that question today, I would tell you that parenting a child like Amelia is still much like being on a rollercoaster. The carriage holding your family might hover on an up-swing for months and you feel that pleasurable excitement of *progress* in the pit of your stomach.

You yell into the oncoming wind: "We're making it, we're really getting somewhere! Upwards and onwards!"

But today, like every day for the past six weeks or so, we're not getting very far. We're deep at the bottom of a trough and the wheels aren't moving anymore.

I think they disintegrated on the way down some invisible ramp and now we're sliding backwards.

In this trough we are locked in yet another lengthy battle of wills with our daughter. It's the Hundred Years War all over again. We might have taken Agincourt but that doesn't mean jack in the long run.

Every day is filled with screaming fits, physical outbursts, nocturnal wanderings and ever more screaming.

We have been here so many times before, but my god it never gets easier. We're nearly seven years in and some days I wonder how much longer I can hold on.

Last night around dinner time when the screaming began for the fourth time, I walked silently into my room and crawled onto my bed in the dark to escape my own child. In that dark I felt no comfort but at least the space was quiet and it was mine.

The dark is the right place for me in those moments. I can't see myself (or her) anymore, I can only hear the sound of my breathing.

The dark is heavy and that is what I want. To allow the blackest thoughts in my head to wash over me as I lie there. There's no use fighting them, pounding as they are to get out. Might as well set them free.

Lying on the bed I curl into a ball and weep. I cry because I am so tired I don't really know how it is that I can function in the day. And because I feel a momentary yet powerful sense of defeat.

In the shadows I know only that I am losing this battle – not the battle to beat Amelia at this relentless 'game'. Nobody's playing around here. No, I am failing to help her handle the frustrations she cannot yet manage on her own. I hear taunting voices in that dark room too.

They say: "There's *nothing* wrong with Amelia. She's only like this because you are a *bad* parent." (Yes, in my head I italicise for emphasis.)

To those voices I say: "Come into the dark with me and see how long you'd last. You know nothing, cruel, hateful voices. Get away from me and never come back."

Then suddenly into the dark comes my real, live daughter, the one I'm taking refuge from. She puts a hand onto my back and holds it there. I reach over my shoulder to touch her, to tell her she is welcome there with me.

Amelia lies down next to me and curls her arm around my neck. The dark brings no true comfort, but her affection does. She kisses my cheek softly and presses herself into me. The darkness shifts a little and loses something of its heaviness.

I'm no superhuman and I'm not a machine either. The more confronting behaviours that define Amelia's autism naturally penetrate the surface of my skin.

My resilience is not bottomless. On such little sleep over so many weeks I can feel myself start to fray at the edges. I forget where I'm supposed to be going. I lose my way.

In this state it's so hard to know what to do to. Sometimes I want to run so far away that no-one will ever find me. But I only ever get as far as that room, where only the dark will do.

And it is here, where all is finally, blessedly quiet that Amelia reaches out and brings me safely back to myself. With empathy and love we hold each other in the dark and start again, as we must, every time.

Spidey sense

5 August, 2015

S o Amelia has discovered superheroes. It was bound to happen. She fancies herself a bit of a muscle-bound crime fighter, so I understand the attraction.

I certainly wouldn't mess with her. I mean, I don't.

Amelia's first superhero love is Spider-Man. He of the red and blue suit, the incredible climbing powers, web-shooting wrists, and sixth 'Spidey' sense.

She runs around the house pretending to be him, flicking her wrist with sound effects and attempting her own death-defying leaps from couch to couch (or from couch to unsuspecting parent).

Daredevil girls have all the fun.

It's always exciting when your child finds passion in something new, whatever it is. So, the other day I bought Amelia a Spider-Man figurine and left it for her to find when she arrived home from school.

Rushing in from the bus, she went straight into her room and saw him. Her very own Spider-Man, replete with an arachnid-embossed button on his chest that when pressed would emit a range of on-brand exclamations and quips.

Amelia pressed the button over and over. "I'm Spider-Man!"

"Like the suit? It comes with the job."

She held the figure up close to her ear. I realised that despite her hearing aids, she might find it hard to make out what Spider-Man was saying.

Amelia looked at me quizzically for a second then walked over to a set of stray headphones lying on our hall table. She held one headphone to her hearing aid on the left and pressed the other into her new friend's chest and pressed the button again.

I was fascinated. She was trying to work out how to direct or amplify the sound being received by her aids via the headphones. They weren't connected to anything, but it was worth a try.

She turned to me with a cheeky little spark in her eyes and said: "Mum, Spider-Man talks to me through my hearing aid."

Pause.

"You're not deaf, so you *can't.*" That last word was the verbal equivalent of a dismissive hair toss over her shoulder.

No I have no such superpower, but I didn't care. I loved watching her ingenuity at work and the connections she was making with her deafness and what her hearing aids can do.

Spider-Man was for her and her alone. He has a Spidey sense, and she does too. There are no limits here, only possibilities.

And me? I was the boring ol' third wheel, ordered into the kitchen for some snacks while they got on with the serious business of being superheroes.

Amelia's midnight garden

She whispered me her nightmare
Crouched in the quiet of the dark
She said
A man-sized cat came out of the garden
And the dirt behind the bushes
Had shifted and lifted up to
Cover her tiny mouth.

Her dark eyes were moon-like
As she clutched my hand
Too hard
And spoke her tale of dread
Of animals not being what they should
And the dirt doing what it could
To cut her voice dead.

My own eyes looked up and out
Beyond the window to the trees
To catch
Signs of the dream in her head
Of lurking feline giant shapes
And murderous soil creeping up
To kill us in our beds.

I whispered softly to my love
It was only a movie in your mind
Not real
Then I signed away her final fears
And sang a song she could not hear
About night-time cats now sleeping
And the garden dirt forever still.

Never say Neverland

9 October, 2015

Questions, always with the questions.
"What's your name?" Amelia asked me for approximately the hundredth time that week.

I am forever* patient. "My name's Melinda. What's your name?" It's always quid pro quo with us.

A shy smile. Amelia answers, "I'm Peter Pan… and I can fly!" She took off then, milky-white arms aloft, reaching for the sky. Well, the ceiling, anyway.

Amelia is Barrie's boy who wouldn't grow up. And she can fly.

The meaning of this fantastical claim was not lost on me. I have carried heavy facts about Amelia around in my head for years, details that told me she was very far from flying.

From walking, from talking. Hearing. Learning. Connecting. Growing apace with her peers.

My Peter Pan was tethered to the tarmac by phrases like "abnormality of development", "lower border of the normal range", "limited", "requiring substantial support".

Those were the diagnostic words. Deaf and autistic was the poster copy.

It's one thing to be told harsh things about your child's development but it is quite another to absorb them. To believe them as the natural order of things.

Her cognitive test scores painted a bleak picture of her abilities when she was four. But who's to say that was the whole story of who she would turn out to be?

Not me. I just held my breath and waited to see what would really happen.

Time has passed and Amelia's progress has stunned us and all the people who love her and work to support her.

She can read. Read! By herself in her room, she reads out loud and asks for help with the tricky words and then goes on. "I can do by myself." Yes, you can.

She can learn, about numbers and rules and abstract things thought beyond her grasp. She is interested in the patterns that shape her world and how things work.

She can sign and speak and tell us a little about her fears and feelings. She can express herself in two languages and through ribald jokes that make me laugh like a drain.

She can listen and hear enough with her hearing aids to learn, to recognise our voices, to feel present in the world. She asks me to sing and holds her ear close to my mouth. Be still my heart.

She can run and jump and do forward somersaults in mid-air and suspend herself in a handstand on the front wall of our house. She is strong and confident in her body, as she proudly tells me with flexed arms, "Me muscles!"

She can, in a quiet voice, ask other children to play with her in the park. Take their hand and show them how to climb. Watch out for the little ones on the slide. Join in.

She introduces herself thus: "My name is Amelia and I wear hearing aids. I'm deaf." Just like that. See, she really *can* fly.

I love her unbridled passion for Peter Pan and all of the whimsy and magic that his story entails. He is brave and so is she, so the velvet-green cap with the feather truly fits.

But part of me wants to tell her that she is better than him, that fictional boy who fears growing old and who is trapped in the arrested development of the endlessly immature.

Amelia in full flight

Peter Pan lives in Neverland, which is a wonderful place for feisty fairies called Tinkerbell and curious children to dream large, but it has its limits, as Barrie himself discovered. Never say Neverland, I reckon.

My Amelia lives in a more wondrous place than that, unimagined when she was two and four and dark limits blocked the sky from view.

Last week she said to me, "Mum, I can't wait to be older." Because life is exciting. Growth and development are a cause for happiness and celebration.

For now she is content to play at being Peter Pan, flying high around the lounge room and leaping from the couch launching pad to the stars.

But in Amelia's ever-expanding world, growing up is the real aim. As time goes on, my quiet faith in this girl grows louder, more insistent. I don't believe in fairy tales anymore, but I do believe in her.

As Barrie wrote so beautifully, "The moment you doubt whether you can fly, you cease forever to be able to do it."

* *This statement is caffeine and sleep dependent.*

Shock and awe

29 October, 2015

I didn't tell her everything.

How could I? It was hard enough to hold the trauma of it in my own head. I didn't tell Amelia that her daddy had collapsed at the hospital, on the hard, cold ground of the car park.

That I thought he'd fallen over behind me until I saw the way he was lying, arched forward in a twisted ball of agony.

I didn't recount for her the sounds coming from his mouth in that moment. His urgent struggle to breathe. Unforgettable sounds that escalated to a primal wailing that ripped through his body and ricocheted through mine.

What use to her would it be to paint a vivid picture of that night, flashing in my mind like a horror movie every time I closed my eyes?

I see it all in colours and let me tell ya, it ain't no rainbow.

There's the white of my tensed knuckles gripping onto her daddy's shirt as three of us tried to keep his convulsing body on its side.

The hideous transition of grey to blue as his face changed hue. That was the moment when his heart stopped. For one minute, then more. Seven all told.

To me, the time stretched into infinity. Seconds expanded into excruciating intervals of pain. I thought he was lost to me forever.

After that there was no colour at all, only panic and movement. Doctors and nurses running into the car park from the hospital corridor with life-saving instruments. I was dragged away.

It turns out it wasn't our sweet man's time to die that night. Maybe Lady Luck was smiling down on us. I'm part-Irish, vaguely Protestant, wholly atheist, but I thanked the Gods with all my heart. Damn it, they owed me one.

Next morning, it was my own mother's job to pass on the news with careful hands to her grand-daughter. I can think of no-one better for such an important task.

She said: "Honey, your dad had a sore heart and he went to the hospital feeling sick but he's much better now. He'll be home in five days."

Amelia paused over her breakfast, eyes suddenly shining with almost-tears but her internal dam walls held them in.

My brilliant Mum recognises that explaining time frames to our girl helps her to feel safe. Together they counted out the days on their fingers, reaching Monday as the likely date of her daddy's return.

Amelia nodded and her eyes cleared; she could cope with that.

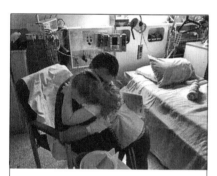

Holding her Dad close to her heart

The note from school the next day read: 'Amelia seemed a little sad today.'

I watched her out of the corner of my eye, looking for signs of melancholy or worry. As usual, Amelia's deepest emotions remained just that, buried in the subterranean depths of her enigmatic heart and mind.

But I know that just because she's not asking questions doesn't mean she's not thinking intensely about the world around her.

So in a light voice, I asked her straight out: "Baby, are you feeling a bit sad that your dad is in the hospital?"

Her reply was prompt and awe-inspiring: "No. I'm strong." She followed this with a typical Popeye flex of her arms.

Conversation over.

No. I'm strong. You could have picked me up from the floor.

Her response signalled two things to me. One was that she really didn't want to talk about what was happening. That her way of dealing with the sudden change in our lives was to soldier on as though all was well. I could only respect that.

On a more literal level, Amelia really was saying to me, "It's okay Mum, I'm tough. I can handle it." This wasn't some statement she'd heard somewhere and was parroting back to me without meaning.

At six, sometimes Amelia's behaviour still resembles that of a three-year-old. But here she understood that strength is something intangible you call upon in the darkest moments to make it through.

I saw this understanding take further shape when she saw her dad in the hospital for the first time. She didn't speak but she held him in one of the gentlest, longest hugs of her life. His silent tears poured into her hair and she held him longer still.

So, I didn't need to tell her everything, did I? There was so much she already knew. Talking was hard enough for me anyway. Eating and sleeping almost impossible.

Amelia's very real strength rose up to bolster my own. At night, I held her body close to mine and she placed a hand tenderly on my cheek. She kissed me there with wet lips but I didn't wipe the moisture away. It made me feel alive.

Soil searching

23 November, 2015

I have something shocking to report. Something disturbing has happened to me in the wash-up of recent traumatic events.

I never thought this would happen to me as we put the pieces of our little family back together and started to breathe again.

Okay, here goes. I have become … an avid gardener. You heard.

I'm the newest green thumb on the suburban block. A woman with soil permanently wedged beneath her previously manicured fingernails and dirt marks smudged proudly on a rouged cheek.

Marks from the earth are my new war paint. I am obsessed and there is no stopping me now I have started.

There is still no cessation of the intense energy (mania) that drives me from morning to night, but you can't have everything. And, after all, how much pruning could I achieve without such boundless energy?

The garden has never looked so luscious and cared for in the ten years I have nurtured and neglected it in equal measure.

It started with small steps out in the backyard. My husband was in hospital and after my daughter Amelia went to sleep at night, I'd find myself sitting on the cool ground outside, tearing out weeds and over-grown tendrils of grass.

My hands needed to work so that my rattled mind could stop churning, even as the daylight faded and I could no longer see the garage for the trees. So work is what I did, for days and nights on end.

I rejected gloves outright, preferring to connect with the often harsh textures of the garden. I endured deep cuts, broken nails, rose thorn splinters, and the pitter-patter of arachnid legs down my arm (eek).

The abrasions on my body at the end of the day satisfied me somehow. They were a positive sign of the exertions that were holding me together.

From weeds, I turned to the wild native shrubs that had suffered from months of inattention. They were locked in a permanently coiled dance, branch arm in tortured arm, plant figures robbed of distinct identities.

I took up my gardening shears and hacked and slashed at these shape-less masses with violent zeal. Sweat ran down my back from the effort, from the sun beating down on my pale skin. But I didn't feel anything. I was too busy to care.

My partner in garden crime

Inside the frenzy of my activity there was always method, always control. A sense of creating something new with my bare hands and sharp steel. Of taming and cultivating. Surviving.

I was an amateur gardener but I felt like an artist. I stood back to survey the landscape; feral forms had been transformed into shapely bushes with breathing space to call their own.

One willowy tree, previously choked by an untamed knot of green mess, was now free to stand tall and swing high in the breeze.

At night I would stand at the back window and press my hands to the glass, looking out at the garden. My garden. I was changing it for the better; my influence was everywhere – in the newly-planted pots of blooming flowers in pink and blue. Or the water trickling down the path post an evening soaking session for my thirsty friends.

In the dark hours of wakefulness over the next few weeks I would imagine new garden beds. And then in the morning I would set about bringing them to life. Hanging terrariums dotted with shells collected from some forgotten beach. Plans to convert an arid corner of our property into a secret succulent garden. The movement created by long-limbed plants covered in bright blooms, tucked beneath our Crepe Myrtle tree.

Once the garden had taken root in my imagination, I couldn't let it go.

Amelia joined me on my intense botanical mission. She lovingly tended to her own little patch of green things; her strawberry plant, the flowers, the tomatoes, mint, kale and parsley (she is a child of Melbourne's hip northern suburbs after all).

And all of this watched over by a cheeky little garden gnome and a solemn statue of a girl who used to care for my Nan's own garden before she died.

Our afternoons of toil would usually end the same way – with us covered in mud and Amelia stripping off her clothes to play under the delicious cold spray from the hose.

We grew things, re-shaped them and made them come alive again. One native shrub received some much-needed pruning and water treatment. Weeks later I spotted glorious, bright pink flowers appear on its spiky branches.

In all the years since it was planted, I have never seen those flowers before. It made me so happy to see them, such a generous response to the love I had finally given it.

And though our world isn't spinning so fast anymore, life is returning to something approaching normal, I feel forever changed by the experience. I *need* to be in the garden now, not just to distract myself from pain or worry. It's a part of me; I've poured my soul into it and so we are bound together.

At night, I am uneasy if I haven't at least dug my hands briefly into the soil or splashed some water over the beds, tucking my plants in for the night.

I step out onto the porch and take my time to look out across the garden towards our worn-out picket fence.

I soak up the warm night air and gaze happily at recent nursery additions now flourishing, and frown over a young plant failing to thrive.

Tomorrow I will endeavour to restore it to good health and hope to find some peace for myself. Just for a little while.

Signing Santa

1 December, 2015

It's that time of year again. Christmas is just around the corner and you can feel the urgency (panic) in the air and on the roads.

I'm steadfastly avoiding the chaos of shopping malls, except in the virtual world where you can shop at ease (and in your underwear) without being elbowed or causing a public scandal.

It was on one of my online voyages that I came across a magical initiative offered by a shopping centre in the UK called the intu Metrocentre. Naturally, Santa was going to be dropping in to make a lot of generous promises for parents to try and keep.

And on two special Sundays, Santa would be signing to deaf children clutching their own dreams of bikes, superheroes and so much more.

I flipped over the sheer coolness of the idea, so unique in my experience as the parent of a deaf nearly seven-year-old who has reached peak Christmas excitement in 2015. I shouted my approval to the company from the rooftops of social media and to my delight, I received a wonderful surprise message in return.

How would we like their signing Santa to make a video message for our daughter Amelia?

Is the Pope a Catholic? You bet your life we would LOVE that, I replied. I was really bowled over by the unexpected generosity of their offer to us. There are so few deaf characters or stories in the mass media, but having the big guy from the North Pole fluent in sign language* seemed like a radical start to our festive season.

About a week later, Amelia's video arrived in my inbox. The proof of its worth is in the stunning, personalised Christmas video pudding, provided by Santa and Mrs Claus.

Christmas morning will be full of lovingly chosen revelations for Amelia. But she has received an early gift this year, and its unique contents made her face shine with joy and unbridled excitement.

Amelia's mouth dropped open when Mrs Claus mentioned her passion for Spider-Man (how did she know?). She followed the message closely and copied the signs she recognised about the reindeer and snacks for Santa and his helpers.

When it had finished, she pressed replay over and over, endlessly enchanted by it all. It's simply a gorgeous video; we absolutely love it. Especially the bit where Santa tells Amelia to be a good girl and go to sleep on Christmas Eve.

If he could write *that* message in the night sky and hang some lights off it, that'd be awesome too.

---

* *Although the message is in British Sign Language and Amelia uses Auslan, many of the signs were familiar to her so she followed it well.*

In dreams, you're mine

11 December, 2015

We were at dinner with friends when I saw the bonny baby at the next table. A new-born covered in a light muslin wrap, protected from the too-cool air inside.

His mother was cuddling him in the warmth of her arms. She rocked him back and forth, swaying rhythmically in her seat.

Her beloved one had just woken without protest, but she was soothing him with the closeness of her body, the soft murmuring on her lips.

I was mesmerised. Trapped in a zone with them I could never truly share.

There were no tears from him, no raucous babble; he simply stared up at her with fixated wonder. His mother.

The yearning inside me was powerful, like I'd been sucker punched without warning. It hurt in a distant part of myself I've tried to bury. But it's always there; it grows stronger with age.

It rears its ugly head sometimes when I pass a pram in the street and glimpse the soft skin of infant feet, bouncing with the movement created by the street. My stomach lurches; I look away.

Or like the day when I was walking behind a man carrying a sleeping child in his arms and I put my hand out as if to touch a silken baby cheek. They moved out of reach and I let my possessed hand fall back by my side.

Every so often I cross the road to save myself the heartache. I don't always have a choice.

This night, I stopped the conversation at our table mid-stream: "Oh god, look at that beautiful baby. Just there. He's so sweet! Look how tenderly she's holding him."

My companions politely indulged me for a moment. I wanted to go over and hold that baby to my chest with a ferocity of feeling that shocked me. It took all of my strength to resist the urge, but I wrangled it, pushed that dreadful longing down into the dark where it belongs. There's no cure for it anyway.

So, I don't tell anyone that it's there. It's a private pain that ebbs and flows.

Instead when I'm asked by strangers for the millionth time why we 'only' have one child, I say: "No, I can't have any more children, but really we were happy to have 'just' one."

Or: "IVF was so very hard that we didn't have the strength to go through it all again."

And: "Our daughter has challenges and needs so much extra help and support. It was meant to be this way."

We are lucky. We live with grief. But we have no regrets.

Toy like her

17 December, 2015

Pre-Christmas discussion around gifts and the tricky scenario of matching the heart's desire of an extremely particular six-year-old with those gifts.

Me: "What do want Father Christmas to bring you this year, chicky?"

Amelia: "I want a Barbie doll with hearing aids like mine."

With hearing aids *like mine*.

Hmm, I thought. I don't know if Mattel has made great strides in the toys-for-kids-with-disabilities space to date. Apart from a few limited edition examples, true diversity in Barbie-land seems a long way off.

But old Saint Nick has but one KPI and that is to deliver special goods to order, so as his best elf-in-training, I took up the challenge on his behalf. And I never fail at things like that. Ever.

Amelia is happy to picture herself as other people, imaginary or real. Some days she gets her super-hero vibe on with a bit of Spider-Man play. Other times she wants to act like a baby and be rocked and sung to, giggling into my chest as we pretend.

Kids are fabulous at dreaming up fantasy worlds. But often the most exciting thing for little people (and big people too) is when they recognise something of themselves in their peers, on television, or in books.

So imagine if you are a proud, bilingual deaf girl – and that fact is rather central to your sense of identity – but you hardly ever see that experience reflected anywhere at all. No characters with hearing aids, or who use sign language.

To understand what a critical deficiency this is, it is important to know that Amelia goes to a school for deaf children, so during the week she is surrounded by other deaf children and adults. It is the norm for her. Yet it's a rarefied environment, specific to her school life. In the bigger, more dominant hearing world, she is more or less on her own.

Thankfully the times are beginning to change a little, and a wonderful social media campaign (founded by journalist Rebecca Atkinson) for diversity in toys called #Toylikeme has paved the way ahead of us.

We don't need to lobby toy companies to make Amelia's doll-with-hearing-aids dream come true, because this movement already has with some success.

My favourite of the companies to jump on board with the idea is called Makies in the UK. They already create gorgeous dolls that can be designed to suit a wide range of looks, clothes (I love the archaeologist career pack) and accessories.

Now they've added a range that allows for another level of choice where hearing aids, cochlear implants, wheelchairs, birthmarks and so on are finally a possibility. I was all over it.

After I lovingly chose the specs for Amelia's doll that shares her name, hair colour, sweet smile and quirky clothes sense, I clicked on 'hearing aids – pink'. CONFIRM ORDER. Done.

On Monday, the doll version of Amelia arrived and she's everything my girl (and I) had hoped for. I am beside myself with excitement to see her face on Christmas Day when they meet for the first time.

Just two cool girls with long blonde hair, dark eyes and hearing aids, hanging out together and wondering how Santa could be so switched on.

*Amelia models her
hearing aids*

*'Amelia', deaf girl in
doll form*

I'm deaf and you're not

21 January, 2015

I watched her playing in the park by the ocean. Another little girl approached and asked her in a tiny voice, "Do you want to play with me?"

Amelia was moving past her and didn't hear the question. The girl was shy and took silence to mean rejection.

I quickly intervened. "Hi there, sweet one. Amelia is deaf so she didn't quite hear you. Come over and ask her again." I translated.

She was called Alexandra. With names and ages hastily exchanged they were off, running and laughing and joking like the oldest of friends.

I sat once more and drank in the simplicity of childish play. The natural rhythm of it. The ease. Alexandra had a wand with magic powers deployed most usefully when she was tagged "it".

Not to be outdone, Amelia held up her hair and declared triumphantly, "I have hearing aids. I'm deaf and you're not."

Her face shone with pride. So did mine.

The greatest show on earth

24 February, 2016

That magnificent girl on the 'flying' trapeze

When I see Amelia swinging atop the trapeze, back straight, eyes clear and true, I think: *Anything is possible.*

I don't think about the time I tried to take her to another class some-place else and they said no. No, because she's deaf and autistic and it was all too hard. My daughter wasn't worth the effort.

I don't even think back to the day I took her to a soccer clinic and she lost it, running across the pitches to avoid me, screaming and yelling.

I kept falling over in my desperate effort to catch her, to get us out of there. My legs were grazed and people stared. Their eyes said, 'Thank god that's not me.'

After an eternity in hell, a burly, tattooed man helped me carry her away to our final point of collapse on the nature strip. I held that stranger's hand so tight and cried enough tears to flood the street.

I forget his name but not his kindness.

My mind has moved on and carried me elsewhere, to human pyramids and balancing acts. To death-defying feats like the tentative first steps taken on a wire. To a place where a young woman has learned some Auslan without being asked just so Amelia can be more involved. I want to hug her for the longest time.

To Thursday nights when we drop her off in the safe hands of her new troupe of friends and we don't worry.

We sneak a peek at her from the doorway, transfixed by her form sitting shoulder-to-shoulder with kids her own age.

She watches everything like a hawk and is not afraid to try. Suspending her strong body from brightly coloured sashes she looks weightless and free. So are we.

We don't want a lot more in life than to see our child happy and healthy and safe. To be able to join in and feel included. They're basic things but what else could be more important?

Nothing. In our world we've learned to appreciate the smallest of triumphs. Like the look on Amelia's face when we pick her up at 6pm and she's flushed from the *fun* of it all.

We dreamed of this for her and now we are here. Our little girl's run away to join the circus but she has our blessing along with our hearts.

The kite runner

22 March, 2016

High as a kite

She only let go of his hand for a moment, all the better to chase the colourful kite sailing above their heads. Her arms are raised, as though she can touch the clouds or pull the kite to her with an invisible string clasped in her hands.

The cool breeze brushes against her bare forearms, her face tilted skywards. There's nothing so perfect as a March day when the heavens are smiling so wide you can almost see their teeth.

The kite is tethered but it is free and so is she. Tethered to her father standing close behind but out of view; free as the kite soaring into the blue.

She follows its path along the clouds, running to catch up but it is forever out of reach. No matter, the joy is in the chasing not the catching.

They had only planned on the park and slides and maybe swings, not kites. Nothing so special as that. They were a surprise bonus.

As was the wonder their simple appearance brought out in her. The thrill in her voice when she came home to tell me that, "We saw kites, Mum! It was a kite *festival*." Festival. It's a new word for her but her voice is clear and true. I understand perfectly.

And the happiness on her dad's face, "She held my hand for ages. She sat and painted her face with the other children. She made a little book inscribed with her name. And danced. We both danced."

They both danced. The kite was reeled in at festival's end but the magic went on in their heads. All night long.

The divine Miss M

30 May, 2016

I love how easily little children fall in love with things; their joy in new experiences and people.

This is especially true of Amelia who hasn't yet learned to play her emotional cards close to her chest.

She crushes hard on her toys, on newly-met kids in the park and writes passionate letters (and emails and text messages) to her teacher: "S, I love you so much."

Our home is littered with tender notes left on side tables, Valentines slipped quietly into pockets and drawers.

Then, there is M, our 16-year-old neighbour. A gentle, dark-haired girl who waves to us in the garden and once picked a red flower, passing it to Amelia over the short fence that separates our houses.

A rose by any other teenage girl would not smell nearly as sweet. And with that flower she did win Amelia's sweet heart. Like, forever.

A few weeks ago, I found Amelia outside, pressed up against the fence, calling M's name into the cooling night air. "M! Where are you?" There was a note of shyness in her voice, but there was hope, too. Lots of hope.

Before I could wrangle her back inside, M suddenly appeared. She said, "I thought I heard you calling me! Let's play a game." And over our little fence, M joined hands with Amelia and showed her how to wrestle thumbs. They chatted and laughed together before parting ways.

It was a fleeting interaction, but it meant so much to Amelia. It solidified something growing steadily inside her. That longed for connection with another human being – friendship. She has so much love to give but not always the facility to show it or receive it.

Soon after, Amelia drew a special picture for her new buddy M. She spent a long time on it and together we put it into a special envelope covered in stickers and hearts. I said, "Should we go and give it to her now?" Did I even need to ask?

M wasn't home, so we left the letter in the safe hands of her younger brother. I forgot about it until the next day after Amelia went to school. I checked the letter box for the daily mail and instead found a small gift box and card inside.

It was addressed to Amelia, from M. I carefully took it out and held it in my hands, as though it was fragile, precious. And it was. I'd been worried Amelia's intensity might be annoying to our teenage neighbour, but I was so, so wrong.

I put the gift inside, ready for its lucky recipient to return home. You'd be forgiven for thinking the present was for me, the way I paced around waiting for the school bus to arrive in our street, desperate to see its secret contents revealed.

Amelia finally came home and I greeted her with the news falling urgently from my lips, "Baby, M left you a present, it's inside!"

Her eyes widened in disbelief. "M? For me?"

"Yes, for you! Let's go!"

We ran together into the house, jostling to reach the little box veritably pulsing with life on the kitchen bench. The card contained a beautifully penned thank you note from M. Amelia's picture had made her day, so here was something in return. Just for her.

Opening a gift of friendship

Inside the box was a silver chain with a pretty circular pendant depicting a tree. A thing that grows. Like the friendship between a loving deaf, autistic girl and her sweet teenage neighbour.

They are separated by nearly ten years of age and the small fence that separates our houses. M doesn't always understand what Amelia is trying to say, and my little one misses plenty of sounds and what they mean.

But these things are not barriers; the distance between Amelia and M is remarkably short. When they touch hands and laugh and send each other letters they are just two girls reaching out to each other and finding a friend.

Epilogue

"Hope" is the thing with feathers -
That perches in the soul -
And sings the tune without the words -
And never stops - at all -

> *− Emily Dickinson,*
> *"Hope" is the thing with feathers*

And then the day came,
when the risk
to remain tight
in a bud
was more painful
than the risk
it took
to Blossom.

> *− Anaïs Nin, Risk*

Reading over the pages of this book which spans more than three years of my family life, I was struck by so many thoughts and feelings. It makes sense to me that the earliest stories are riven with the grief that was still very close to the surface for me in 2013. I'm also reminded of the hours I spent devouring everything about deafness, then autism, trying to bend those diagnoses to my data-driven will. Information helped me to understand but it could not calm the panic I felt inside me. What was going to become of my dear little girl?

What I see now in these vignettes about Amelia is the gradual erosion of that paralysing fear and the growth of something far more hopeful. My anger and grief has given way to a strange sense of almost-peace. Where I had obsessed over the *why* these things had happened and *what* it all meant, I finally made my way back around to wondering about *who* Amelia was. Amelia the girl. The person. The humourist. The dancer. The soulful one. The real her.

I'm not sure that even in my darkest moments I wanted to change my daughter into someone else, but I'll admit I couldn't always see her clearly. I sometimes saw her the way less-than-charitable observers did, but I think my judgement was clouded by my own feelings of failure. Amelia was not a *bad* child, I was a *bad* mother. And if I said to myself once or twice that there were things about her that I wished were more *normal* (that dreadfully loaded word), I know that I was terrified that she would never be able to enjoy her life to the fullest.

So for me, the destination at the end of this particular road is signposted by *acceptance*. There was a point, and I can't exactly recall the time or the place, where I let go of a lot of pain and stopped battling against the situation I was in; I stopped resisting Amelia and I let her in. It shifted in my body like the release of a great weight. Yes, she is still deaf and autistic and these are defining things in her life and ours. But my job is not to try and change those things about her, only to find the best people and programs to help her grow and achieve her dreams. Realising that I had come to terms with this reality within myself through my writing has been one of the singular joys of working on this book.

It is fitting to finish here with another quote from Andrew Solomon, whose book *Far From The Tree* is partly about the degree to which families like mine can reach that place of acceptance. About one mother of a child with autism, Icilda Brown, Solomon writes: "A lifetime of non-choices had given her a gift for acceptance. She demanded good services for her son, but did not expect those services to turn him into someone else. The story of middle-class and affluent parenting of autistic children is an interminable saga of tilting at windmills; in contrast, I admired both Icilda's acquiescence and the happiness that was its corollary." [9]

Acquiescence and happiness. No more tilting at windmills. To me, this is the opposite of living in denial about the challenges facing your child or the hard times that lie ahead. It means finding a way, in time, to reconcile this life with the one you thought you'd be living. In the space that is created by this process of giving in (rather than giving up), you can and will celebrate the unique abilities your child brings to the world. They might be different but that doesn't mean they're not wonderful. Every single one.

---

9   Solomon, p.552.

Useful contacts

There is an overwhelming amount of information that parents of children with special needs have to absorb, especially in the early years following diagnosis. Here are some of the autism and deafness- related organisations, websites and resources that I have gathered for ease of use (details correct at time of publication):

Organisations – Autism

Amaze (Autism Victoria)
Victoria's peak body for autism.
Ph: 1300 308 699
Email: info@amaze.org.au
Webpage: www.amaze.org.au

Australian Advisory Board on Autism Spectrum
The national peak body (formerly The Autism Council of Australia).
Ph: +61 2 8977 8300
Fax: +61 2 8977 8399
Postal address: PO Box 361, Forestville NSW 2087
Webpage: www.autismadvisoryboard.org.au

Autism Association of the Australian Capital Territory
ACT's peak body for autism.
Ph: +61 2 6176 0514
Fax: +61 2 6281 2834
Email: admin@autismaspergeract.com.au
Webpage: www.autismaspergeract.com.au

Autism Association of Queensland
Queensland's peak body for autism.
Ph: +61 7 3273 0000
Fax: +61 7 3273 0093
Email: admin@autismqld.com.au
Webpage: www.autismqld.com.au

Autism Association of South Australia
SA's peak body for autism.
Ph: +61 8 8379 6976
Info line: 1300 288 476
Fax: +61 8 8338 1216
Email: admin@autismsa.org.au
Webpage: www.autismsa.org.au

Autism Association of Western Australia
WA's peak body for autism.
Ph: +61 8 9489 8900
Regional: 1800 636 427
Email: autismwa@autism.org.au
Webpage: www.autism.org.au

Autism Northern Territory
NT's peak body for autism.
Ph: +61 8 8948 4424
Email: autismnt@autismnt.org.au
Webpage: www.autismnt.org.au

Autism Spectrum Australia (Aspect)
NSW's peak body for autism. Includes Autism Launchpad, a resource for
young people with autism and their families to help with leaving school
and leading your own life.
Ph: 1800 277 328
Webpage: www.autismspectrum.org.au

Autism Tasmania
Tasmania's peak body for autism.
Ph: 1300 288 476
Email: autism@autismtas.org.au
Webpage: www.autismtas.org.au

Organisations – Deafness

Canberra Deaf Children's Association
A non-profit community organisation that endeavours to provide support and information to parents and families on issues affecting deaf and hearing-impaired children.
Ph: +61 2 6284 8143
Webpage: www.canberradeafkids.org.au

Deaf Australia
Deaf Australia (formerly the Australian Association of the Deaf) is the national peak body managed by deaf people that represents, promotes, preserves and informs the development of the Australian Deaf community, its language and cultural heritage. It works towards a vision of an Australia where deaf people have no barriers.
Ph: +61 7 3357 8266
TTY: +61 7 3357 8277
Fax: +61 7 3357 8377
Email: info@deafau.org.au
Website: www.deafau.org.au

Deaf Can:Do
Provides a range of services to the South Australian adult Deaf and hard of hearing community.
Ph: +61 8 8100 8200
Fax: +61 8 8346 9625
Webpage: www.deafcando.com.au

Deaf Children Australia
Deaf Children Australia is a national not-for-profit organisation representing the needs of deaf and hard of hearing children and their families across Australia.
Ph: +61 3 9539 5300
TTY: +61 3 9510 7143
Fax: +61 3 9525 2595
Email: helpline@deafchildren.org.au
Webpage: www.deafchildrenaustralia.org.au

Deafness Forum of Australia

Deafness Forum is the peak body for deafness in Australia.
Ph: +61 2 6262 7808
TTY: +61 2 6262 7809
Fax: +61 2 6262 7810
Webpage: www.deafnessforum.org.au

DeafNT

Provides support to deaf and hard of hearing adults, children and young
people in the Northern Territory.
Ph/Fax/TTY: +61 8 8945 2016
Mobile/SMS: +61 0 429 452 016
Email: Betty.Franklin@deafnt.org.au
Webpage: www.deafnt.org.au

Deaf Services Queensland

Provides a range of services to the deaf and hard of hearing communities
in Queensland.
Ph: +61 7 3892 8500
TTY: +61 7 3892 8501
Fax: +61 7 3392 8511
Email: dsq@deafsq.org
Webpage: www.deafservicesqld.org.au

Disability Discrimination Commissioner

Alastair McEwin (appointed July, 2016)
Australian Human Rights Commission
Ph: +61 2 9284 9600
National: 1300 656 419
TTY: 1800 620 241
Fax: +61 2 9284 9611
Email: infoservice@humanrights.gov.au
Webpage: www.humanrights.gov.au/our-work/disability-rights

Hear For You

Hear For You is a mentoring program for young deaf people. It provides
e-mentoring and group workshops aimed at helping young deaf people
in mainstream schools to engage fully in life and realise their potential.
Phone: +61 0 407 722 985

Email: info@hearforyou.com.au
Webpage: www.hearforyou.com

Parents of Deaf Children (PODC)

Formerly Parent Council for Deaf Children, PODC provides families of
deaf and hard of hearing children in New South Wales with independent
and unbiased information and support. Collaborates with parents, profes-
sionals, other organisations and government departments to promote
equity of access to services and opportunities.
Ph: +61 2 9871 3049
TTY: +61 2 9871 3193
Fax: +61 2 9871 3193
Email: info@podc.org.au
Webpage: www.podc.org.au

Tasdeaf

The Tasmanian Deaf Society's works to minimise the impact of hearing
loss on individuals while improving the quality of life for those who are
deaf and as a result may face barriers to participate in community life.
Ph/TTY: +61 3 6228 1955
Fax: +61 3 6228 1966
FREECALL: 1800 982 212
Email: info@tasdeaf.org.au
Webpage: www.tasdeaf.com.au

Vicdeaf

The Victorian Deaf Society provides information, programs and educa-
tion to over 16,000 deaf and hard of hearing adults each year through
its diverse range of services across Victoria.
Ph: +61 3 9473 1199
TTY: +61 3 9473 1111
Fax: +61 3 9473 1122
Email: info@vicdeaf.com.au
Webpage: www.vicdeaf.com.au

WA Deaf Society

A non-profit organisation providing services to deaf and hard of hearing
people in Western Australia.
Ph: +61 8 9441 2677

TTY: +61 8 9441 2655
Fax: +61 8 9441 2616
Email: wadeaf@wadeaf.org.au
Webpage: www.wadeaf.org.au

Websites

www.aussiedeafkids.org.au
Resources, stories and online discussion groups for parents.

www.autismspectrum.org.au
Autism Spectrum Australia (Aspect) is Australia's largest service provider for people on the autism spectrum.

www.autismeurope.org
An international association advancing the rights of people on the autism spectrum by influencing European decision-makers.

www.autism-society.org
The official site of the main US autism organisation.

www.autism.org.uk
The official site of the UK's NAS – one of the largest autism organisations.

www.ndis.gov.au
Information about the National Disability Insurance Scheme (NDIS), with links to State and Territory trial sites.

www.hearing.com.au
Australian Hearing is the nation's leading hearing specialist and largest current provider of Government funded hearing services.

www.otaus.com.au
Occupational Therapy Australia; information about professional development, support, and access to profession-specific information.

PlayConnect
Provides playgroups suited to the needs of children aged 0-6 years with ASD or ASD like symptoms.

www.speechpathologyaustralia.org.au
The national peak body for the speech pathology profession in Australia

www.deafchildrenaustralia.org.au
Resources, stories and online discussion groups for parents and deaf youth.

www.parentline.com.au
Another great parent support option.

www.raisingchildren.net.au
Resource for Australian parents, including information about pregnancy to newborns to teenagers.

www.artsaccessaustralia.org
News, connections and information about the Australian arts and disability sector.

www.deafchildworldwide.info
Ideas, discussions, research and information on all aspects of childhood deafness on a global scale.

www.ndcs.org.uk
The National Deaf Children's Society in the UK.

www.nad.org
The National Association of the Deaf in the United States of America.

www.eud.eu
The European Union of the Deaf.

www.innovativeresources.org
Sells conversation-building resources that might be useful for parents.

www.autismawareness.com.au
Providing parents and carers with quality information, resources and targeted educational programs to families, professionals and the broader community.

www.wom.com.au
Supplier of assistive devices for Deaf and Hard of Hearing people in Australia.

www.auslan.org.au
Language resources site for Auslan (Australian Sign Language).

www.hearingdogs.asn.au
Soundfield systems for schools from Lion's Hearing Dogs.

www.phonak.com/au/en/support/children-and-parents.html
Practical hints and tips on hearing aids for children and parents.

www.mindsandhearts.net
Training Events and Psychology Services for Asperger's Syndrome and Autism Spectrum Conditions.

www.experiencebooks.co.uk
Books can be personalised for children with autism, those who wear hearing aids, have cochlear implants or who are wheelchair users. Each unique book is designed to explain how a child communicates and experiences the world. Parents can share information to new support workers, child minders or teachers so won't have to repeat the same things over again.

www.toylikeme.org
A wonderful creative collective celebrating diff:ability in toys and calling on the global toy industry to positively represent 150 million kids with disability and difference worldwide.

Glossary of terms

Art Therapy promotes mental and emotional growth through art making. Unlike art instruction, art therapy is conducted with the aim of building life skills, addressing deficits and difficult behaviours, and promoting healthy self-expression. Clients are encouraged to explore and express themselves using art materials.

Attention deficit hyperactivity disorder (ADHD): Disorder in children associated with three main kinds of problems: overactive Behaviour (hyperactivity), impulsive Behaviour, and difficulty in paying attention.

Audiogram is a standard way of presenting a person's hearing loss. It is represented as a picture or a graph.

Audiology is a branch of science that studies hearing, balance, and related disorders. Its practitioners, who treat those with hearing loss and proactively prevent related damage are **audiologists**. Employing various testing strategies (e.g. hearing tests), audiology aims to determine whether someone can hear within the 'normal' range, and if not, which portions of hearing (high, middle, or low frequencies) are affected and to what degree. If an audiologist determines that a hearing loss is present he or she will provide recommendations to a patient as to what options (e.g. hearing aid, cochlear implants, appropriate medical referrals) may be of assistance.

Auditory Brainstem Response (ABR) testing is a screening test to monitor for hearing loss or deafness, particularly for newborn infants. For this test, sounds are played to the baby's ears. Band-aid-like electrodes are placed on the baby's head to detect responses and can measure up to a 90 decibel loss.

Auslan (Australian sign language) is the preferred method of communicating among members of the Deaf community in Australia. It is the national sign language of Australia and is officially recognised as a separate language. It is a unique visual gestural language with its own grammar and ensures full and complete communication.

The signing is not in English word order and is distinct from English. It allows deaf children to communicate from a young age, easily and completely with other people who know Auslan.

Autism is a complex neurodevelopmental disorder which affects the brain's growth and development, with symptoms appearing in early childhood. It has an impact on, among other things, the way an individual relates to his or her environment and their interaction with other people. Autism is characterised, in varying degrees, by difficulties in social interaction, verbal and nonverbal communication and repetitive behaviours.

Baby Sign Language is the use of manual signing allowing infants and toddlers to communicate emotions, desires, and objects prior to spoken language development. Baby sign is distinct from sign language (e.g. Auslan). It is used by hearing parents with hearing children to improve communication.

Bilateral versus unilateral hearing loss: Unilateral hearing loss is hearing loss in only one ear. This can cause great difficulty in hearing background noise and makes localising the source of a sound difficult. Bilateral hearing loss is hearing loss in both ears. In addition to hearing speech at reduced volume, bilateral sensorineural hearing losses can cause sounds to be distorted. Putting sounds together meaningfully can be a difficult task. Medical intervention is not usually possible and the loss is permanent. Hearing aids are frequently fitted to assist the child to hear, depending on the degree of hearing loss.

Bilingual means being able to use more than one language. Deaf children may struggle to learn English because they do not hear English well enough to become fluent. On the other hand, deaf children can learn Auslan naturally and easily if they are exposed to it. The Bilingual-Bicultural (BLBC) approach is an educational communication program for deaf children which uses Auslan. Acknowledging Auslan and English as two distinct languages, it instructs a child in Auslan as a first language to communicate with the Deaf community and other Auslan speakers and teaches English as a second language. The child learns English through reading and writing and their teacher explains to them in Auslan how English fits together – the sentence structures, vocabulary etc.

Cochlear implant (bionic ear) is a surgically implanted electronic device providing sound to a profoundly or severely deaf or hard of hearing person. People with mild or moderate sensorineural hearing loss are generally not candidates for cochlear implants. Unlike hearing aids, the cochlear implant does not amplify sound, but works by directly stimulating any functioning auditory nerves inside the cochlea with electric field stimulated through an electric impulse. External components of the cochlear implant include a microphone, speech processor and an RF transmitter. Similarly, an RF receiver is implanted beneath the skin. The transmitter has a piece of magnet by which it attaches to another magnet placed beside the receiver. When the receiver gets a signal, it transmits to the implanted electrodes in the cochlea. The speech processor allows an individual to adjust the sound level of sensitivity.

A cochlear implant will not cure deafness or hearing impairment, but is a prosthetic substitute for hearing. Some recipients find them very effective, others somewhat effective, and some feel overall worse off with the implant than without. For people already functional in spoken language who lose their hearing, cochlear implants can be a great help in restoring functional comprehension of speech, especially if they have only lost their hearing for a short time.

Deaf community: The Deaf community in Australia is a diverse cultural and linguistic minority group that encompasses a vast network of social, political, religious, artistic and sporting groups that use Auslan as their primary mode of communication. Accepting one's deafness as part of a person's identity is the core element in identification into the Deaf community who are often described as Deaf with a capital 'D' to emphasise their deaf identity; 'deaf' (with a small 'd') is used in this book to include all people who are deaf or hard of hearing. Identification with the Deaf community is a personal choice and it does not depend on one's degree of deafness, rather on identifying with the cultural model of deafness. Culturally Deaf people, whether they have hearing aids, cochlear implants or use sign language, view themselves not as disabled, but as a normal, linguistic minority group. Being proud of one's Deafness now takes full force in a variety of ways – such as the Deaf festivals that are fostered each year across Australia throughout the National Week of Deaf people.

Deafness and hearing loss: Deafness constitutes a hearing impairment or hearing loss in which a person's ability to detect or understand sounds is fully or partially decreased. People are classified as having different levels of hearing loss. These are: mild, moderate, severe and profound. 'Mild hearing loss' is defined as having hearing problems at around 26 to 40 decibels. People in this category may have difficulties keeping up with conversations, particularly in noisy conditions. 'Moderate hearing loss' classifies difficulty in hearing quiet sounds heard by people between 40 and 70 decibels. People in this category also have difficulty keeping up with conversations and find both a hearing aid and lipreading useful. 'Severe hearing loss' is encountered by people who find it difficult to hear at 70 to 95 decibels. People in this category will benefit from powerful hearing aids, but often they rely heavily on lipreading even when they are using hearing aids. Some also use sign language. 'Profound hearing loss' is defined as a hearing threshold greater than 90 decibels. People in this category are very hard of hearing and rely mostly on lipreading and/or sign language. The written word may be the only way that some of the people in this category can communicate.

There are two types of hearing loss: **conductive** and **sensorineural**.

Conductive hearing loss is caused by problems in the outer or middle ear which prevent the sound from being 'conducted' to the inner ear and hearing nerves. The hearing may fluctuate and may affect one of both ears to varying degrees. Conductive problems usually affect the quantity (loudness only) of the sound that is heard. It is usually medically or surgically treatable. A common cause of conductive loss in children is middle ear infection.

Sensorineural hearing loss is due to a problem in the cochlear (the sensory part of the ear) or the hearing nerve (the neural part). It can be acquired or be present at birth. There is usually a loss of clarity as well as loudness, i.e. the quality and the quantity of the sound is affected. It is possible to have both a conductive and a sensorineural hearing loss. This type of loss is called a mixed hearing loss.

Developmental disorder: A disorder that interrupts normal development in childhood. A developmental disorder may affect a single area of development (specific developmental disorder) or several (pervasive developmental disorder).

Early intervention centres aim to offer specialist support to all children with additional needs (in this case deafness and/or autism) and their families, prior to school entry. Evidence has shown that support given to children from birth through to the early years of formal education has a significant effect on their development. Early intervention includes: identification of children and families who may require specialist support, building parents' skills in caring for their children with special needs, promoting the development of children across all areas, promoting independence and family ability to make informed decisions in all aspects and stages of intervention, and encouraging participation of all children in the local community.

Fine motor skills: Activities which require the co-ordination of smaller body muscles, for example, writing.

FM units (radio aids, FM systems, microlinks) work in partnership with a hearing aid or cochlear implant. They are often given to children to use in school. The teacher wears the microphone and the child the transmitter. The FM is designed to help minimise background noise, allow the teacher's voice to be heard more clearly and the child to hear from a distance. Hearing aids by themselves have three major problems: firstly, they don't work very well over a distance; secondly, they amplify everything so background noise is a problem; and thirdly, reverberation can cause sound to be distorted. FM systems overcome all these problems so they may assist the deaf child in the classroom.

Gross motor skills: Body movements which utilise larger muscle groups such as sitting, kicking and jumping.

Hearing aid is an instrument that amplifies sound to assist people with hearing loss. They are distinguished by where they are worn: in the ear (ITE), in the canal (ITC), completely in the canal (CIC), behind the ear (BTE), or on the body. The hearing aid microphone picks up the sound, makes it louder and then transmits the louder sound (or parts of the sound) down through the hearing aid mould into the ear. Hearing aids can be analogue or digital. Each suits the level of your child's hearing loss.

Hearing loop is a loop of wire installed around the perimeter of an area, such as a cinema or a church, and connected directly to an audio amplifier, to assist people with hearing loss.

High functioning autism: Autism in individuals with normal/ near-normal IQ.

In Vitro Fertilisation is a process by which an egg is fertilised by sperm outside the body: *in vitro* ("in glass"). The process involves monitoring and stimulating a woman's ovulatory process, removing an ovum or ova (egg or eggs) from the woman's ovaries and letting sperm fertilise them in a liquid in a laboratory. The fertilised egg (zygote) is cultured for 2–6 days in a growth medium and is then implanted in the same or another woman's uterus, with the intention of establishing a successful pregnancy.

Low-functioning autism: Autism associated with an intellectual disability.

Mainstreaming: The concept that students with special needs should, when appropriate, be integrated with their non-disabled peers to the maximum extent possible.

Neurological: Having to do with the nerves or the nervous system.

Obsessive compulsive disorder (OCD): Disorder where a person has recurrent unwanted ideas (obsessions) and an urge (compulsion) to do something to relieve the obsession.

Occupational Therapy (OT) is the use of assessment and treatment by an **occupational therapist** to develop, recover, or maintain the daily living and work skills of people with a physical, mental, or cognitive disorder. Occupational therapy is a client-centred practice that places emphasis on the progress towards the client's goals. Among these clients, occupational therapists assist children and their caregivers to build skills that enable them to participate in meaningful occupations. They also address the psychosocial needs of children and youth to enable them to participate in meaningful life events. These occupations may include: normal growth and development, feeding, play, social skills, and education.

Oral method, aural/oral and Cued Speech: The oral methodology consists of three different approaches. In the auditory verbal method, the child is taught through intensive teaching to use their remaining hearing to learn to speak. No visual cues, such as lipreading, facial expressions or natural gestures are used. Emphasis is placed on the child's personal amplification system and/or cochlear implant.

The aural/oral method also aims to teach deaf children to speak and lipread, but this method accepts the use of lipreading and natural gestures. Children will use their hearing aids and/or cochlear implant.

Cued Speech is a system of hand movements near the mouth to assist lipreading. Many sounds look the same on the lips and Cued Speech is used to assist the deaf and hard of hearing child to distinguish between them. Children will also use their hearing aids and/or cochlear implant to aid communication. The aim of Cued Speech is to assist communication through speech and lipreading. Cued speech is not a sign language and is very rarely used by deaf adults. It is generally used in educational settings only.

Processor is part of a cochlear implant that converts speech sounds into electrical impulses to stimulate the auditory nerve.

Self-stimulatory Behaviour: Commonly referred to as a 'stim'. Any kind of repetitive or stereotypic Behaviour (for example, staring at lights, flapping hands, rocking etc), which is believed to provide some form or sensory stimulation.

Sensory Processing Disorder (SPD) is a neurological condition that impairs the functional skills of 1 in 20 children. People with **Sensory Processing Disorder (SPD)** misinterpret everyday sensory information, such as touch, sound and movement. They may feel overwhelmed by sensory information, may seek out sensory experiences or may avoid certain experiences.

People with **SPD** experience their world as either Hypersensitive (over reactive, sensory avoidance) or Hyposensitive (under reactive, sensory seeker). They may also present with motor skill problems. They may react with strong emotional behaviours and experience what may be described as 'melt downs'.

Signed English is a made-up, hand-expressed code for English, which is not used outside of educational settings. Unlike Auslan, it is not a separate language. It was introduced into the Australian education system in the 1970s to try and improve the literacy, communication and reading skills of deaf children. People speak and sign at the same time when Signed English is used. Deaf adults rarely use Signed English.

Speech pathology is a field of expertise practiced by a clinician known as a **speech pathologist**. Speech pathologists study, diagnose and treat communication disorders, including difficulties with speaking, listening, understanding language, reading, writing, social skills, stuttering and using voice. They work with people who have difficulty communicating because of developmental delays, stroke, brain injuries, learning disability, intellectual disability, cerebral palsy, dementia and hearing loss, as well as other problems that can affect speech and language. People who experience difficulties swallowing food and drink safely can also be helped by a speech pathologist.

Theory of mind: Ability to attribute mental states to oneself and others and to understand what another person thinks, feels, desires, intends or believes.

Visual communication is simply communication in the form of visual aid. It allows the conveyance of ideas and information in forms that can be read or looked upon. It relies entirely on sight and can include signs, typography, drawing, graphic design, illustration and colour.

Visual supports: The presentation of information in a visually structured manner to make it easier to understand, for example, a daily schedule may be shown by photographs or cartoons.

About the author

Melinda Hildebrandt is a former film researcher and cinephile with a doctorate in British cinema. She has contributed to key texts such as The Oxford Companion to Australian Film (1999) and The Encyclopedia of British Film (2003). The seeds of her passion for the movies were sown from early childhood with parent-sanctioned screenings of films like Lawrence of Arabia, Seven Samurai, Psycho, The Searchers and Duck Soup.

She has worked for over fifteen years as a senior administrator in the university sector. Long before disability became a part of her family life, her work was driven by a commitment to equity and access in higher education and student-centred projects for young people at risk.

Melinda loved writing from a young age, but it wasn't until she started blogging about raising her deaf and autistic daughter Amelia in 2013, that she discovered the power of words to express the turmoil, grief, wonder and hope of her daily life.

Posts from her blog 'Moderate-severe/profound... quirky' have been published by Mamamia, ABC Ramp Up, Catherine Deveny and The Limping Chicken (UK deaf news and deaf blogs). Other pieces have been featured in parent support-group publications by Aussie Deaf Kids, Parents of Deaf Children and Aurora School Early Intervention.

Melinda lives in the gentrified northern suburbs of Melbourne with Amelia and her husband. Her interests include gardening, distance running, Pilates, alt-country music (especially with fiddles), German football, Marlon Brando and loud soprano singing in the shower. Sometimes Amelia makes it an operatic duet.

Acknowledgments

Heartfelt thanks belong to so many lovely people.

My husband Tim was by my side from the beginning of my blog to the creation of this book, providing advice and the ever-valuable skills of the professional sub-editor. He always trusted me to share the private details of our family life with care. I have no greater champion.

To my parents, who have only ever offered unconditional love and support from the moment Amelia was born. Their love is like the spine that keeps my body upright and allows me to keep on walking, ever forward.

Our wonderful family and friends who have listened and learned with us and never judged, with love to: my dear departed Nan, Gen and Nick, the Romans, the Reeves, Jeff and Karen, Andrew and Turiya, Ange, Corrie, Peter H, Val and Carl, Brian and Gerie, Belinda T, Sarah S, Sally, Vicki, Janet, Mike, Denise, Cathy and Jim, Hayley A, Christine W, Melissa A, Kathy R, Jo M, Jacqui, Jude, Jill, Helen, Christel, Rob, Dee, Peggy, Bronwyn and everyone at Athleticka.

The one-in-a-million Catherine Deveny, whose wonderful writing class and forthright encouragement changed my life and gave me the confidence to stop dreaming, to just get on with it and to finish this book.

Julie Postance for taking me by the hand and guiding me expertly through the self-publishing process. Her own book on deafness, 'Breaking the Sound Barriers' is very special to me. Our collaboration was meant to be.

Amanda Spedding, my trusted editor, whose substantial skills and faith in my work helped me take my blog and turn it into a book.

The creative experts who designed my layout, logo and cover. Special mention belongs to both Nelly Murariu (graphic designer, PixBeeDesign) and my talented friend Lynette Zeeng for her beautiful photography (back cover and contact page).

Lots of people read my blog-then-book and offered me helpful advice and encouragement along the way, including: Amanda A (the first stone in the pond), Hannah and Kathryn (my gorgeous beta readers), Sally, Ann P (thank you for your most generous foreword), Belinda B, Miki, Donna, Nicole R, Charlie and Andy, and Jane B.

The membership of Team Amelia has changed over time, but I would not be standing today without the commitment of this collective to give

Amelia and our family the best possible care: Pragashni, Kerryn and Gillian, Irma and Loretta (Australian Hearing), Christine N, Janine, Mario and Theresa, Ann L, Meg M, Megan A, Gabi, Katrina and Laura (Northcote Aquatic and Recreation Centre), Aurora School Early Intervention, Casa Bambini Coburg, St Martin's Youth Arts Centre (Drama Play Program), Westside Circus and every amazing person (staff and students) at Furlong Park School for Deaf Children.

And to my dear girl Amelia, whose little kite-heart picture graces the pages of this book. I love you to the moon and back.

Contact Melinda

Please contact Melinda directly at
melinda.hildebrandt@gmail.com

See Melinda's website for more information:
www.melindahildebrandt.com.au

Follow Melinda on Twitter: *@DrMel76*

Follow Melinda on Instagram: *@mhildebr76*

Like Melinda on Facebook:
www.facebook.com/melindahildebrandtauthor/

22792657R00165

Printed in Great Britain
by Amazon